Kindle Fire HDX for Seniors

Studio Visual Steps

Kindle Fire HDX
for Seniors

Step-by-step instructions to work with the Kindle Fire HDX tablet

Visual Steps™
www.visualsteps.com

This book has been written using the Visual Steps™ method.
Cover design by Studio Willemien Haagsma bNO

© 2014 Visual Steps
Author: Studio Visual Steps

First printing: March 2014
ISBN 978 90 5905 100 3

Resources used: A number of definitions and explanations of computer terminology are taken over from the *Kindle Fire HDX User Guide.*

Do you have questions or suggestions?
Email: info@visualsteps.com

Would you like more information?
www.visualsteps.com

Website for this book:
www.visualsteps.com/kindlefirehdx

Subscribe to the free Visual Steps Newsletter:
www.visualsteps.com/newsletter

Table of Contents

Appendices

Foreword

Kindle tablets have become increasingly popular not only for reading e-books but also for surfing the Internet, sending emails, working with photos, video and music, downloading apps and more.

Amazon offers a huge amount of digital content that can be viewed or downloaded on the Kindle. There are literally thousands of e-books as well as a growing variety of movies, TV episodes, games and other apps available. You can also transfer your own files such as photos or PDF documents directly from your computer to your Kindle.

This book features step-by-step instructions and well-illustrated, full-color screen shots that will guide you as you learn the basic features of the Kindle. Practical and efficient, this is the best book to get you started with this user-friendly tablet.

Discover the possibilities of a Kindle with this handy book!

Yvette Huijsman
Studio Visual Steps

PS We welcome your comments and suggestions. Our email address is: info@visualsteps.com

Visual Steps Newsletter

All Visual Steps books follow the same methodology: clear and concise step-by-step instructions with screen shots to demonstrate each task. A complete list of all our books can be found on our website **www.visualsteps.com**

You can also sign up to receive our **free Visual Steps Newsletter**.
In this Newsletter you will receive periodic information by email regarding:
- the latest titles and previously released books;
- special offers, supplemental chapters, tips and free informative booklets.
Also, our Newsletter subscribers may download any of the documents listed on the web pages **www.visualsteps.com/info_downloads**

When you subscribe to our Newsletter you can be assured that we will never use your email address for any purpose other than sending you the information as previously described. We will not share this address with any third-party. Each Newsletter also contains a one-click link to unsubscribe.

Introduction to Visual Steps™

The Visual Steps handbooks and manuals are the best instructional materials available for learning how to work with mobile devices, computers and software applications. Nowhere else can you find better support for getting to know a tablet such as the Kindle, iPad, Samsung Galaxy Tab or Google Nexus tablet, or an iPhone, *Windows* computer, Mac, the Internet and various computer programs.

Properties of the Visual Steps books:
- **Comprehensible contents**
  Addresses the needs of the beginner or intermediate computer user for a manual written in simple, straight-forward English.
- **Clear structure**
  Precise, easy to follow instructions. The material is broken down into small enough segments to allow for easy absorption.
- **Screen shots of every step**
  Quickly compare what you see on your screen with the screen shots in the book. Pointers and tips guide you when new windows are opened so you always know what to do next.
- **Get started right away**
  All you have to do is turn on your computer or device and have your book at hand. Sit some where's comfortable, begin reading and perform the operations as indicated on your own device.
- **Layout**
  The text is printed in a large size font and is clearly legible.

In short, I believe these manuals will be excellent guides for you.

Dr. H. van der Meij
Faculty of Applied Education, Department of Instructional Technology, University of Twente, the Netherlands

What You Will Need

To be able to work through this book, you will need a number of things:

A Kindle Fire HDX tablet.

A computer or laptop to transfer files to your Kindle. If you do not own a computer or laptop, you may be able to transfer these files using a computer from a friend or family member.

How to Use This Book

This book has been written using the Visual Steps™ method. The method is simple: you put the book next to your Kindle and perform each task step by step, directly on your Kindle. With the clear instructions and the multitude of screen shots, you will know exactly what to do. By working through all the tasks in each chapter, you will gain a thorough understanding of your Kindle.

In this Visual Steps™ book, you will see various icons. This is what they mean:

Techniques
These icons indicate an action to be carried out:

 The index finger indicates you need to do something on the Kindle's screen, for instance, tap something, or type a text.

 The keyboard icon means you should type something on the keyboard of your Kindle or your computer.

 The mouse icon means you should do something on your computer with the mouse.

 The hand icon means you should do something else, for example rotate the Kindle or turn it off. The hand can also indicate a series of operations which you learned at an earlier stage.

In some areas of this book additional icons indicate warnings or helpful hints. These are to help you avoid making mistakes and will alert you when you need to make a decision about something.

Help
These icons indicate that extra help is available:

 The arrow icon warns you about something.

 The bandage icon will help you if something has gone wrong.

 Have you forgotten how to do something? The number next to the footsteps tells you where to look it up at the end of the book in the appendix *How Do I Do That Again?*

The following icons indicate general information or tips concerning the Kindle.

Extra information
Information boxes are denoted by these icons:

 The book icon gives you extra background information that you can read at your convenience. This extra information is not necessary for working through the book.

 The light bulb icon indicates an extra tip for using the Kindle.

Website

On the website that accompanies this book, **www.visualsteps.com/kindlefirehdx**, you will find more information about this book. This website will also keep you informed of changes you need to know as a user of the book. Visit this website regularly and check if there are any recent updates or additions to this book, or possible errata.

Test Your Knowledge

After you have worked through this book, you can test your knowledge online, on the **www.ccforseniors.com** website.

By answering a number of multiple choice questions you will be able to test your knowledge. If you pass the test, you can also receive a free *Computer Certificate* by email. Participating in the test is **free of charge**. The computer certificate website is a free Visual Steps service.

For Teachers

The Visual Steps books have been written as self-study guides for individual use. They are also well suited for use in a group or a classroom setting. For this purpose, some of our books come with a free teacher's manual. You can download the available teacher's manuals and additional materials from the website:
www.visualsteps.com/instructor
After you have registered at this website, you can use this service for free.

The Screen shots

The screen shots in this book indicate which button, file or hyperlink you need to tap or click on your Kindle screen or computer. In the instruction text (in **bold** letters) you will see a small image of the item you need to tap or click. The black line will point you to the right place on your screen.
The small screen shots that are printed in this book are not meant to be completely legible all the time. This is not necessary, as you will see these images on your own Kindle screen in real size and fully legible.

Here you see an example of such an instruction text and a screen shot of the item you need to tap. The black line indicates where to find this item on your own screen:

In some cases, the screen shot only displays part of the screen. Below you see an example of this:

At the bottom of the screen:

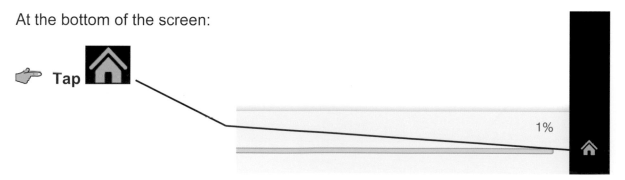

We would like to emphasize that we **do not intend you** to read the information in all of the screen shots in this book. Always use the screen shots in combination with the display on your Kindle screen.

1. The Kindle Fire HDX

The Kindle Fire HDX from Amazon is not just an e-book reader. This light, easy-to-use tablet computer comes with a beautiful, high resolution display and has many great features. It runs Amazon's own operating system, a modified version of Google's *Android* operating system.

You can easily surf the Internet and send emails with the Kindle. You can even keep a calendar, play games, watch videos and read newspapers or magazines.

You can do all of this by using various *apps*. These are the programs that are installed on the Kindle Fire HDX. You can add additional (free and paid) apps by visiting the *Amazon Appstore*, the web shop where an ever-increasing variety of apps can be found.

In this chapter you will get to know the Kindle Fire HDX and learn the basic operations necessary for using it along with the onscreen keyboard.

In this chapter you will learn how to:

- turn on or unlock the Kindle Fire HDX;
- set up and register the Kindle Fire HDX;
- distinguish the main components of the Kindle Fire HDX;
- handle the basic operations of the Kindle Fire HDX;
- lock the screen rotation;
- adjust the brightness and show more settings;
- connect the Kindle Fire HDX to a wireless network (Wi-Fi);
- connect the Kindle Fire HDX to a 3G or 4G/LTE network;
- update the Kindle Fire HDX;
- lock or turn off the Kindle Fire HDX.

1.1 Turning On or Unlocking the Kindle Fire HDX

The Kindle Fire HDX may be turned off or be in sleep mode. If your Kindle Fire HDX is turned off, you can turn it on using the button on the back:

☞ **Press the Power button ⏻ and keep it pressed in until you see the Kindle Fire HDX logo on the screen**

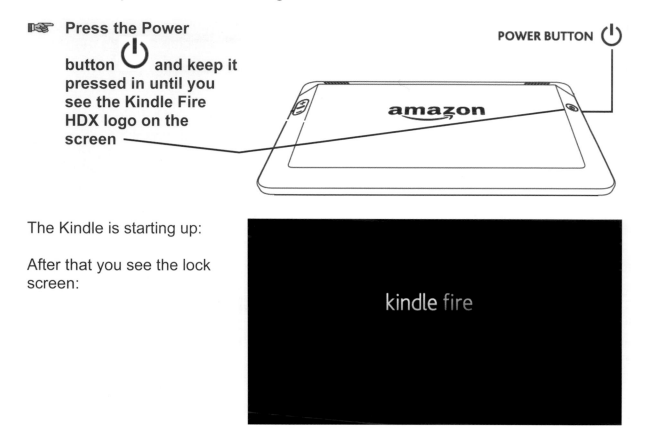

The Kindle is starting up:

After that you see the lock screen:

The Kindle may also be in sleep mode. The screen is dark and it does not respond to touch gestures. If that is the case, you can wake the Kindle like this:

☞ **Briefly press the Power button ⏻**

You can unlock the screen like this:

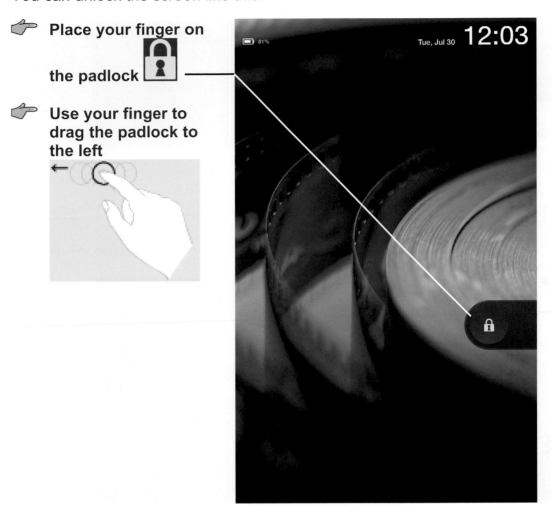

☞ **Place your finger on**

the padlock

☞ **Use your finger to drag the padlock to the left**

If this is the first time you start up your Kindle, you will see a number of set-up screens. In the next section you can read how to adjust these settings and register your Kindle Fire HDX.

If you have previously used your Kindle, you can continue with *section 1.3 The Main Components of the Kindle Fire HDX*.

1.2 Setting Up and Registering Your Kindle Fire HDX

The screens you see when you start you Kindle Fire HDX for the first time may vary. This depends on whether the Kindle has already been registered to an *Amazon* account or not. If you bought the Kindle online using your *Amazon* account, Amazon may already have registered it to your account.

If that is the case, you will be asked to set up a Wi-Fi connection:

☞ **Tap the network you
want to use, for
example**

If you see a list of languages instead of the screen above:

☞ **Continue reading on page 22**

You may need to enter a password. In that case the onscreen keyboard appears:

⌨ **Type the password** ⎯⎯⎯⎯⎯

Does the password contain
capital letters or numbers?
You can refer to the *Tip* on
page 37 to see more about
how to type with the onscreen
keyboard.

☞ **Tap**

Connect

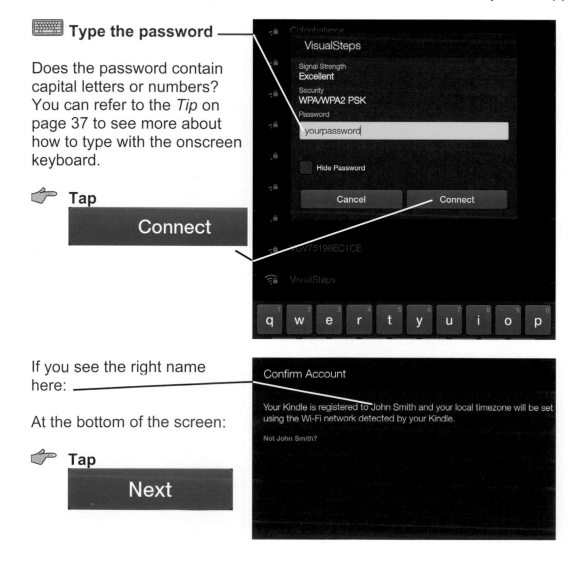

If you see the right name
here: ⎯⎯⎯⎯⎯

At the bottom of the screen:

☞ **Tap**

Next

If you have received the Kindle as a gift for example, you may see the name of the buyer in this screen. In that case:

 Tap
Not John Smith?

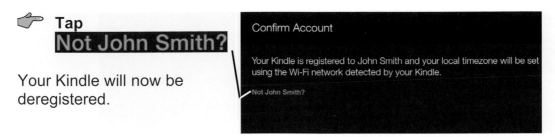

Your Kindle will now be deregistered.

You see the screen where you can register the Kindle using your own *Amazon* account:

Tap the box below
Email Address

Type your email address

Tap the box below
Password

Type your password

Tap

Register

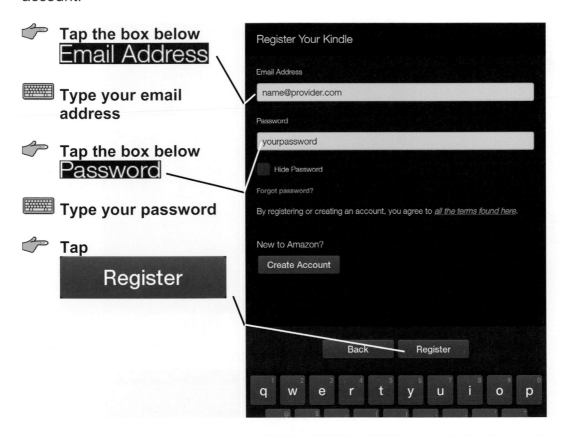

☞ **Continue reading on page 27**

✂ HELP! I do not have an Amazon account.

You need an *Amazon* account to be able to register and use your Kindle. If you do not have an *Amazon* account, you can create one now.

☞ **Continue reading on page 24**

If your Kindle has not been registered to an *Amazon* account yet, you start by selecting the language:

👉 **Tap the language, for example**
English (United State

👉 **Tap**

Next

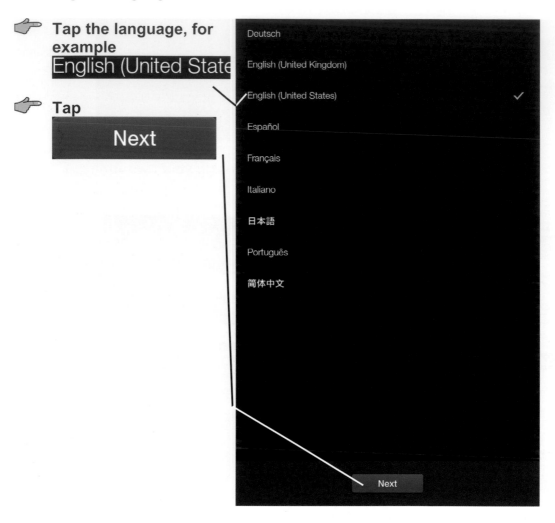

You will be asked to set up a Wi-Fi connection:

👉 **Tap the network you want to use, for example**
VisualSteps

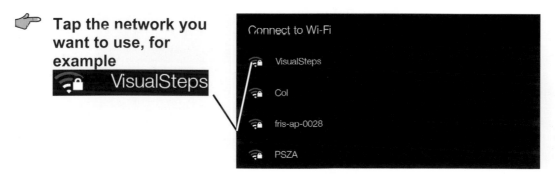

You may need to enter a password. In that case the onscreen keyboard appears:

⌨ **Type the password** ⸺

Does the password contain capital letters or numbers? Please refer to page 37 to see how to type them.

☞ **Tap**

Connect

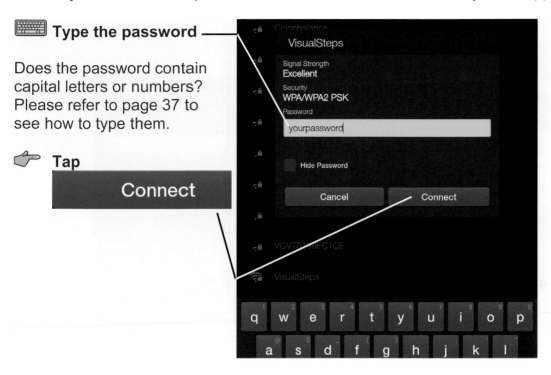

You see the screen where you can register the Kindle. If you already have an *Amazon* account:

☞ **Tap the box below Email Address**

⌨ **Type your email address**

☞ **Tap the box below Password**

⌨ **Type your password**

☞ **Tap**

Register

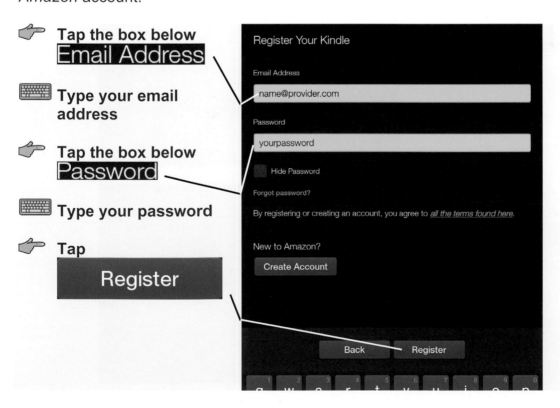

☞ **Continue reading on page 27**

You need an *Amazon* account to be able to register and use your Kindle. If you do not have an *Amazon* account yet, you can create one now:

☞ **Tap**
> **Create Account**

First you enter your country or region:

☞ **Tap**
> **Tap to select**

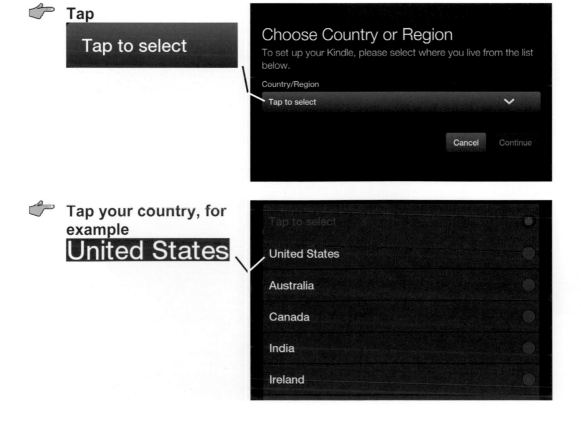

☞ **Tap your country, for example**
> **United States**

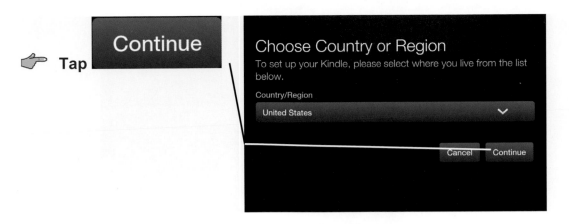

☞ **Tap** **Continue**

An *Amazon* account consists of an email address and a password:

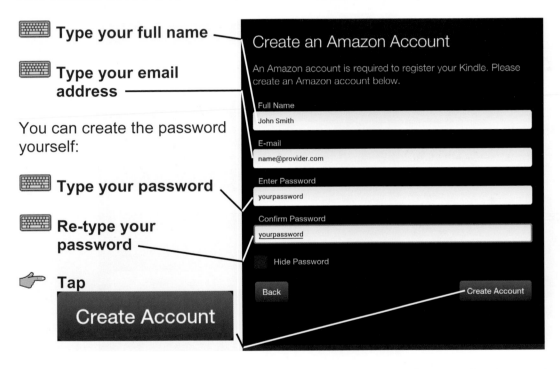

⌨ **Type your full name**

⌨ **Type your email address**

You can create the password yourself:

⌨ **Type your password**

⌨ **Re-type your password**

☞ **Tap** **Create Account**

Now Amazon asks for your payment information. Even if you only plan to download free books and apps, you have to add a credit card to your account:

☞ **Tap** **Amazon.com Visa**

☞ **Tap the credit card you want to use**

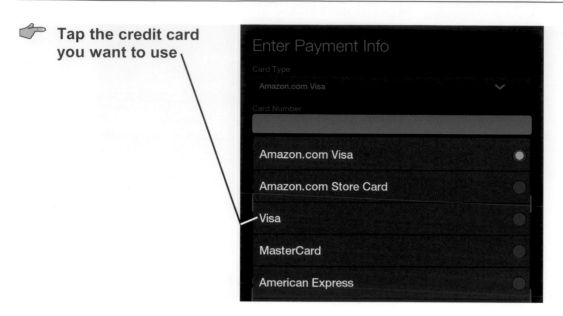

Enter your credit card information:

⌨ **Type your 16 digit credit card number**

Enter the expiration date:

☞ **Tap 01**

☞ **Tap the correct month**

☞ **Tap 2015**

☞ **Tap the correct year**

⌨ **Type your name exactly as it appears on your credit card**

☞ **Tap Continue**

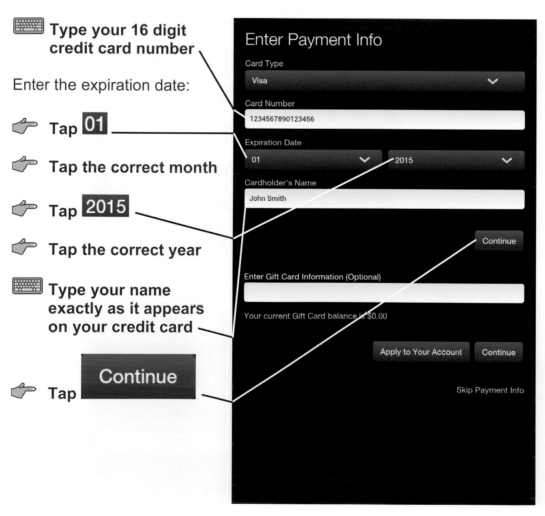

Amazon also needs you billing address:

☞ **Enter the required information**

👉 **Tap**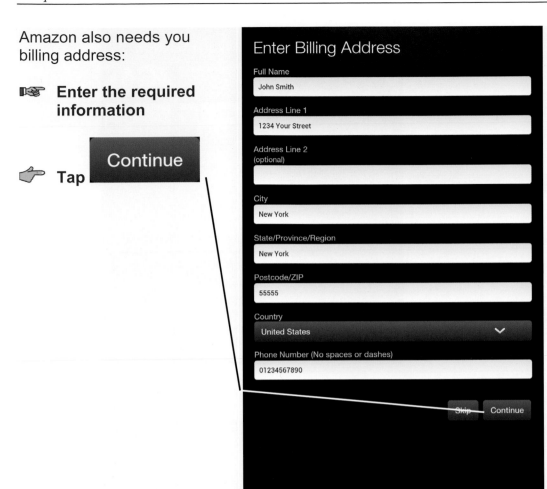

Now you can confirm that the Kindle is registered correctly:

At the bottom of the screen:

👉 **Tap**

You may see a screen promoting the use of Amazon Prime for a free 30-day trial:

In this example we will not be using this offer:

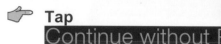 **Tap**

You are asked if you want to connect your Kindle to *Facebook* and *Twitter*:

You do not need to do that now:

At the bottom of the screen:

 Tap

You will now see a few screens offering a quick guide to the Kindle Fire HDX:

 **Tap**

The information on these screens is also covered in this book, but in more detail. On the next few screens:

 Swipe the screen in the direction the arrow shows

In the last screen:

 **Tap**

The device has been set up and is ready for use:

You see the Home screen of the Kindle Fire HDX:

HELP! My Kindle Fire HDX is locked.

If you do not use the Kindle for a short while, it may automatically lock. By default, this is set to happen after five minutes. This is how you unlock the Kindle:

☞ **Press the Power button** ⏻

👉 **Swipe the padlock** 🔒 **to the left**

1.3 The Main Components of the Kindle Fire HDX

In the diagram below you see the main components of the Kindle Fire HDX. When we describe how a specific component operates in this book, you can always refer back to this diagram to find its location on the tablet.

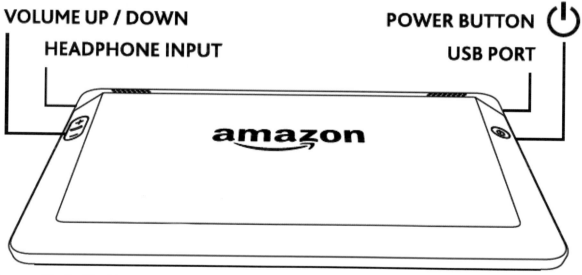

Source: Kindle Fire HDX User Guide

On the Home screen you see the following items:

Status bar:

Search button:

Navigation bar with links to libraries:

Carousel:

The Carousel displays your most recently viewed books, videos, music and apps. If you have not used your Kindle before, it may be completely empty.

At the bottom of the screen the favorite items are shown:

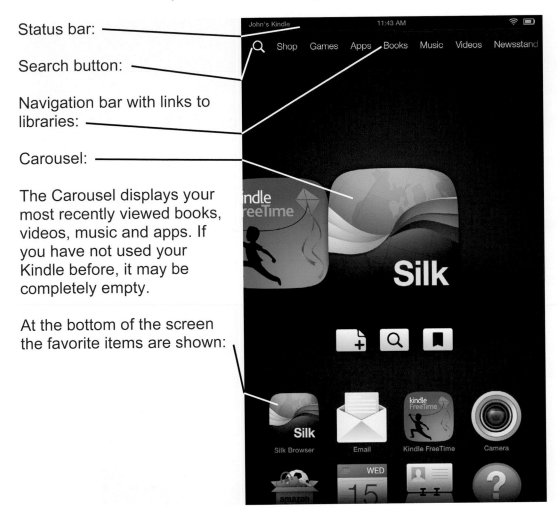

The current time is displayed in the center of the status bar and on the left and right you will see other small icons. These icons indicate information about the status of the Kindle and its connections. Here is a quick overview of the icons:

 Notifications: messages generated by games and applications.

 Wireless: the number of bands represents the strength of the Wi-Fi signal at your current location.

 Bluetooth: the Bluetooth-icon will appear when Bluetooth is on, and it will turn blue when your Kindle is paired with another Bluetooth device.

 Location based services: a compass icon will appear when your Kindle is using Wi-Fi to estimate your location. This happens when you are using a location-based application and have enabled Location-Based

Services in the *Settings* screen.

This icon will show you the amount remaining in your battery charge.

Source: Kindle Fire HDX User Guide

1.4 Basic Operations on the Kindle Fire HDX

The Kindle is very easy to use. In this section you are going to practice some basic operations and touch gestures. If necessary, first unlock the Kindle:

🖝 **If necessary, unlock the Kindle** 🐾¹

You will see the Home screen with favorite items on the bottom of the screen. If you have not used your Kindle before, you will see some default items.

To show all the favorite items at the bottom of the screen:

☞ **Swipe the screen**

   upwards

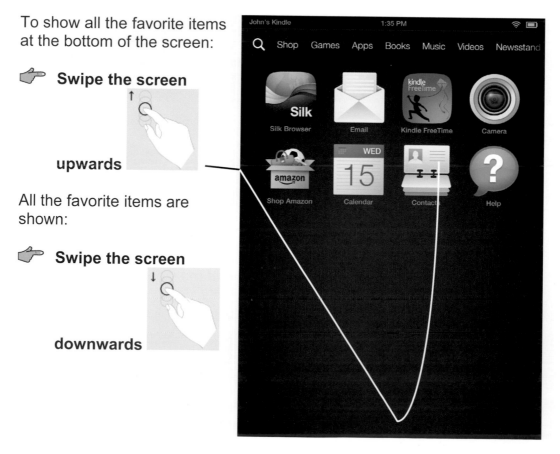

All the favorite items are shown:

☞ **Swipe the screen**

   downwards

You will see the regular Home screen again.

It is very easy to add your favorite apps, e-books and web pages to this section of the Home screen. Try that with an app from the *Apps* library:

To open the *Apps* library:

☞ **Tap** Apps

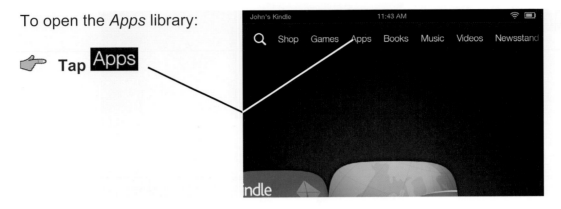

You see the app icons for the default apps on the Kindle:

☞ **Place your finger on**

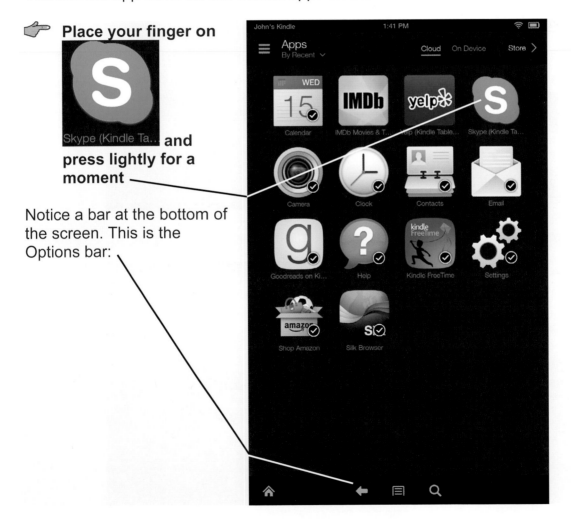

Skype (Kindle Ta... **and press lightly for a moment**

Notice a bar at the bottom of the screen. This is the Options bar:

After a few seconds a menu option appears:

☞ **Tap**
Add to Home

At the bottom of the screen you can go back to the Home screen:

☞ **Tap** 🏠

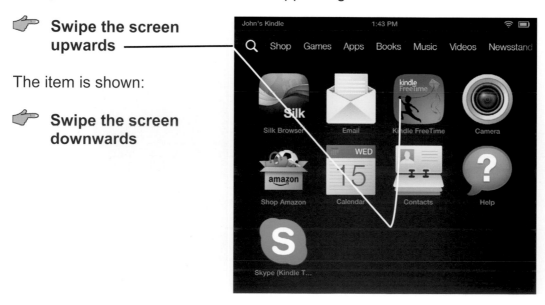

Now you will see a new favorite item appearing at the bottom of the Home screen:

☞ **Swipe the screen upwards**

The item is shown:

☞ **Swipe the screen downwards**

You can access the search function from the Home screen:

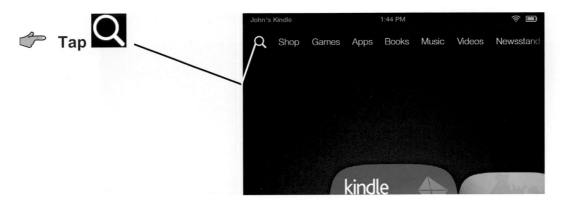

☞ **Tap**

You will see the search page with the onscreen keyboard. This keyboard works the same way as a regular keyboard. The only difference is that you tap the keys instead of pressing them. Just try it:

Type: `cal`

The libraries, the *Appstore* and the Internet are searched for anything that starts with 'cal':

For example, the *Calendar* app is found right away:

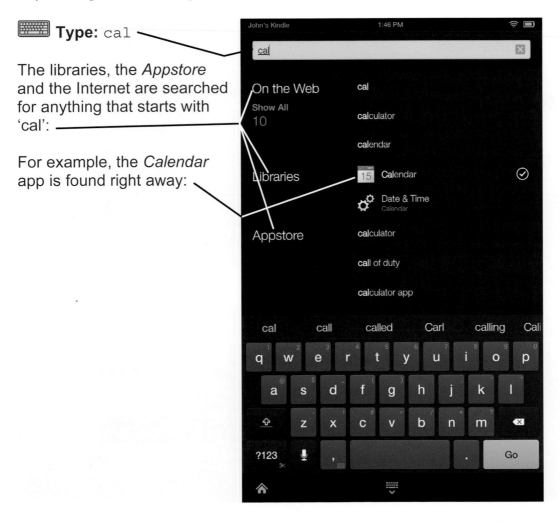

You can use the 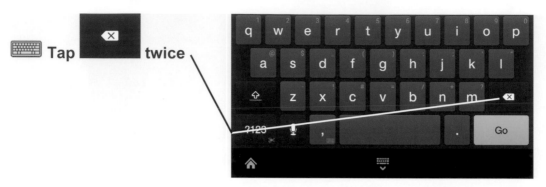 key to remove letters you typed one-by-one:

⌨ **Tap** 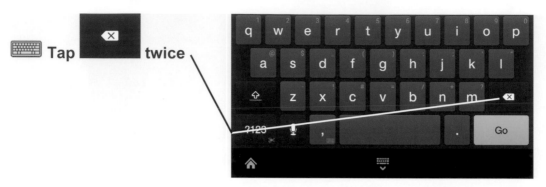 **twice**

The search result is adapted to the new search term 'c':

You can see that more results are found by **Libraries**:

If necessary, you can tap **4 results** to show all the results.

For now, that is not necessary and you can empty the search box:

☞ **Tap**

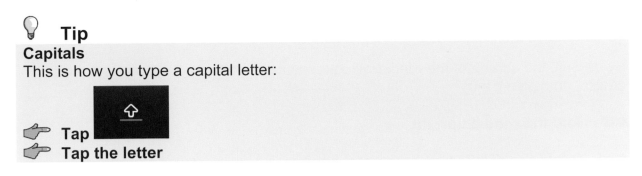

Tip

Capitals

This is how you type a capital letter:

☞ **Tap**

☞ **Tap the letter**

In the default view of the keyboard on the Kindle you will not see any numbers or special characters. You need to use a different view of the onscreen keyboard for that:

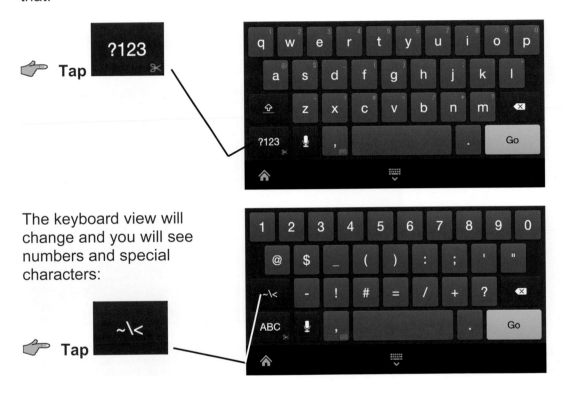

☞ **Tap**

The keyboard view will change and you will see numbers and special characters:

☞ **Tap**

Now you see even more special characters. To go back to the default view:

☞ **Tap**

1.5 Locking the Screen Rotation

By default, the screen of the Kindle will automatically rotate when you rotate the device. Just give it a try:

☞ **Hold the Kindle upright**

☞ **Rotate the Kindle to a horizontal position**

☞ **Hold the Kindle upright**

☞ **Rotate the Kindle to a horizontal position**

The Kindle contains a hidden menu where you can adjust various settings. To display this panel:

☞ **Swipe your finger from the top of the screen downwards**

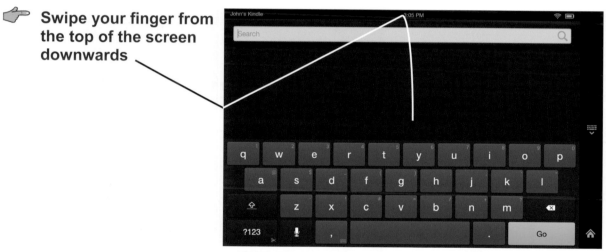

You will see the *Quick Settings* menu:

You can use this panel to quickly adjust the various settings on your tablet.

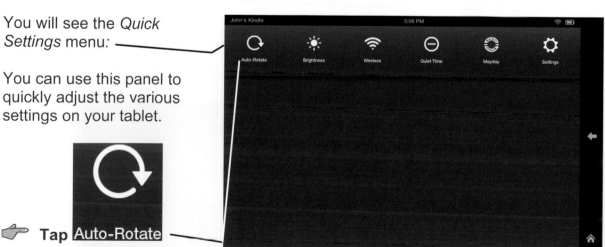

☞ **Tap Auto-Rotate**

The button has changed to

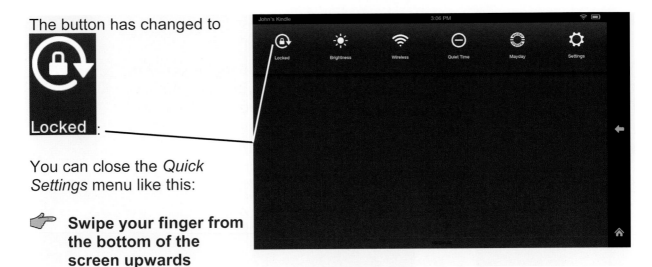

 :

You can close the *Quick Settings* menu like this:

 Swipe your finger from the bottom of the screen upwards

You can check to see if this works:

 Hold the Kindle upright

Now you will notice that the Kindle's image no longer rotates with the device. The image has been locked in landscape mode.

 Rotate the Kindle to a horizontal position

Please note:

In this book we hold the Kindle in a horizontal position. We recommend you do the same while performing the exercises described in this book. Otherwise images on your Kindle will appear differently than the screen shots shown in this book.

💡 **Tip**

Unlocking the screen rotation

If you do want to auto-rotate the image on the Kindle, just change the setting:

 Swipe down from the top of the screen

 Tap Locked

 Swipe up towards the top of the screen

1.6 Adjusting the Brightness

You can also use the *Quick Settings* menu to adjust the brightness of the screen. For example when you read a book in a dark room, you do not want the screen to be too bright. Also, the brighter the screen, the more battery power will be used.

☞ **Open the *Quick Settings* menu**  ²

☞ **Tap Brightness**

The brightness can be adjusted using a slider:

☞ **Drag the slider to the left**

You see that the screen becomes darker.

You can also use the Auto-Brightness option. This function automatically adjusts the brightness of the screen to the available light:

The Auto-Brightness option:

You can set the brightness with the slider:

☞ **Drag the slider to the desired position**

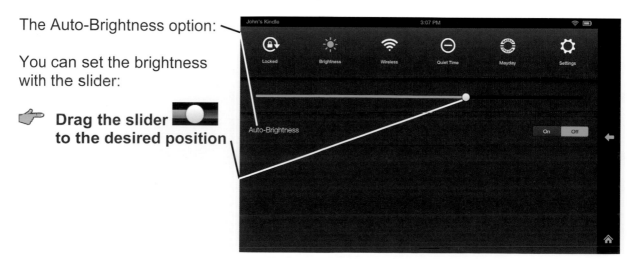

You can use the Options bar to go back to the Home screen from anywhere on the Kindle:

☞ **Swipe your finger up towards the top of the screen** ───────

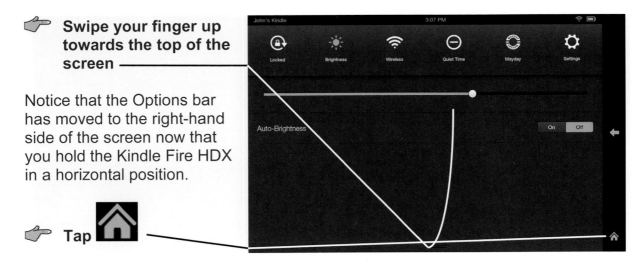

Notice that the Options bar has moved to the right-hand side of the screen now that you hold the Kindle Fire HDX in a horizontal position.

☞ **Tap** ───────

The *Quick Settings* menu is closed. You see the Home screen.

1.7 More Settings

From the *Quick Settings* menu you can access even more settings:

☞ **Open the *Quick Settings* menu** 👣²

☞ **Tap** Settings ───────

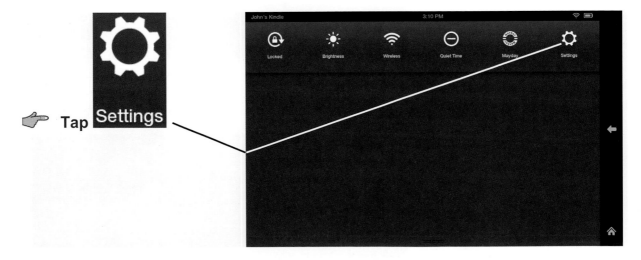

The *Settings* screen contains lots of other options, too many to display on a single screen. This is how you view the rest of the settings list:

👉 **Gently drag the list upwards**

By doing this you drag the list upwards a little bit at a time. This touch gesture is also called *scrolling*.

👉 Tap Device

You see various general settings for the device. If you would like to display the battery status percentage in the status bar:

👉 Tap On

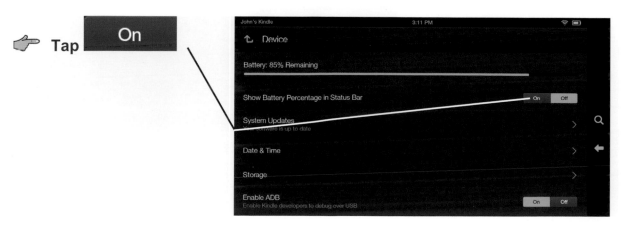

Now the percentage of battery time left is shown in the status bar: ———

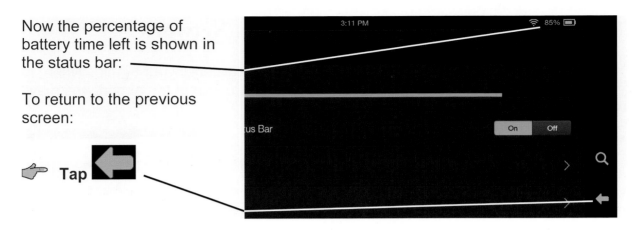

To return to the previous screen:

 **Tap** ⬅

You can also scroll in the opposite direction:

👉 **Gently drag the list downwards** ——

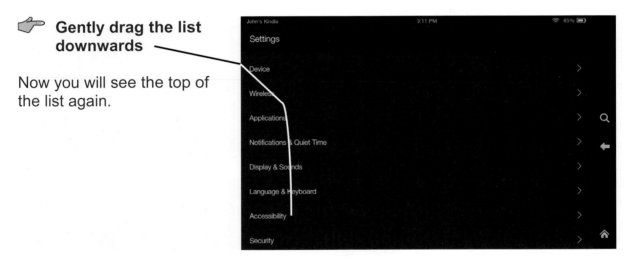

Now you will see the top of the list again.

This is how you quit the *Settings* screen and go back to the Home screen:

👉 **Tap** 🏠

By now you have practiced a few basic operations and touch gestures. Of course there are lots of other touch gestures, such as scrolling sideways, and zooming in and out. These gestures will be discussed in the appropriate chapters, as soon as you need to make use of them.

1.8 Connecting to a Different Wireless Network

You already connected to a Wi-Fi network when you registered your Kindle. When you use your Kindle at a different location, such as at work or at the airport, you may want to connect to a different wireless network.

 Please note:

In order to follow the steps in this section you will need to have access to a different wireless network (Wi-Fi). If you do not (yet) have access, you can just read through this section.

☞ **Open the *Quick Settings* menu** 𝄞²

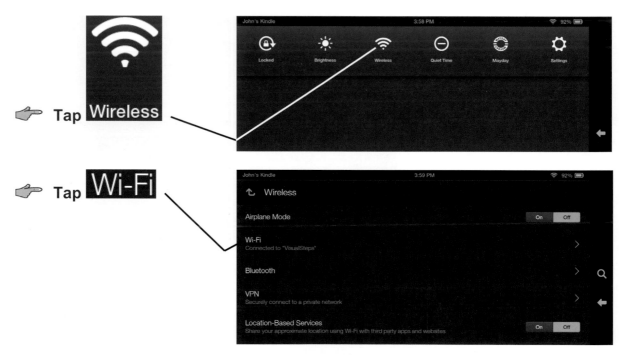

☞ Tap Wireless

☞ Tap Wi-Fi

You see the settings for wireless Internet access:

If necessary, turn Wi-Fi on:

☞ Tap On

👉 **Tap the network you want to use** ⸺

If necessary:

👉 **Enter the required password**

You will be connected to the wireless network:

The [icon] icon on the status bar indicates that there is a connection with a wireless network: ⸺

Here you see which network you are connected to: ⸺

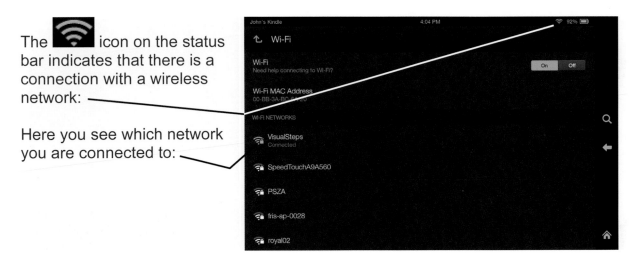

When you turn on Wi-Fi in the future, the system will try to connect automatically to known wireless networks. You can check this by first turning Wi-Fi off:

👉 By **Wi-Fi**, tap **Off**

The Wi-Fi icon  has disappeared from the status bar:

☞ By **Wi-Fi**, tap
On

Wi-Fi will be turned on again.

A connection will be established automatically with the wireless network previously used in your current location:

If you had to enter a password before, it will usually be remembered.

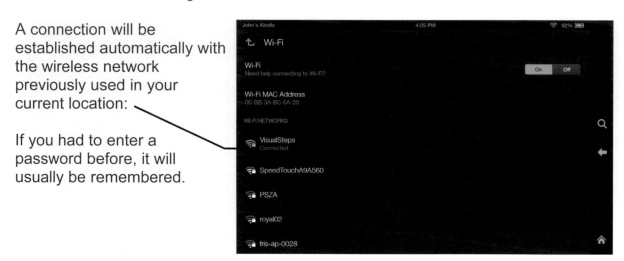

☞ **If you wish, you can turn Wi-Fi off again** 𝒮𝒮4

 Tip

Leaving Wi-Fi turned on
It is a good idea to leave the Wi-Fi connection enabled. This way, you have a permanent Internet connection and will receive all current updates, email messages, etcetera.

☞ **Go back to the Home screen** 𝒮𝒮3

1.9 Connecting to a 3G/4G LTE Network

If your Kindle Fire HDX tablet is suitable for a mobile data network (3G/4G LTE models) you can connect to the Internet using a 3G or 4G network as well.
The 4G network is available in the United States and other countries. Connecting to the mobile data network can be useful when you are in a location where there is no Wi-Fi. You will need to have a data plan or contract set up. If you do not (yet) have this, you can just read through this section.

 Tip

Mobile Internet
Since the Kindle does not have a simlock, you are free to select a mobile Internet provider. Many providers such as AT&T, Verizon Wireless and British Telecom offer data plans for the Kindle, including a micro SIM card. For prepaid mobile Internet plans you can use Virgin Mobile USA, AT&T, Verizon and Vodafone, among others. The prices and conditions are subject to change. Check out the websites of various providers for more information.

A Kindle that is suitable for Wi-Fi and a mobile data network will be fitted with a SIM card tray.

☞ **Place the SIM card in the SIM card tray**

Usually, the Kindle will connect to the network automatically. You may see a few onscreen instructions.

☞ **If necessary, follow the instructions onscreen**

If necessary, you can enable the connection as follows:

☞ **Open the *Quick Settings* menu** ᐭᐭ²

☞ Tap

☞ Tap **Mobile Network**

☞ By , tap **On**

When you disconnect the mobile data network, the Kindle Fire HDX will automatically switch to a Wi-Fi network if available.

Vice versa, when Wi-Fi is disabled, the Kindle automatically switches to the mobile data network. So if you use mobile data, please pay attention to the type of activity you are using it for. Downloading apps or videos can result in high costs.

 Please note:

If you are using cellular data, make sure the data roaming function is disabled. Data roaming means that you can use the network of a different Internet service provider, whenever the network of your own provider is out of reach. If you enable this option abroad, this may result in extremely high costs!

1.10 Updating the Kindle Fire HDX

Amazon updates the Kindle software on a regular basis. These updates may include solutions to several problems, or new features and functions.

Usually these updates are installed automatically. As soon as an update is available, and your Kindle is connected to a Wi-Fi network, the download starts in the background. The update installs after the download is complete and the device is asleep. Your Kindle will restart during the software update. After the restart, the message 'Kindle is upgrading' might appear on the screen.

If you see on the Amazon website or in the news that a new Kindle update is available, you can start the download yourself:

☞ Open the *Quick Settings* menu $\mathscr{B}^2$

☞ Tap **Settings**

☞ **Tap Sync All Content**

You will see the arrows in the icon revolve once. The software update automatically downloads in the background and installs after the download is complete and the device is asleep.

You can also manually check for updates:

☞ **Tap Device**

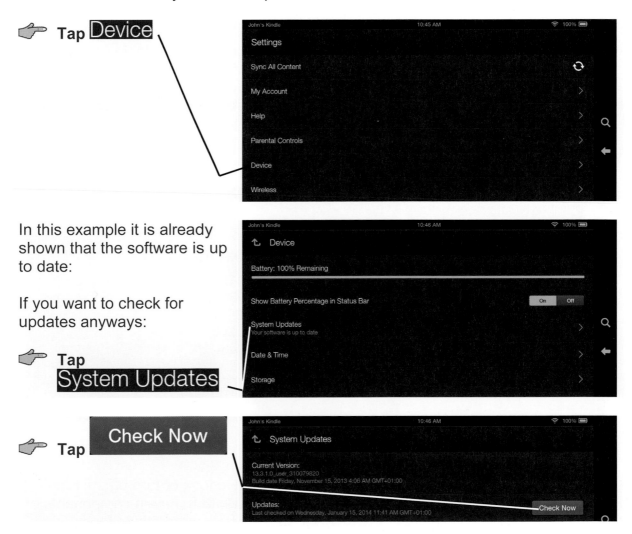

In this example it is already shown that the software is up to date:

If you want to check for updates anyways:

☞ **Tap System Updates**

☞ **Tap Check Now**

If an update is found, this is shown onscreen. In that case, you can follow the instructions.

☞ **Tap**

1.11 Locking or Turning Off the Kindle Fire HDX

If you no longer want to use the Kindle, you can lock the device or completely turn it off. If you lock the device, the Kindle will still be active, but consume less battery power. If you have turned off Wi-Fi, it will hardly use any power at all. This is how you lock the Kindle Fire HDX:

☞ **Briefly press the Power button** ⏻

The screen will be turned off and no longer react to touch gestures.

If you want to turn off the Kindle Fire HDX altogether, you need to do this:

☞ **Press the Power button** ⏻ **and keep it pressed in until you see the *Do you want to shut down your Kindle?* window**

You need to confirm this action:

☞ **Tap**

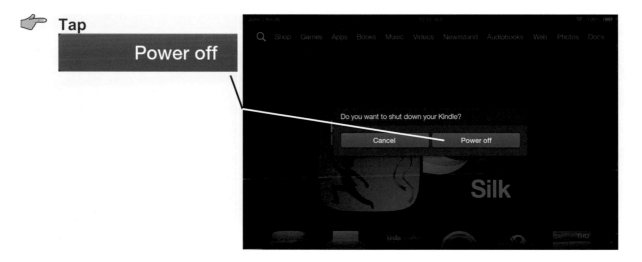

Power off

The Kindle Fire HDX will be turned off.

In future, you can decide for yourself whether you want to lock or turn off the Kindle Fire HDX. In this chapter you have become acquainted with the main components of the Kindle Fire HDX. You have learned how to use the basic operations for working with the device, such as turning it on and off, adjusting settings, using the onscreen keyboard, and how to connect it to the Internet. In the *Background Information* and the *Tips* on the next pages you will find additional information.

1.12 Background Information

Dictionary

Airplane mode	In this mode your Kindle Fire HDX can no longer transmit or receive Wi-Fi or Bluetooth signals.
Amazon account	A combination of an email address and a password, that provides access to the Amazon stores and services.
Android	A mobile operating system used for smartphones, tablets and other types of devices. *Android* is not connected to a specific manufacturer, *Google* offers free use of the *Android* software to manufacturers of mobile devices. Like many manufacturers, Amazon has built its own user interface for the Kindle to make it look like the well-known Kindle e-reader. Due to the variations in user interfaces, the tablets of different manufacturers will look different and operate in different ways, even though they use the same version of the *Android* operating system.
Appstore, Amazon Appstore	An online shop where you can acquire new apps (paid or for free) for the Kindle Fire HDX.
App	Short for *application*, a program for the Kindle Fire HDX.
Bluetooth	An open communication standard for short-distance wireless connections between devices. For example, with Bluetooth you can connect a wireless keyboard or a headset to the Kindle Fire HDX.
Carousel	The Carousel on the Home screen displays your most recently viewed books, videos, music and apps.
E-book	An electronic book is a book-length publication in digital form, consisting of text, images, or both, that can be read on computers or other electronic devices like e-readers.

- Continue on the next page -

E-reader	An e-book reader, also called an e-book device or e-reader, is a mobile electronic device that is designed primarily for the purpose of reading digital e-books and periodicals.
Home screen	The first screen you see when you turn on and unlock the Kindle Fire HDX.
Kindle Fire HDX	Third generation of Amazon's Kindle Fire line of color touchscreen tablet computers. It is available in two models, 7" and 8.9". The Kindle Fire HD and Kindle Fire are the previous editions.
Library	The section of the Kindle Fire HDX where you store and manage your content. The Kindle Fire HDX has separate libraries for games, apps, books, music, videos, newsstand, audiobooks, web, photos, docs and offers.
Location based services	Various apps use location services to collect and use information about your geographical location. The location information that is collected is not linked to your personal data.
Lock	You can lock the Kindle Fire HDX by turning off the screen with the Power button, if you do not want to use the device for a certain period of time. When the Kindle Fire HDX is locked, nothing will happen when you touch the screen. The playback of music files will continue as usual and you can also use the volume control buttons.
Lock screen	The screen that appears when you turn on the Kindle Fire HDX. You will need to unlock the Kindle Fire HDX on the Lock screen in order to use the device. The Lock screen displays a different advertisement every time you wake the Kindle, if you have the "Special Offers" version. Otherwise you will see a different Lock screen picture.
Notifications	Messages generated by games and apps.
Options bar	The Options bar appears when you are viewing a content library and when you are using an app. It is located at the bottom of the screen, or on the right-hand side when you hold the Kindle Fire HDX in a horizontal position. It may be hidden when some apps are running. You will see different options depending on the library or app you are using.

- Continue on the next page -

Power button   The ⏻ button which you can use to lock, unlock, turn on and turn off the Kindle Fire HDX.

Quick Settings   Hidden menu bar for frequently used settings.

Screen Timeout   A default function in the Kindle Fire HDX that turns off the screen and locks the device if it is not used for a period of five minutes or longer.

Sleep mode   When the screen is turned off and locked. The screen is dark and it does not respond to touch gestures. See also: Lock.

Status bar   Located at the top of the screen. It displays the time, notifications, Bluetooth indicator, Wi-Fi indicator, Location Based Services indicator and battery information.

Tablet, tablet PC   A tablet PC is a computer that does not have a case or keyboard and is operated by a touchscreen.

Wi-Fi   A wireless network for the Internet.

3G   The third generation of standards and technology for mobile phone connections. The higher speed of 3G offers many more options than previous standards. With a 3G connection, you can make and receive phone calls over the Internet.

4G   4G is the fourth generation of standards and technology for mobile phone connections. With 4G connection, you can make and receive phone calls over the Internet, among other things, and it is even faster than 3G. At the time of this writing, 4G was available in the USA and was slowly being introduced to the European market.

Source: Kindle Fire HDX User Guide, Wikipedia

1.13 Tips

 Tip

Display sleep
By default, your Kindle Fire HDX will automatically lock after five minutes of inactivity. This setting saves battery power, but you may prefer to have your tablet stay active a little while longer:

☞ **Open the *Quick Settings* menu** 𝜚𝜚²

👉 **Tap** Settings, Display & Sounds

👉 **Drag the list upwards**

👉 **Tap**
Display Sleep

You will see a screen in which you can set a different duration for the time-out screen to appear:

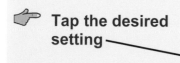 **Tap the desired setting**

Tip

Mute or change notification sounds

Your Kindle will make a sound when a notification is received. A notification is a message generated by an app or a game. For instance, you will be notified when an email is received. You can determine which sounds you want to hear and which sounds you want to turn off. Use the *Settings* screen to change these settings:

☞ **Open the *Quick Settings* menu** 👣²

If you want to turn off all notification sounds:

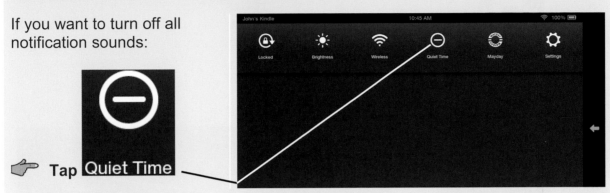

☞ Tap **Quiet Time**

If you want to select the sound that is played when you receive a notification:

☞ **Open the *Quick Settings* menu** 👣²

☞ Tap **Settings**, **Display & Sounds**, **Notification Sound**

You see a long list of sounds:

When you tap a sound, it is played.

☞ **Tap the desired sound**

Tip

Lock with a PIN or password

By default, your Kindle Fire HDX is protected from unintentional data entry. When you turn on the tablet, you need to swipe the padlock to the left to unlock the device. Anyone can do this, of course. But you can protect your tablet even better by using a PIN or password. Here is how you do that:

☞ **Open the *Quick Settings* menu** $\mathscr{QP}^2$

☞ Tap 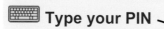 Settings, Security

☞ By
Lock Screen Passw

tap On

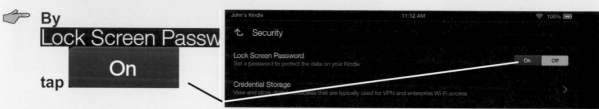

You enter your new PIN. The PIN should have at least four digits:

⌨ **Type your PIN**

☞ Tap **Next**

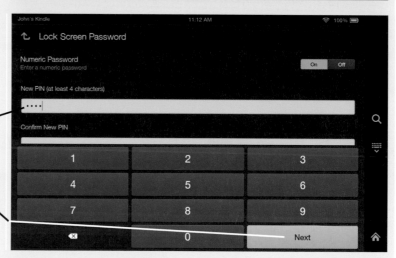

To confirm the PIN:

⌨ **Re-type your PIN**

☞ Tap **Done**

- Continue on the next page -

You have changed the security settings on your tablet. Now you can check to see if this works:

☞ **Tap**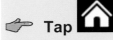

☞ **Lock your Kindle Fire HDX** ⅙⅙5

☞ **Unlock your Kindle Fire HDX** ⅙⅙1
⌨ **Type your PIN**

Instead of a PIN, you can also use a password. In the *Lock Screen Password* window:

☞ **By** , **tap** [Off]
⌨ **Type your password**

Please note: be sure to write this PIN or password down and save it somewhere, in case you forget it.

To remove a PIN or password:

☞ **Open the *Security* screen as described at the beginning of this *Tip***

☞ **By** 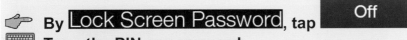, **tap** [Off]
⌨ **Type the PIN or password**
☞ **Tap**

💡 **Tip**

Removing a favorite item
Is an item on the bottom of the Home screen no longer your favorite? Then you can remove it like this:

☞ **Swipe the screen upwards**

☞ **Tap and hold the icon of the item**

☞ **Tap**

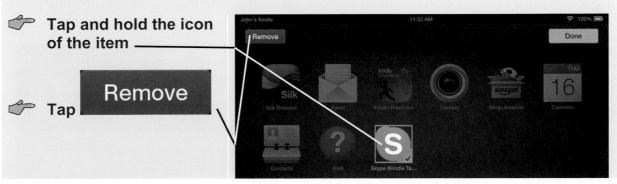

Tip

Airplane Mode
During a flight, you will most likely need to turn Wi-Fi and/or Bluetooth off. At the time of writing, some airlines were offering Wi-Fi on selected flights. In *Airplane Mode*, all signal transmitting functions are suspended. Here is how you activate it:

☞ **Open the *Quick Settings* menu** &⁹²

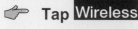

☞ **Tap** Wireless

☞ **By** Airplane Mode**, tap** On

 Tip

Typing hidden special and accented characters
In the default view the letter keys also have a faint character in the top right-hand

corner: . To type @:

 Tap gently on

 **and hold it for a moment**

As soon as you see @ :

☞ **Let the key go**

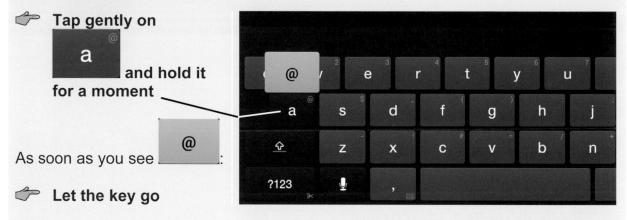

If you hold the key too long, a small window appears with other special characters. To type one of these:

☞ **Tap the character you want to use**

To close the window:

☞ **Tap** ⊗

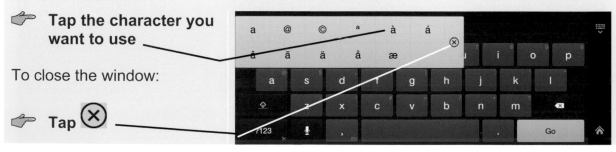

2. Downloading and Reading Books

The very first Kindle developed by Amazon was an e-reader for e-books, newspapers and magazines. The Kindles that came out after that had improved screens and more functions. Today, the Kindle Fire HDX is a multifunctional tablet computer with so many features that you might forget its roots as an e-reader. But the e-reader is still there. Everything that made the previous Kindle e-readers so special has been incorporated in the Kindle Fire HDX.

In this chapter you will learn how to download books from the Kindle *Bookstore* where you have direct access to millions of paid and free titles. You will see how easy it is to read a book, adjust the book settings and add bookmarks.

In this chapter you will also get acquainted with the Cloud Drive, Amazon's free unlimited online storage space for all digital content purchased from the Kindle *Bookstore* and other Amazon.com stores. With the Cloud Drive, you will never run out of storage space on your Kindle Fire HDX.

Tired of reading? Then start listening to your favorite books. In this chapter you will learn about downloading and playing audiobooks.

In this chapter you will learn how to:

- search for books in the *Bookstore*;
- download a free book;
- read and navigate through a book;
- adjust book settings;
- add a bookmark;
- use more ways to navigate;
- download a paid book;
- use the *Books* library;
- remove a book from the device and download it again from the Cloud Drive;
- add highlights and notes;
- use narration.

2.1 Searching for Books in the Bookstore

When you start using your Kindle Fire HDX, the *Books* library is empty. From the *Books* library you can access the full range of e-books in the *Amazon Kindle Bookstore*. This store contains millions of books that you can buy or download for free. If you want to search for a book, you start by opening the *Books* library:

☞ **Unlock or turn on the Kindle Fire HDX** ✂¹

☞ **Tap** Books

In this example, the *Books* library is empty. The *Bookstore* is shown automatically:

You see the top categories in the *Bookstore*:

You will probably see different books on your screen because the online *Bookstore* changes regularly.

☞ **Swipe your finger upwards across the page**

 HELP! I do not see the Bookstore.

If you have already downloaded one or more books to your Kindle, than you will see the *Books* library first. To go to the *Bookstore*:

☞ **Tap** Store >

More books are shown.

👉 **Swipe your finger upwards across the page**

You can also display books per category. To see all categories:

👉 **Tap** **☰ Bookstore**

👉 **Tap** **Browse Categories**

You can scroll down to see more categories:

👉 **Swipe upwards over the list**

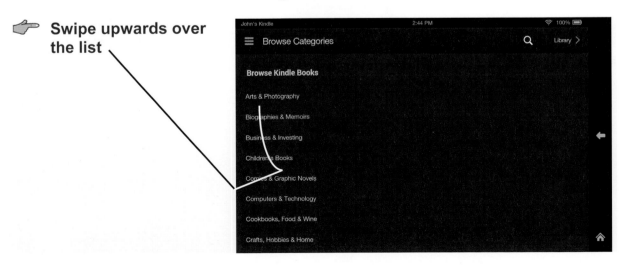

To see all books in a particular category:

☞ **Tap**
Literature & Fiction,
for example

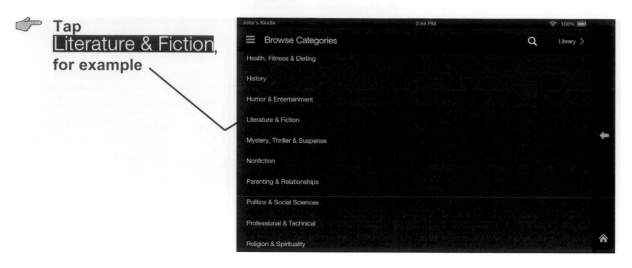

You will see the first books in the category Literature & Fiction. You can scroll down to see more books, but that is not necessary now.

Below each book the price is listed:

★★★★★ (2,472) is the rating for the book given by readers. The number of readers that have rated it is shown in parentheses:

You can use the Search icon to look for a different book category:

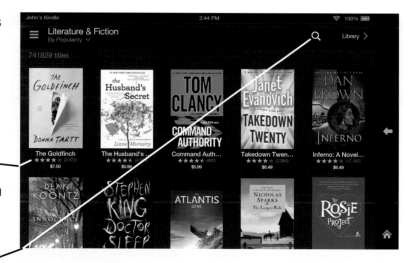

☞ **Tap**

Type: `free classics`

As you type, you will see suggestions for search terms appear:

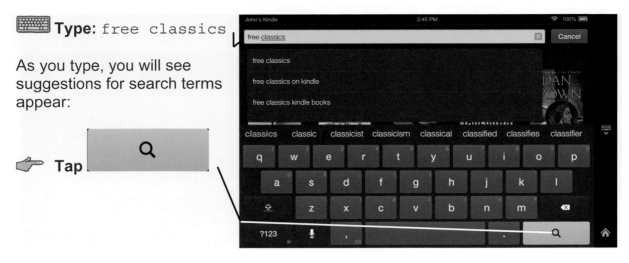

☞ **Tap** Q

💡 **Tip**

List of suggestions
Do you see the search term you need in the list of suggestions, tap it and the search will be performed right away.

In the search results you will find the book *Les Misérables*. *Les Misérables* is the classic work that the successful musical and movie were based on. If you cannot find the book, you can select another free book. You can recognize free books by the label **Free**.

☞ **If necessary, swipe your finger upwards**

☞ **Tap** Les Misérables (...

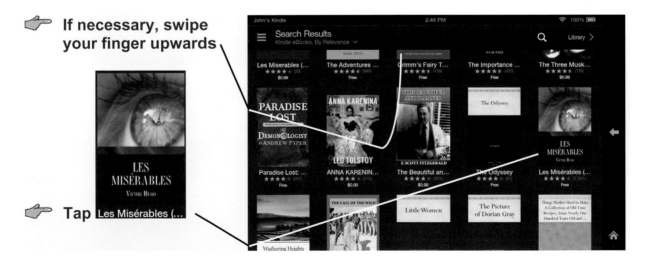

To download this free book:

☞ **Tap**

> **Buy for Free**

If you wish, you can find
more information about the
book here:

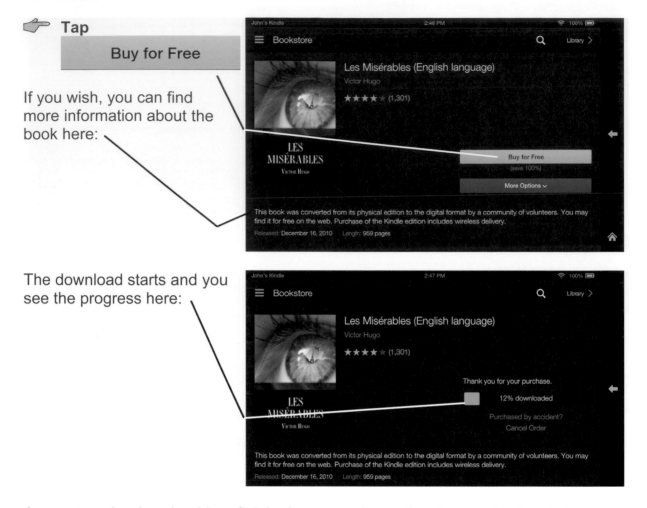

The download starts and you
see the progress here:

As soon as the download has finished, you can leave the store and return to the
Home screen:

☞ **Tap** 🏠

The book has been added to the Carousel:

2.2 Reading a Book

Reading a book on the Kindle Fire HDX is very easy. First you open the book:

 Tap

You see the title page:

To go to the next page:

 Tap the right-hand side of the page

VOLUME I.—FANTINE.

PREFACE

So long as there shall exist, by virtue of law and custom, decrees of damnation pronounced by society, artificially creating hells amid the civilization of earth, and adding the element of human fate to divine destiny; so long as the three great problems of the century—the degradation of man through pauperism, the corruption of woman through hunger, the crippling

Learning reading speed   1%

You can also use a swiping or flicking gesture to go to the next page:

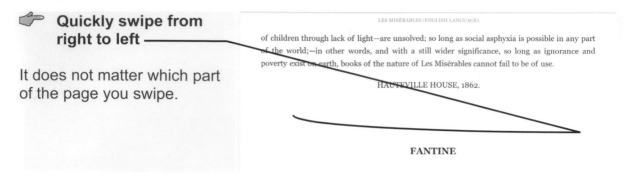

☞ **Quickly swipe from right to left**

It does not matter which part of the page you swipe.

You see the next page. To go back one page, either tap the left-hand side of the page or reverse the swiping gesture:

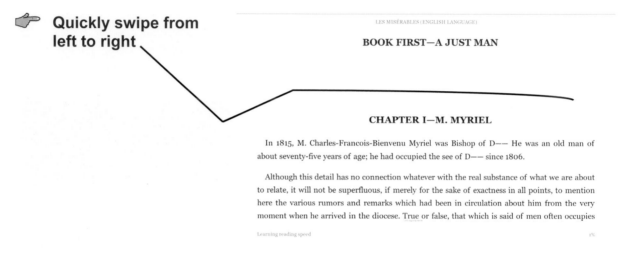

☞ **Quickly swipe from left to right**

2.3 Adjusting Book Settings

You can customize the way the book is displayed on screen. This is how you display the menu bar:

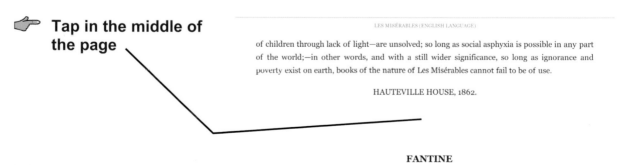

☞ **Tap in the middle of the page**

Two new bars will appear, one at the top and one at the bottom:

Menu bar:

Location bar:

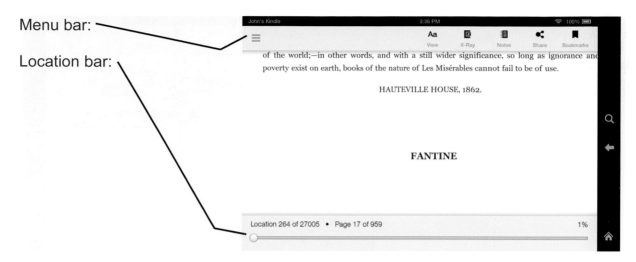

Location numbering

Instead of page numbers, Amazon uses *Location numbering*: Location 264 of 27005. Page numbers do not work well in an e-book. For example, if you hold the Kindle upright (portrait mode) while reading, page 26 fits on one page. But if you hold it sideways, the page is shorter, and you need two pages for page 26. The same thing applies when you increase or decrease the font size, or read the book on a smaller device.

With Location numbering, an e-book file is divided into small parts of 128 bytes (about 125 characters) that are all numbered. When you look up a location number in the same book on different devices, you will see the same part of the book.

Some publishers do offer page numbering in their Kindle books. In that case you see both the location number and the page number that corresponds with the page in the actual book: Location 264 of 27005 • Page 17 of 959.

You can use the Menu bar to adjust the font size and several other settings:

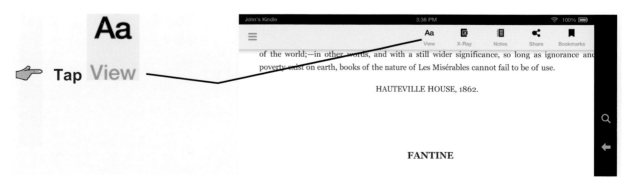

You can increase the font size like this:

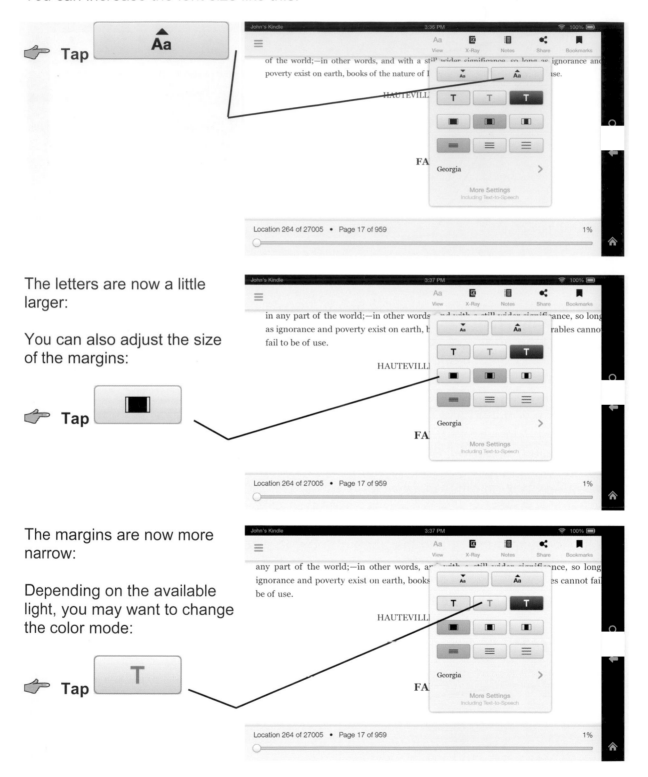

☞ **Tap**

The letters are now a little larger:

You can also adjust the size of the margins:

☞ **Tap**

The margins are now more narrow:

Depending on the available light, you may want to change the color mode:

☞ **Tap**

The page color has changed to beige with dark brown letters. You can close the settings panel:

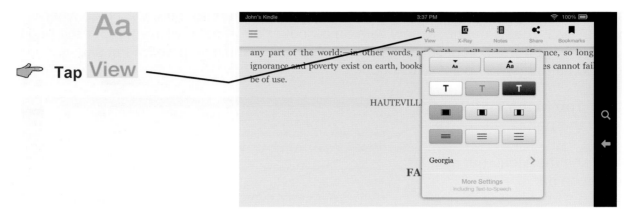

👉 **Tap** View

You can hide the Menu and Location bar like this:

👉 **Tap in the middle of the page**

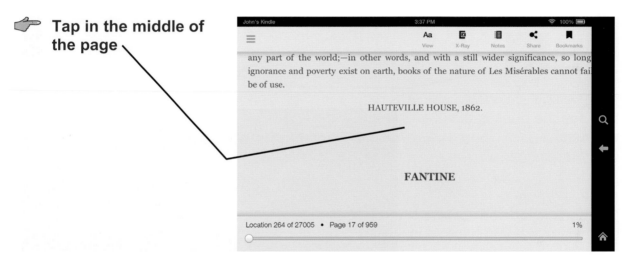

Now you see the full page with the new settings:

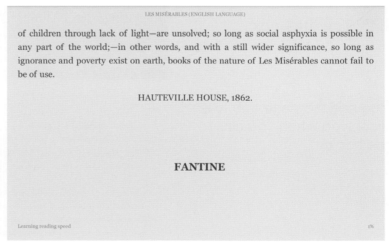

2.4 Adding a Bookmark

When you read a regular book, you can insert a bookmark to mark the place where you are at. That is not necessary with an e-book. Your Kindle will remember the page you had open when you closed the book. You can test this yourself. First skip ahead to about the halfway point of this book:

☞ **Tap in the middle of the page**

You see the Menu bar and Location bar:

☞ **Drag the slider ◯ to the middle**

☞ **Tap**

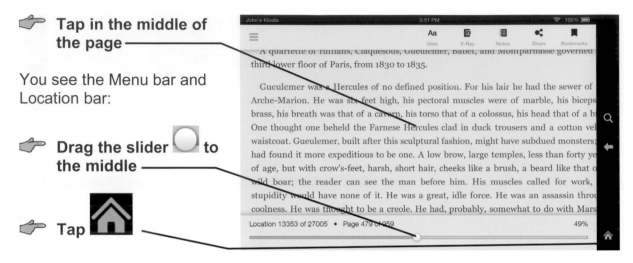

You see the book in the Carousel:

The book is labeled **49%** to indicate that you have read half of it:

☞ **Tap the book**

You see the page that was displayed when you closed the book:

LES MISÉRABLES (ENGLISH LANGUAGE)

A quartette of ruffians, Claquesous, Gueulemer, Babet, and Montparnasse governed the third lower floor of Paris, from 1830 to 1835.

Gueulemer was a Hercules of no defined position. For his lair he had the sewer of the Arche-Marion. He was six feet high, his pectoral muscles were of marble, his biceps of brass, his breath was that of a cavern, his torso that of a colossus, his head that of a bird. One thought one beheld the Farnese Hercules clad in duck trousers and a cotton velvet waistcoat. Gueulemer, built after this sculptural fashion, might have subdued monsters; he had found it more expeditious to be one. A low brow, large temples, less than forty years of age, but with crow's-feet, harsh, short hair, cheeks like a brush, a beard like that of a wild boar; the reader can see the man before him. His muscles called for work, his stupidity would have none of it. He was a great, idle force. He was an assassin through

Still it is sometimes handy to add a bookmark yourself such as when you want to mark a specific part of the book. To place a bookmark on this page:

👉 **Tap in the middle of the page**

👉 **Tap** Bookmarks

👉 **Tap** ⊕ Add Bookmark

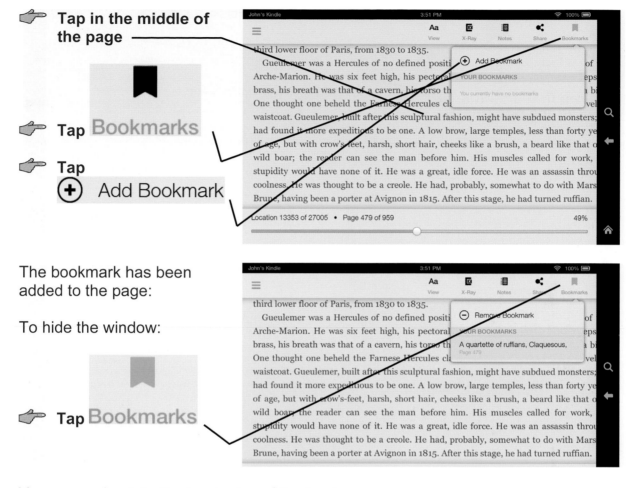

The bookmark has been added to the page:

To hide the window:

👉 **Tap** Bookmarks

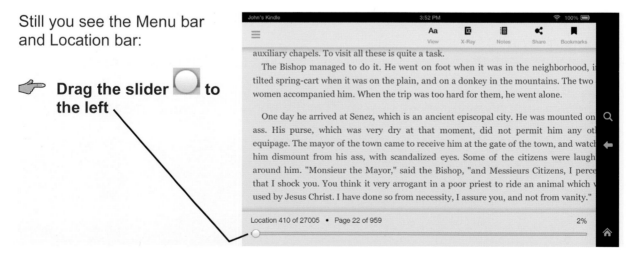

You can go back to the beginning of the book:

Still you see the Menu bar and Location bar:

👉 **Drag the slider ◯ to the left**

The Kindle Fire HDX keeps track of all the bookmarks you add to a book. You can look up a bookmark like this:

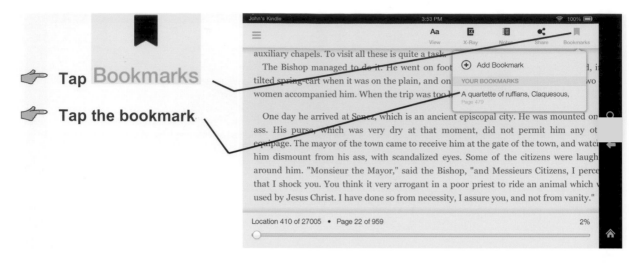

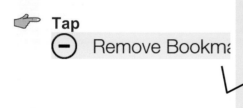 👉 Tap Bookmarks

👉 **Tap the bookmark**

The Kindle jumps to the page you bookmarked:

To remove the bookmark:

👉 **Tap**
   ⊖ Remove Bookmark

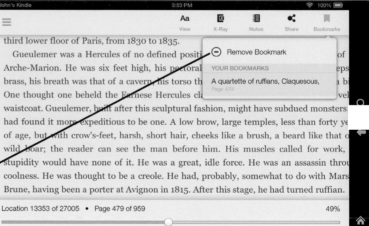

 Tip
Bookmark icon
When you are reading a book and the Menu bar and Location bar are not shown,

you can see the blue bookmark icon 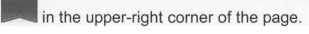 in the upper-right corner of the page.

2.5 More Ways to Navigate

So far you have learned how to flip through the pages of a book and how to use the Location bar, but there is even another way of navigating through a book:

☞ **Tap**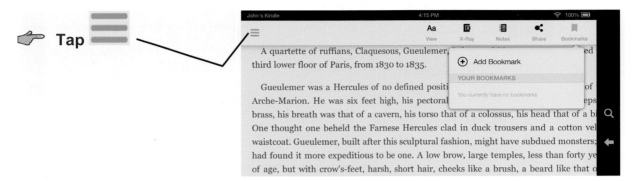

You will see a navigation screen based on the table of contents of the book. Most publishers add a similar table of contents to their e-books.

☞ **Tap**
BOOK THIRD. — THE GR

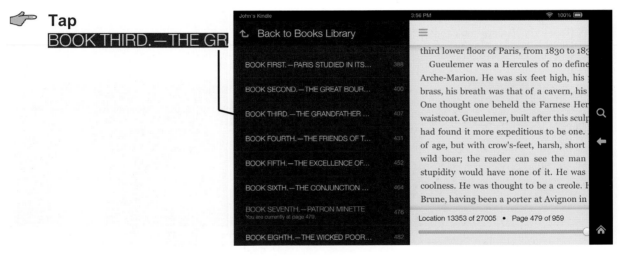

The book opens at the beginning of the part you selected:

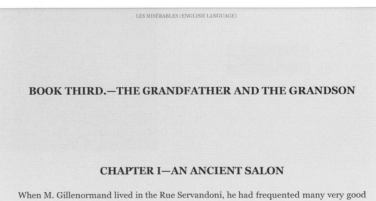

You can go back to the Home screen:

☞ **Tap in the middle of the page** ——

☞ **Tap** 🏠

You will see the Home screen again.

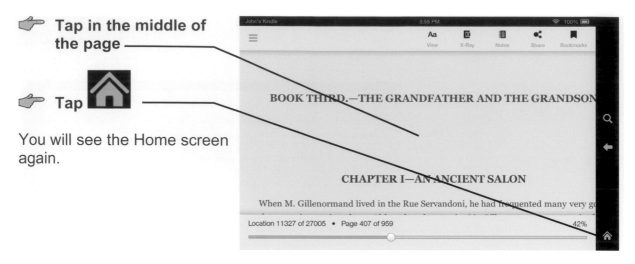

2.6 Downloading a Paid Book

Even though there are a lot of free e-books for your Kindle Fire HDX, you will probably want to buy a new book at some point. Here is how you do that:

☞ Tap **Books**

You see one book in the library:

☞ Tap **Store ›**

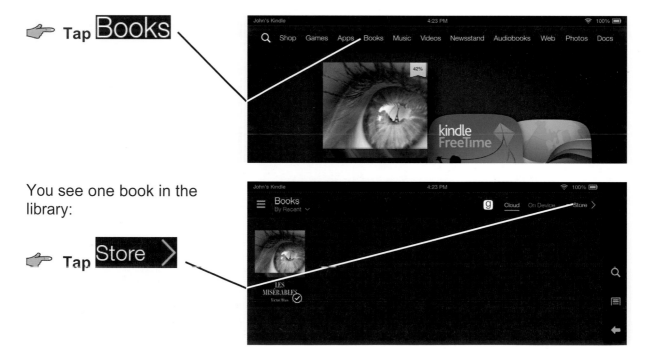

You can search for a particular writer:

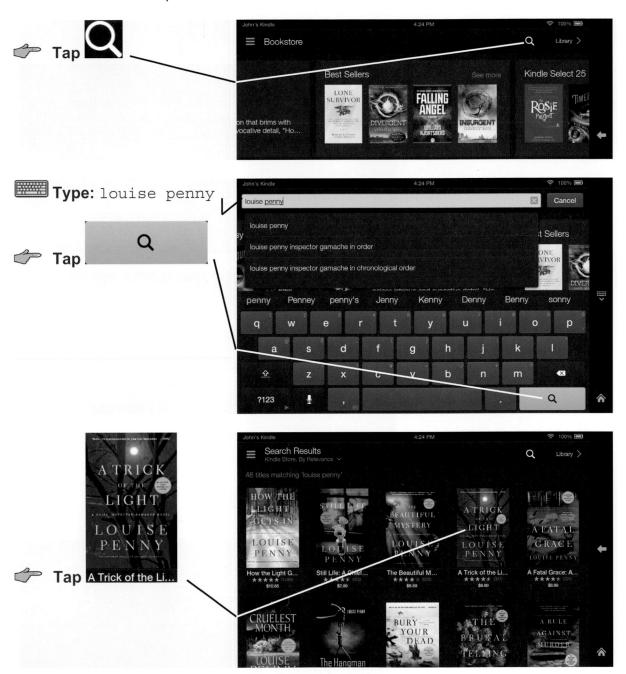

☞ Tap 🔍

⌨ Type: `louise penny`

☞ Tap 🔍

☞ Tap A Trick of the Li...

➥ Please note:

In the next section we will actually purchase a book. You can decide for yourself if you want to continue with the steps to purchase the book. Of course, you do not need to buy the exact same book as in this example. You can also just continue reading to understand how purchasing and downloading a book works or buy another free book.

Please note:

You can only follow the steps explained below if you have added a credit card or credit from a gift card to your *Amazon* account.

☞ **Tap**   Buy for $8.89

Your purchase is processed and downloaded:

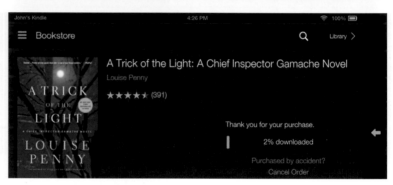

As soon as you see the button 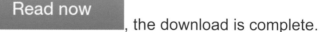, the download is complete. You can return to the library:

☞ **Tap** Library >

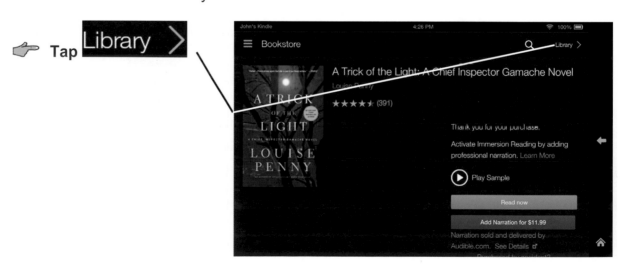

The book has been added to your library:

 Tip

Returning a purchase

Kindle books you purchase from the *Bookstore* are eligible for return and refund if you return the book within seven days of the date of purchase. Once a refund is issued, you will no longer have access to the item. In the *Tips* at the end of this chapter you can read how to return a book.

2.7 Using the Books Library

The *Books* library has various handy features that are especially interesting when you have a lot of books.

By default, your books are sorted by the date they were added, the most recent first:

You can also sort your books by author or by title:

 Tap

The books are now sorted by last name of the author, in alphabetical order. Instead of the default grid view that looks like a bookshelf, you can also display the books in a list:

☞ **Tap**

☞ **Tap** List view

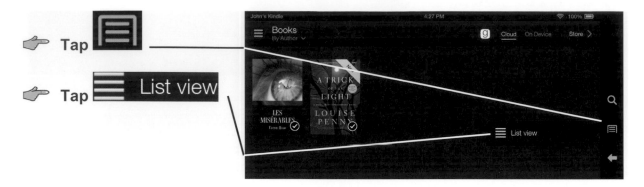

The books are displayed in a list. To go back to the grid view:

☞ **Tap**

☞ **Tap** Grid view

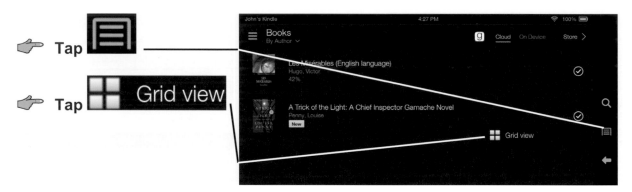

In the library, you can open a book like this:

☞ **Tap a book, for**

example

You will see the first page of the book. To go back to the library:

👉 **Tap**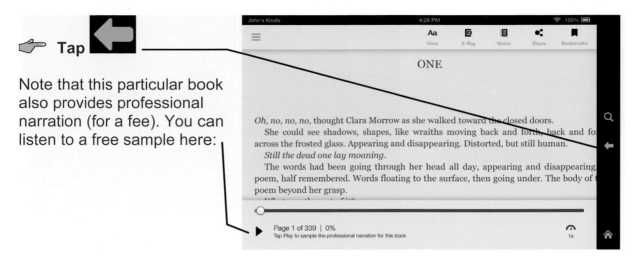

Note that this particular book also provides professional narration (for a fee). You can listen to a free sample here:

You see the library again.

At the top of the page you see the buttons **Cloud   On Device**:

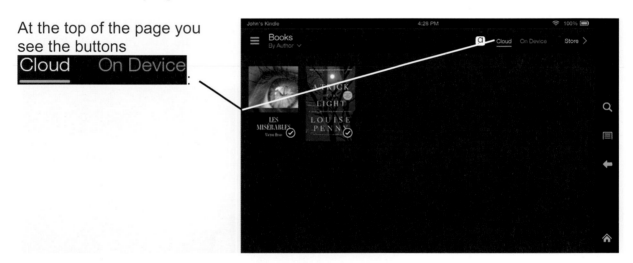

These buttons indicate the two locations where your e-books can be stored. *On Device* means the internal memory of your Kindle Fire HDX. *Cloud* means the Cloud Drive, the free unlimited online storage for all digital content purchased from Amazon that comes with your *Amazon* account. If you use your *Amazon* account with other devices, you will see the books you downloaded with those devices in the *Cloud Books* library as well.

The two books you
downloaded are stored in the
cloud:

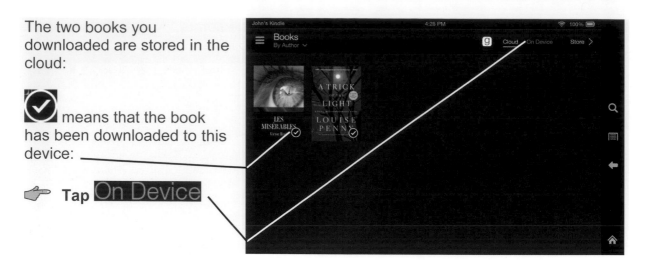

✅ means that the book
has been downloaded to this
device: ————————

☞ Tap On Device

💡 Tip

Cloud Drive

In addition to the unlimited free space for digital items you purchase from Amazon,
you can also add your own files to the Cloud Drive. Your Cloud Drive has 5GB of
free space for that. In *Chapter 6 Transferring Files to the Kindle Fire HDX* you can
read more about the Cloud Drive.

In the *On Device* library you
see two free dictionaries that
are pre-loaded on your Kindle
Fire HDX: ————————

These dictionaries cannot be
saved to your cloud.

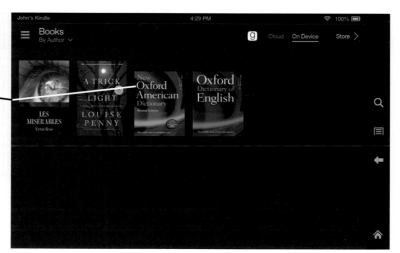

2.8 Removing a Book

You can keep your Kindle Fire HDX organized by removing the books you have read from your *Books* library:

☞ **Tap and hold**

A menu appears:

☞ **Tap**

Remove from Dev

The book is removed from the device:

Open the cloud:

☞ **Tap** Cloud

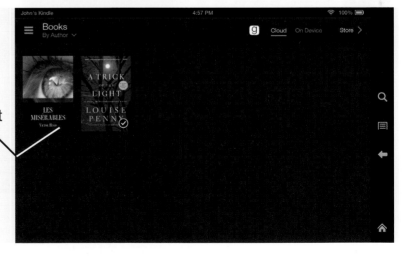

As you see, the book is still available in the cloud:

The book does not have a checkmark ✅, indicating it is not stored on your device:

If you want to read the book again, you have to download it to your device:

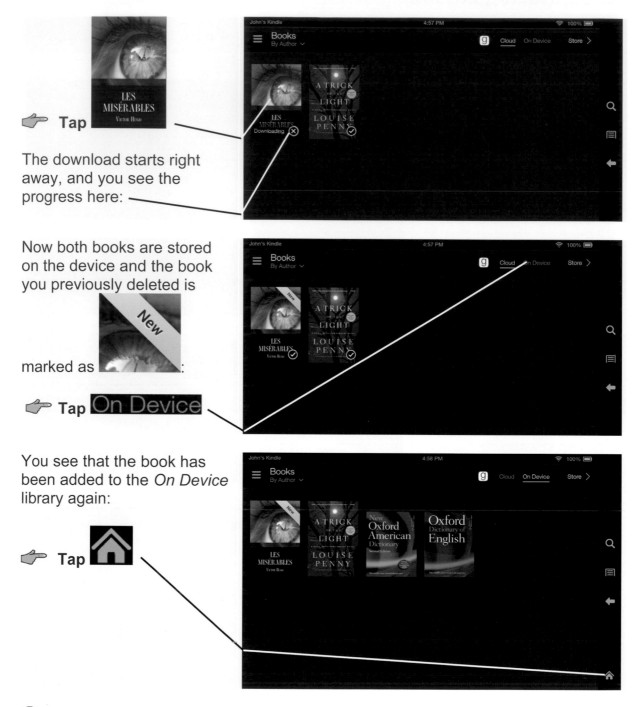

☞ **Tap**

The download starts right away, and you see the progress here:

Now both books are stored on the device and the book you previously deleted is marked as   :

☞ **Tap** On Device

You see that the book has been added to the *On Device* library again:

☞ **Tap**

💡 **Tip**

Permanently remove book from Cloud Drive
In the *Tips* at the end of this chapter you can read how to permanently remove a book from the *Cloud Books* library on the Cloud Drive.

2.9 Adding Highlights and Notes

Aside from bookmarks, you can also add highlights and notes to a book. First you need to select the text you want to highlight:

☞ **Open the *Les Misérables* book** ✂⁶

Select a few words or a sentence so that you have something to practice with. In the example shown, we have selected the first sentence from Chapter 1:

☞ **Tap and drag over the text you wish to select**

For a more precise selection:

☞ **Drag ◣ and ◢ to the desired location**

To add a highlight:

☞ **Tap the desired color**

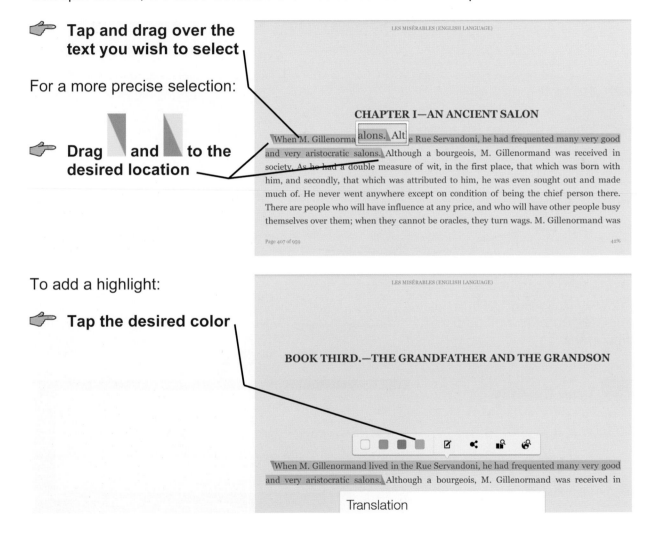

The selection is highlighted:

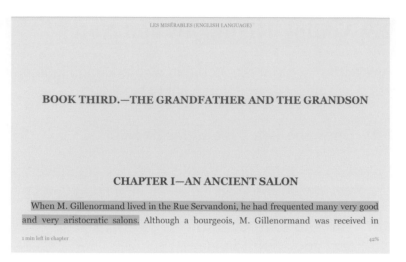

☞ **Go to the next page** 🐾⁷

☞ **Select another bit of text**

To add a note:

👉 **Tap**

Note that in this example the text is also searched by Wikipedia, the free online encyclopedia as well as a dictionary:

⌨ **Type the note**

To hide the keyboard:

👉 **Tap** ∨

👉 **Tap**

Save

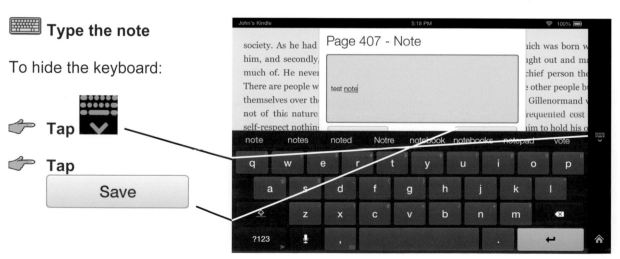

The section is automatically highlighted in yellow and a small icon 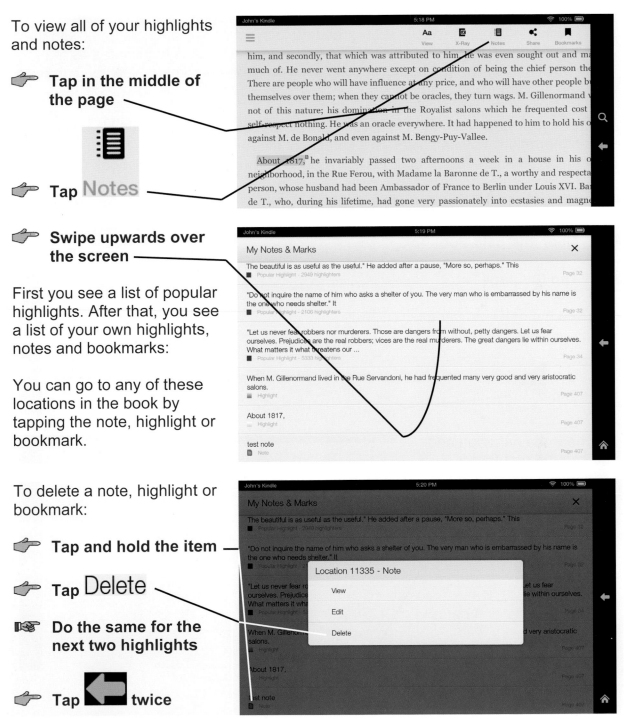 is added. You can tap to view and edit your note.

To view all of your highlights and notes:

☞ **Tap in the middle of the page**

☞ **Tap Notes**

☞ **Swipe upwards over the screen**

First you see a list of popular highlights. After that, you see a list of your own highlights, notes and bookmarks:

You can go to any of these locations in the book by tapping the note, highlight or bookmark.

To delete a note, highlight or bookmark:

☞ **Tap and hold the item**

☞ **Tap Delete**

☞ **Do the same for the next two highlights**

☞ **Tap ⬅ twice**

The highlights have been deleted and you will see the library once more.

2.10 Narration

Amazon is working together with *Audible* to add paid professional narration to a growing selection of Kindle books. A new option has become available called *Immersion reading*. It basically allows readers to synchronize a Kindle book with the *Audible* audio version of that work. While you read, the book is highlighted as the audio track moves along. On the website www.amazon.com/immersion you can read more about immersion reading.

The book that was purchased in *section 2.6 Downloading a Paid Book* also offers this form of narration. You can listen to a sample of the narration for free. If you want to hear more, you can decide later to download the narration for the full book (for a fee).

You can listen to the free sample like this.

☞ **Open the paid book** ✂️⁶

👉 **Tap the page**

You see the option to sample the professional narration.

👉 **Tap** ▶️

You hear the narration and you see the real-time highlighting on the page:

To pause the narration:

👉 **Tap** ⏸️

To hide the Location bar and Menu bar:

👉 **Tap in the middle of the page**

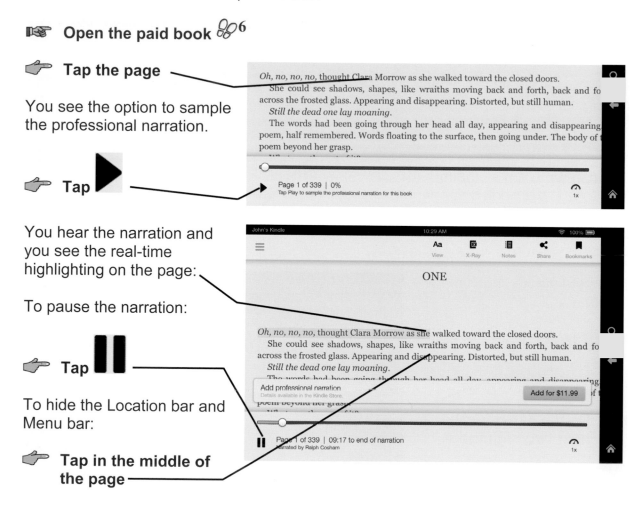

If you wish to purchase the narration for the complete book, tap **Add for $11.99**. The download will be started and when it is completed, the time shown until the end of the sample narration will be removed.

It is not necessary to keep the *Books* app open to be able to listen to the audiobook. If you go back to the Home screen and open another app, the narration will continue. Even if you lock the screen, you can still listen to the audiobook.
If you read without narration, no matter what page you are on when you click the play button again, immersion reading will start from where you left off reading. This new function called *Whispersync for voice* lets you switch back and forth between a Kindle book and the *Audible* audiobook without losing your place. You can read more about *Whispersync for voice* in the *Tips* at the end of this chapter.

☞ **Go back to the Home screen** 🐾³

☞ **Lock or turn off the Kindle Fire HDX** 🐾⁵

In this chapter you have learned how to download, read and organize books on your Kindle Fire HDX.

2.11 Background Information

Dictionary

Audible	Audible.com is an Internet provider of spoken audio entertainment, information, and educational programming. *Audible* sells digital audiobooks, radio and TV programs, and audio versions of magazines and newspapers. *Audible* is a subsidiary of Amazon.
Audiobook	A recording of a book or text being read.
Bookmark	Feature you can use to mark a page of a book for further analysis.
Books library	The section of the Kindle Fire HDX where you store and manage your e-books. The Kindle Fire HDX has separate libraries for games, apps, books, music, videos, newsstand, audiobooks, web, photos, docs and offers.
Cloud, Cloud Drive	The section of the Cloud Drive where your e-books are stored. It contains free unlimited online storage for all digital content purchased from Amazon that comes with your *Amazon* account. The Cloud Drive also contains 5GB free storage for files you upload yourself.
Immersion Reading	Reading and listening to professional narration (an audiobook version) at the same time. Real-time highlighting makes it easy to keep your place in the book.
Kindle Bookstore	Part of the Amazon.com web store dedicated to Kindle books.
Location, Location bar	The location on a Kindle is a way to keep track of your reading progress in a book in the absence of page numbers. The Location bar can be displayed at the bottom of the screen on each e-book page. As you read the book, the progress bar will display a percentage that indicates how much of the book you have read.

- Continue on the next page -

Menu bar	Bar with different options that can be displayed at the top of the screen on each e-book page.
Whispersync for Voice	Function that allows you to read or listen to a book on multiple devices without losing your place. *Whispersync for Voice* syncs your Kindle book and *Audible* audiobook positions to the cloud. In addition to remembering position, *Whispersync for Voice* keeps your notes and bookmarks across devices as well.
X-Ray	Function that quickly scans a book for characters, places and other terms that are often mentioned in the book. You can see where these items are mentioned and also view more detailed information from Wikipedia.

Source: Kindle Fire HDX User Guide and Wikipedia

Whispersync for Voice
With *Whispersync for Voice*, you can read or listen to a book on multiple devices, without losing your place. *Whispersync for Voice* syncs your Kindle book and *Audible* audiobook positions to the cloud. In addition to remembering position, *Whispersync for Voice* keeps your notes and bookmarks across devices as well.

Whispersync for Voice is available when reading on:
- all Kindle e-Ink readers
- all Kindle tablets
- all Kindle reading apps

And when listening on:
- the *Audible* app for iPhone and *Android*
- all Kindle tablets

2.12 Tips

 Tip

Exploring a book using X-Ray

With *X-Ray* you can easily find chapters and locations about the characters, places and other terms mentioned in the book. You can also view more detailed information from Wikipedia and Shelfari, Amazon's community-powered encyclopedia for book lovers. This is how it works:

 Tap in the middle of the page

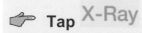 **Tap** X-Ray

You see the characters and locations that are mentioned on this page:

To show all the characters and locations in the book:

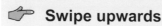 **Swipe upwards**

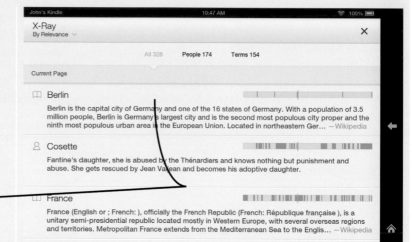

You see a list of all the characters in the book:

The grey/blue bar shows where the character in the book is mentioned:

 Tap a character

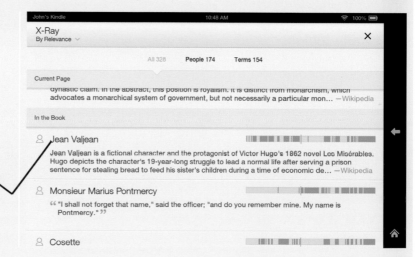

- Continue on the next page -

You see a description of the character, with a link to the ⓒ Full Wikipedia Article:

Here you see a list of excerpts in the book that mention the character:

👉 **Tap** ⬆

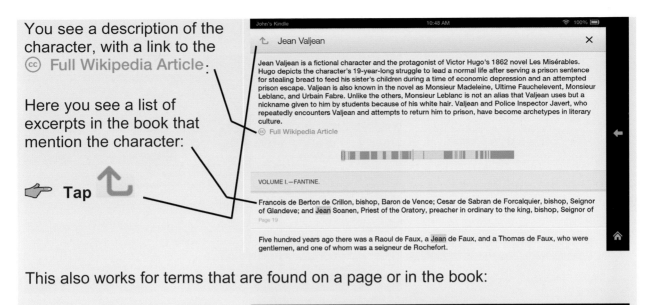

This also works for terms that are found on a page or in the book:

👉 **Tap Terms 154**

If you tap a term, you see a description of the term:

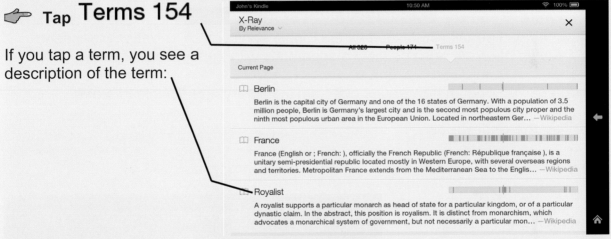

Please note: X-Ray is not available for all Kindle books.

 Tip

Audiobooks
Your Kindle Fire HDX contains a separate library for audiobooks with a link to the *Audiobooks Store*. To open the *Audiobooks Store* from the Home screen:

👉 Tap **Audiobooks**
👉 Tap **Store >**

The *Audiobooks Store* looks a lot like the *Bookstore.* It can be navigated and searched in the same way.

- Continue on the next page -

Once you have found the audiobook you are interested in:

To sign up for a paid subscription:

☞ **Tap**

> Get this Free

Or to buy the audiobook:

☞ **Tap**

> Buy for $27.54

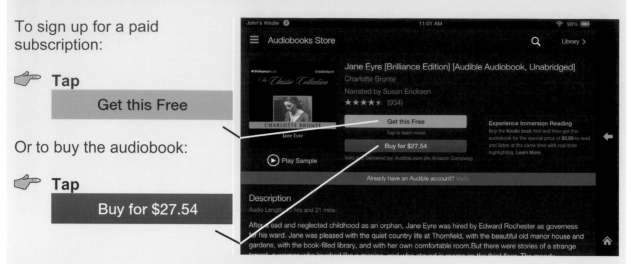

Please note: if you see **Experience Immersion Reading**, you can get a better deal on the audiobook when you buy the Kindle book first. A narration purchased with a Kindle book can also be played separately with the audiobook player.

As soon as you open a new audiobook from the library, the download starts:

☞ **Tap the audiobook**

You see the audiobook player:

Drag the slider ⬤ in the scrubber bar to find the desired position in the book:

Use 🔄 to go back 30 seconds:

Pause the audiobook with ⏸ :

Use 🔖 to add a bookmark:

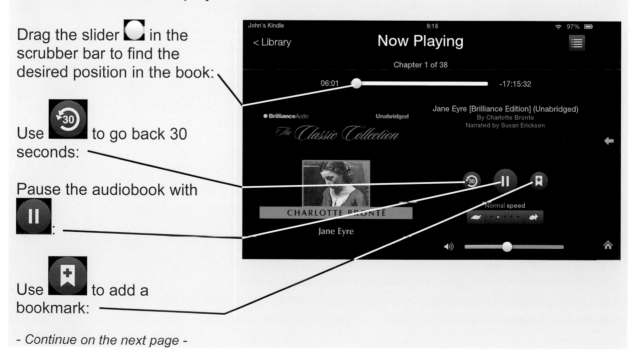

- Continue on the next page -

: display chapters.

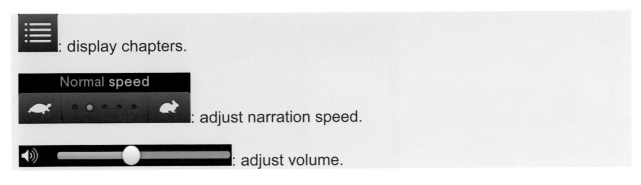 : adjust narration speed.

: adjust volume.

💡 Tip

Newsstand

The *Newsstand* library is the place to read magazines and newspapers that you buy and download from the *Newsstand* store. You can buy separate issues or start a subscription and have each edition delivered to you automatically.

👉 Tap

👉 **If necessary, tap** Store ⟩

The *Newsstand* contains two types of content: Kindle editions and apps.

You see that the *Newsroom* store looks a lot like the *Bookstore*:

Apps are denoted by square icons:

Kindle editions are rectangular:

Apps are custom-built readers especially designed for the Kindle. These readers have good-looking graphics, comfortable navigation and often offer extra's like video. You can download the app of the magazine or newspaper for free, then download separate issues or start a subscription from within the app. In *Chapter 8 Downloading and Managing Apps* you can read more about downloading apps.

- Continue on the next page -

To download a Kindle edition newspaper:

☞ **Tap**

> **Buy Issue $0.75**

The download starts right away. To read the newspaper after that:

☞ **Tap**

> **Read now**

Kindle editions are limited in their design. In this newspaper you see a list of articles:

☞ **Tap**

☞ **Tap an article**

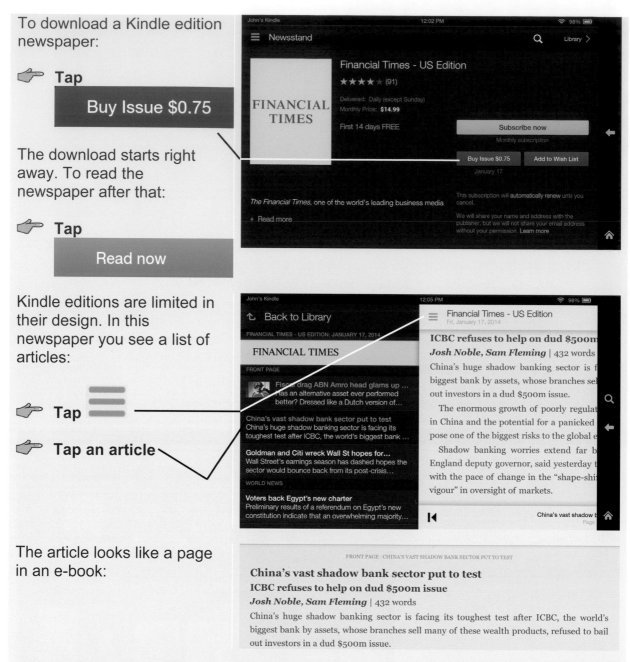

The article looks like a page in an e-book:

A Kindle edition magazine is shrunk to fit on the screen. You can zoom in on a page the same way you zoom in on a website (see *Chapter 3 Surfing with Your Kindle Fire HDX*).

You can flip through the pages the same way you turn the pages of an e-book.

☞ **Tap in the middle of the screen**

- Continue on the next page -

With 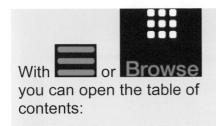 or you can open the table of contents:

On a page with a lot of text, you can zoom in like this:

 Double-tap the page

Please note: double-tap means tap the same location twice in rapid succession.

The text will now fill the screen.

To return:

 Double-tap the page

the road less traveled, **you'll get more out of your trip by using Chase Sapphire** *Preferred®* **and earning 2X the points on travel and dining.**

AUSTRALIAN URBANITY

Vibrant Melbourne might not see the visitor traffic of Sydney, but it has all the attributes of a world-class city: a wealth of culture, charming streets to stroll, sophisticated restaurants, and a high-energy hipster buzz. Focus on music and shopping and you will come away loving this town. Plan your trip to coincide with one of the city's many music festivals. You'll discover great homegrown talent here. Boutiques brim with fashions produced by young Melbourne designers while craft galleries showcase the work of regional artisans. Be sure to hit the Block Arcade, an extravaganza of 19th-century architectural design as well as retail bliss, with shop windows dressed to the nines. Come Sunday morning, hop on a tram and head to Camberwell Market, a patchwork of more than 350 vendors offering up all manner of collectibles. Besides being a shopping wonderland, Camberwell is about heart. Donations made at the gate go straight to charity,

BHUTAN MOUNTAINS

Tucked into the eastern stretch of the Himalaya, the best way to explore Bhutan—one of the planet's most well-preserved ecotourism areas—is to hike its wonderful terrain. With villages that hold on to tradition and monasteries that embody serenity, the bustle that has become Asia is held at bay. Make your home base in Phobjika, a lush high-country valley (10,000 feet) favored by the endangered black-necked cranes that winter here. Spend a morning at the Gangtey Gonpa monastery, where the skills of Bhutan's greatest artisans are in full flower. Continue the thread of authenticity by staying at the 16-room, no TV, no Wi-Fi Dewachen Hotel, whose staff can lead you to the best treks. At the end of the day, unwind with a traditional hot stone bath and dinner at the hotel, where the chef can be relied upon for tasty traditional Bhutanese fare. Nutty red rice, which can be cultivated only in high-altitude locations, and chili peppers—you will

CHILEAN WINE COUNTRY

Begin in thoroughly modern, skyscraper-studded Santiago, a capital city that has more than its fair share of charming boutique hotels. Dine out (late, as is the local custom), mindful that the fine Chilean wine being served will be spotlighted during the rest of your visit. Wine grapes have been grown here since the 16th century. Today some 250 vineyards flourish, producing fine wines that are more than holding their own at international wine competitions. Within a three-hour drive of Chile's bustling capital is the postcard-pretty Colchagua Valley, where some of the country's most prized grapes grow. Wine, though, is but one facet of the area's offerings. Also on the list are exhilarating outdoor activities, from hiking and fishing to horseback riding and, yes, surfing. Thermal springs and spas add a delightfully indulgent note to a wine-country adventure. You can relax knowing you'll earn 2X points on travel and dining with **Chase** Sapphire *Preferred®*, no matter where

---

💡 **Tip**

Removing a book from the Cloud Drive

In this chapter you have learned how to delete a book from your device and how to download it again from your Cloud Drive. It is also possible to remove a book from the Cloud Drive. You can do that using the *Silk* app (See *Chapter 3 Surfing with Your Kindle Fire HDX* for more information using the Internet):

 Open the www.amazon.com website in the *Silk* app 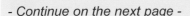[8]

- Continue on the next page -

👉 **Tap**
Hello, John
Your Account ▾

A menu appears:

👉 **Tap**
Manage Your Kindle

You see the login page of the Amazon website:

⌨ **If necessary, type your email address and password**

👉 **Tap**

Sign in using our secure

You see all items in your Kindle library:

Next to the item you want to delete:

👉 **Tap** **Actions... ▾**

👉 **Tap**
› Delete from libra

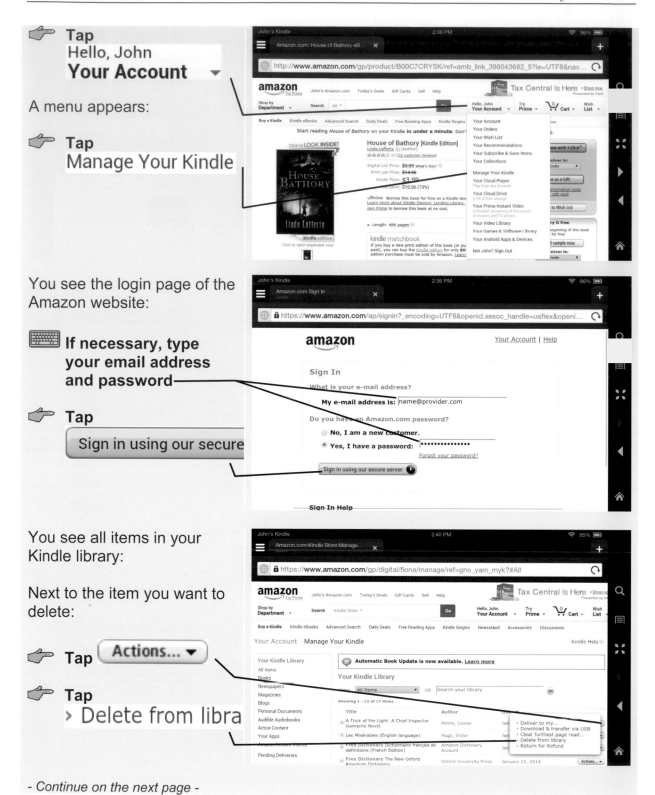

- Continue on the next page -

You need to confirm this action:

 Tap Yes

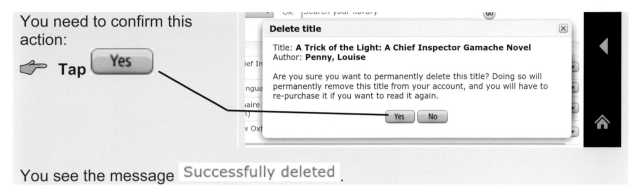

You see the message Successfully deleted .

💡 Tip

Returning a book for a refund

Kindle books you purchase from the *Bookstore* are eligible for return and refund if Amazon receives your request within seven days of the date of purchase. Once a refund is issued, you will no longer have access to the item. In general, other digital content purchased and/or downloaded from Amazon.com is not returnable. To return a book you can use the *Silk* app (See *Chapter 3 Surfing with Your Kindle Fire HDX* for more information using the Internet):

☞ **Follow the first few steps from the previous tip**

Next to the item you want to return:

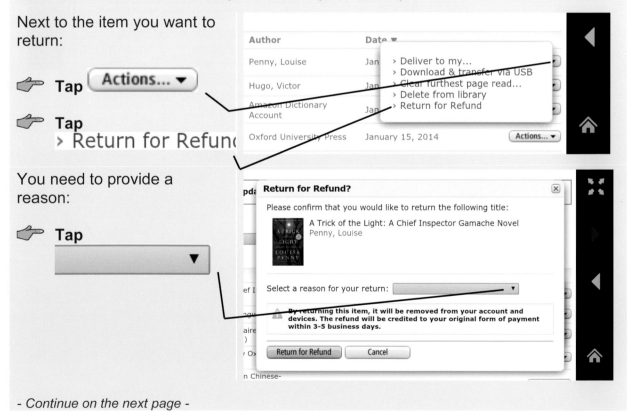

☞ **Tap** Actions... ▼

☞ **Tap**
> Return for Refund

You need to provide a reason:

☞ **Tap** ▼

- Continue on the next page -

Tap a reason

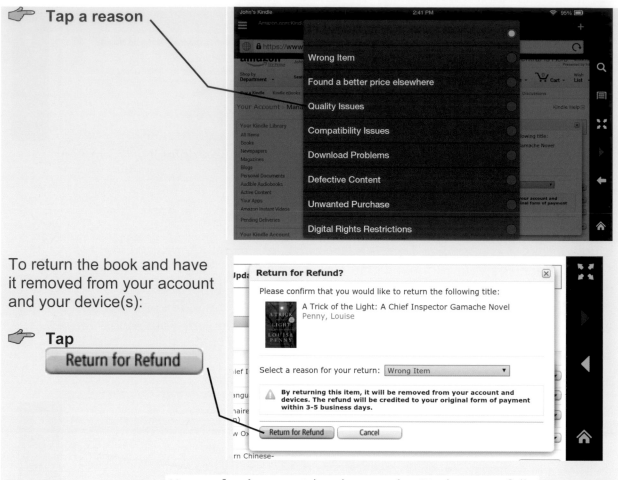

To return the book and have it removed from your account and your device(s):

Tap

Return for Refund

You see the message Your refund request has been submitted successfully.

3. Surfing with Your Kindle Fire HDX

In this chapter you will get to know the *Silk* app. *Silk* is the default web browser application that is installed on your Kindle Fire HDX. You can use this app to surf the Internet. If you are already familiar with surfing the Internet on a computer, you will notice that surfing the web on your Kindle Fire HDX is just as easy. The main difference is the mouse; with a tablet you do not need a mouse. You surf by using touch gestures on the screen.

By learning how to open web pages, you will also get acquainted with some additional touch gestures that allow you to zoom in, zoom out and scroll. Later, you will learn how to open linked pages (also called hyperlinks) and how to work with saved web pages.

The *Silk* app allows you to open a maximum of ten web pages simultaneously. We will show you how to switch between these opened pages.

In this chapter you will learn how to:

- open the *Silk* app;
- open a web page;
- zoom in and zoom out;
- scroll;
- open a link on a web page;
- open a link in a new tab and switch between tabs;
- skip to the previous or next page;
- add a bookmark;
- search.

3.1 Opening the Silk app

This is how you open *Silk*, the app which lets you surf the Internet:

☞ **Unlock or turn on the Kindle Fire HDX** 🦶**1**

You can open the *Silk* app like this:

☞ Tap **Web**

You will see the browser. When you use the *Silk* app for the first time, you see rows of most visited, selected and trending websites.

After using *Silk* for a while you will see the websites that you have visited the most while using your Kindle Fire HDX.

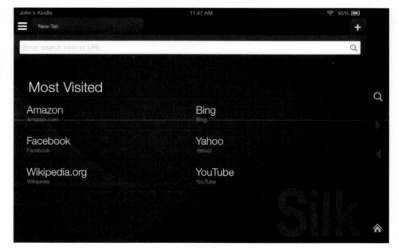

3.2 Opening a Web Page

If you want to enter a web address you need to display the onscreen keyboard first:

☞ **Tap the address bar**

The onscreen keyboard appears at the bottom of the screen:

If you are using the *Silk* app for the first time, you can start typing a web address right away:

By way of practice you can take a look at the Visual Steps website:

⌨ **Type:** www.

By default, you will see one or more suggestions for the web address:

In this example only the Amazon website is suggested.

The more characters of the address you type, the more specific the suggestions will become.

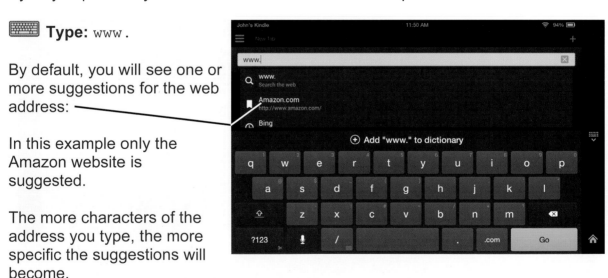

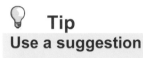 **Type:**
`visualsteps.com`

After you have finished
typing:

☞ **Tap**

Go

💡 **Tip**

Use a suggestion

Of course, you can also tap **Visualsteps** http://www.visualsteps.com/ in the suggestions list.

You will see the Visual Steps
website:

3.3 Zooming In and Zooming Out

If the letters and images on a website appear too small, you can zoom in. You do this by double-tapping the desired spot twice, in rapid succession:

Double-tap the menu on the left-hand side

HELP! A different web page is opened.

If double-tapping is a bit difficult at first, you may have just opened another window.

In that case you need to tap ◀ on the right-hand side and try again. You can also practice double-tapping on a blank section of the screen.

Now you will see a larger view of the web page:

Double-tap the menu once again

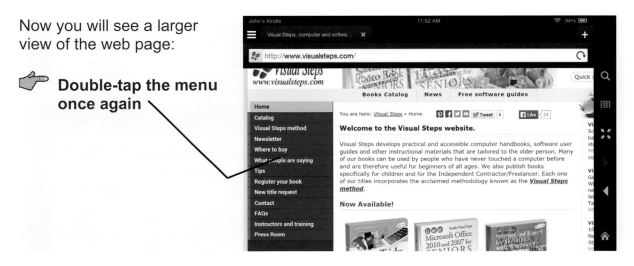

Now you can zoom out again, back to the regular page view. There is also another way to zoom in. With this method you use two fingers:

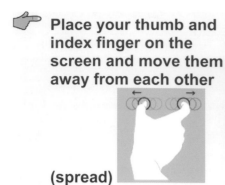

Place your thumb and index finger on the screen and move them away from each other

(spread)

You can zoom in even further, if you like.

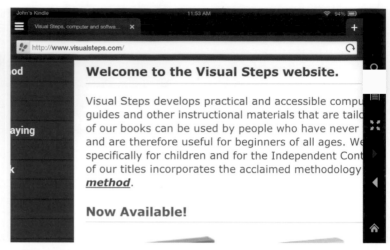

You can zoom out by moving your fingers the other way round:

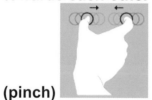

Place your thumb and index finger on the screen and move them towards each other

(pinch)

Now you can return to the regular view:

Double-tap the page

You will see the regular page view once more:

3.4 Scrolling

Scrolling means to navigate through a web page. In this way you can take a look at all sections of a web page. On your Kindle Fire HDX you use your fingers to scroll through a web page:

 Drag the screen upwards a bit

You will see that as you scroll upwards, you are actually moving down to the bottom of the page:

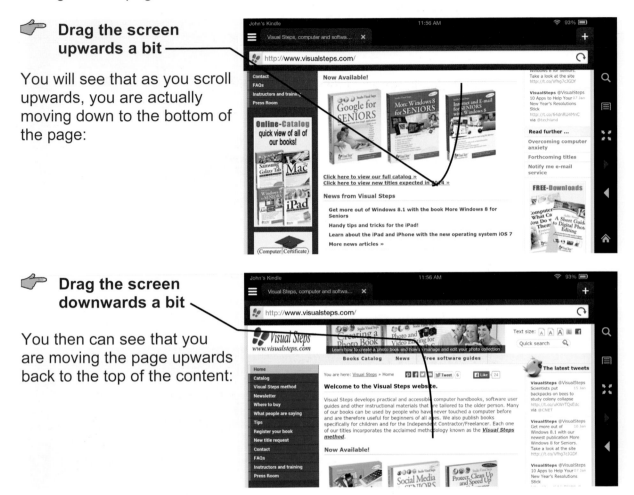

 Drag the screen downwards a bit

You then can see that you are moving the page upwards back to the top of the content:

💡 **Tip**
Scrolling sideways
On a very wide web page you can also scroll sideways, by moving your finger from right to left or from left to right, across the screen.

If you want to quickly scroll through a lengthy page, you can use a swiping or flicking gesture:

 Quickly swipe the screen upwards

This allows you to rapidly scroll down to the bottom of the page:

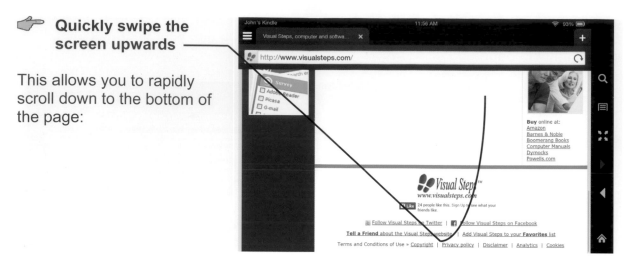

💡 **Tip**

Moving in other directions
You can also use the swiping gesture to quickly go to the top, or to the left or right side of the screen.

To go quickly to the top of the page:

 **Quickly swipe the screen downwards**

You will see the top of the page again:

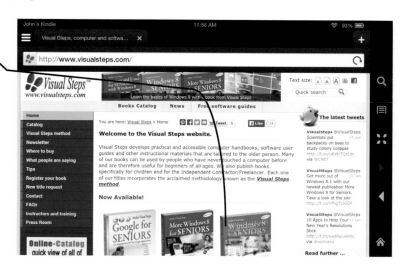

3.5 Opening a Link on a Web Page

If a page contains a link (also called hyperlink) you can open this link by tapping it:

 Tap **Where to buy**

HELP! I am not able to tap the link.

If you find it difficult to tap the right link, you can zoom in on the page first. This way, the links will become larger and easier to tap.

Here you can see the web page about where to find the Visual Steps books:

3.6 Opening a Link in a New Tab

You can also open a link in a new tab:

Place your finger on Catalog and press gently

After a few moments a menu will appear:

☞ Tap
Open in New Tab

If you select
Open in Background Tab
the linked page will be
opened in a new tab behind
the current tab.

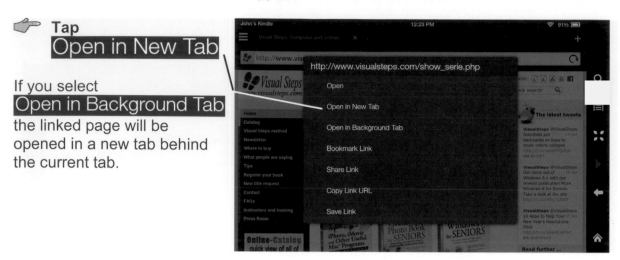

The linked page will be opened in a new tab. This is how you go back to the first tab:

☞ Tap the first tab

Where to find our produc...

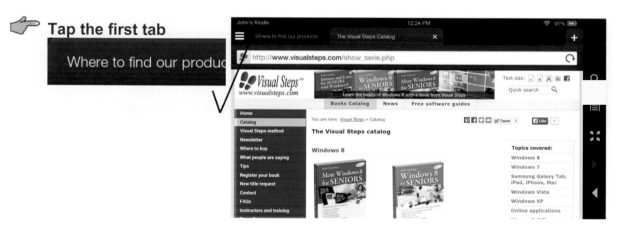

You will see the Where to find our products web page again.

☞ Go to the second tab 👣⁹

This is how you close an open tab:

☞ Tap ✖

Once more, you will see the Where to find our products web page:

💡 Tip

Open a new blank tab
This is how you open a new, blank tab in the *Silk* app:

☞ **Tap** ➕

You will see the new tab with the default Start page.

3.7 Skipping to the Previous or Next Page

You can return to the page you previously visited. Here is how to do that:

☞ **Tap** ◀

Now you will see the Visual Steps Home page again. You can also skip to the next

page. You can use the ▶ button to do this, but for now that is not necessary.

3.8 Adding a Bookmark

If you intend to frequently visit a certain page you can add a bookmark for this page. In the *Silk* app, a bookmark is a website you want to save, in order to visit it later on. This will save you the trouble of typing the full web address each time you want to visit the site. This is how you add a bookmark:

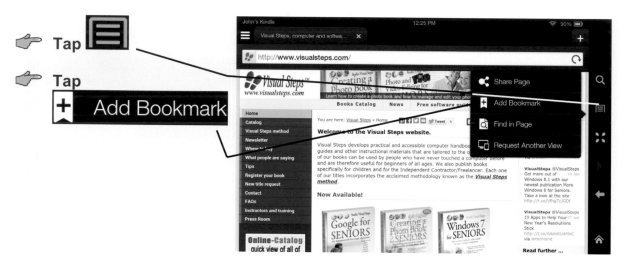

☞ Tap

☞ Tap

In the *Add bookmark* screen you can also enter an easily identifiable name for the web page. For now this will not be necessary:

To show the buttons that are hidden under the onscreen keyboard:

☞ Tap

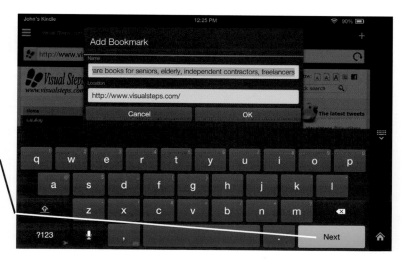

To save the bookmark:

☞ **Tap**

Now the web page has been added to your bookmarks. You can verify this:

☞ **Tap** ☰

☞ **Tap Bookmarks**

You see that the Visual Steps website has been added to your Most Visited websites:

Amazon has already added its own website as a favorite:

☞ **Tap**

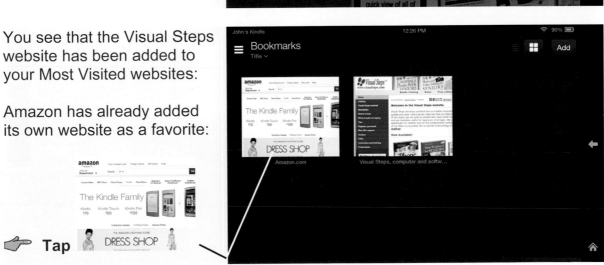

You see the Amazon website in a new tab:

To close the new tab:

☞ **Tap** ✖

You will see the Visual Steps webpage again.

3.9 Searching

The address bar doubles as a search box. *Silk* app uses the *Bing* search engine. Using the search box to search for keywords or names will not be any different from the way you may have already searched the Internet with different Internet browsers on your computer. You start like this:

☞ **Tap the address bar**

This will select the current web address.

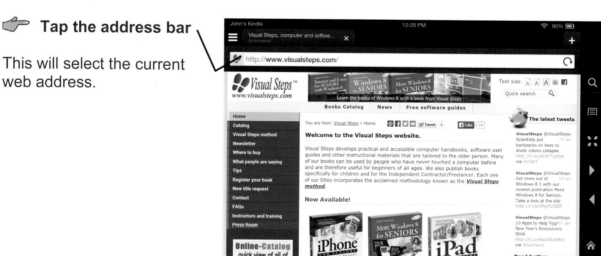

The onscreen keyboard appears and you can start typing right away. The current address is then overwritten. Now you can type your keywords:

Type: `kindle fire hdx sleeve`

While typing you will see various keyword suggestions:

You can use a suggestion by tapping it. For now this will not be necessary.

☞ **Tap** [Go]

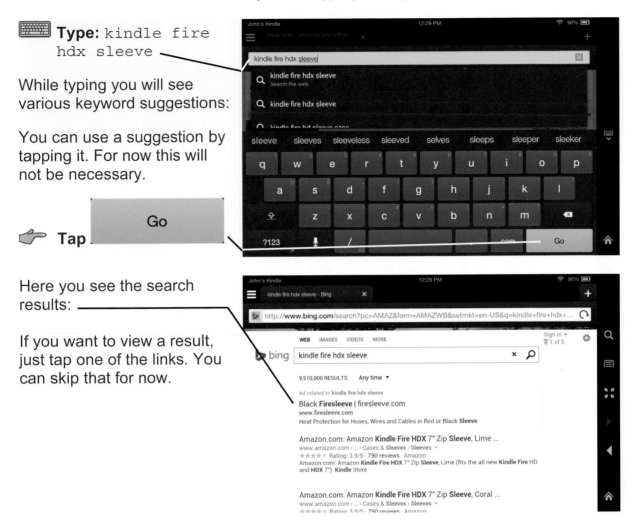

Here you see the search results:

If you want to view a result, just tap one of the links. You can skip that for now.

☞ **Go back to the Home screen** 👣³

☞ **If you wish, lock or turn off the Kindle Fire HDX** 👣⁵

3.10 Background Information

Dictionary

Bing	A search engine from Microsoft.
Bookmark	A reference to a web address stored in a list, which makes it easy to find the web page later on.
Google	*Google,* mainly known as a search engine, offers all kinds of other services as well, such as *Google Maps.*
Link	A link is a navigational tool on a web page, which automatically leads the user to the information when clicked. A link can consist of text or an image, such as an illustration, a button or an icon. It is also called a hyperlink.
Reading view	Reading view can make web content easier to read without all the ads, graphics and other distractions. It allows you to format web articles to look like an e-book.
Scroll	Moving a web page on the screen upwards, downwards, to the left or to the right. On the Kindle Fire HDX you use touch gestures to do this.
Yahoo!	A search engine from *Yahoo!.*
Zoom in	Take a closer look at an item, the letters and images will become larger.
Zoom out	View an item from a distance, the letters and images will become smaller.

Source: Kindle Fire HDX User Guide, Wikipedia

3.11 Tips

 Tip

Full screen
You can view a website full screen, without the status bar and menu bars like this:

☞ **Tap**

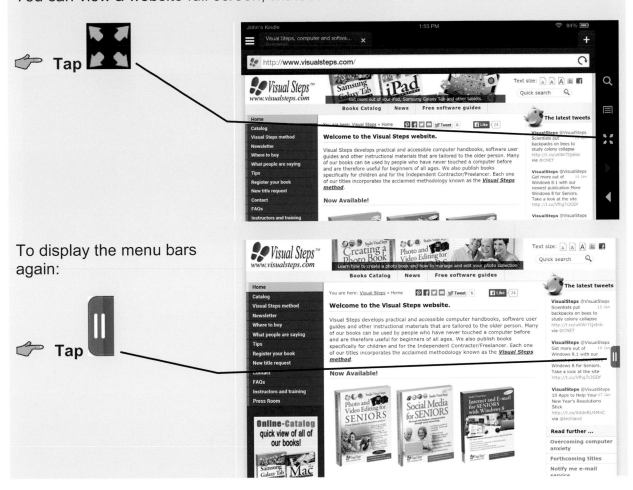

To display the menu bars again:

☞ **Tap**

 Tip

Delete a bookmark
If you no longer want to use a bookmark you can delete the link in the following way:

☞ **Tap**

☞ **Tap** Bookmarks

- Continue on the next page -

After a short while you will see a menu:

☞ **Tap** Delete

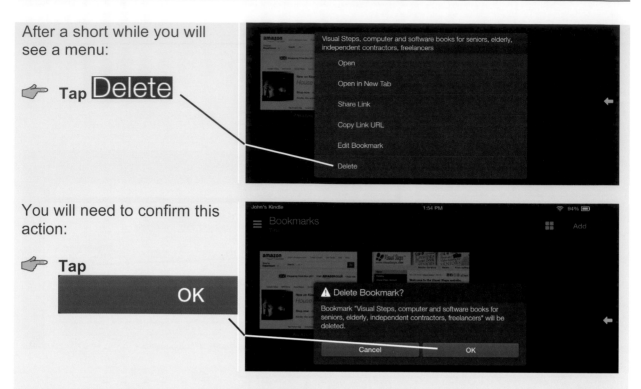

You will need to confirm this action:

☞ **Tap**

OK

The bookmark has been deleted. To go back to the web page you were previously viewing:

☞ **Tap**

💡 **Tip**

View and delete browsing history
The history contains a list of all the websites you have recently visited. This is how you view the history:

☞ **Tap** ≡

☞ **Tap** History

You will see the list of recently visited pages. You can delete this history:

☞ **Tap** Clear All

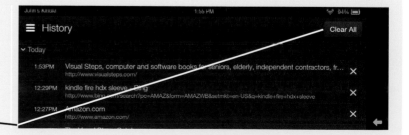

- Continue on the next page -

You will need to confirm this action:

 **Tap**

The history will be deleted.

You can return to the page you were previously viewing:

 Tap

Tip
Reading View
The *Reading View* is a handy option to remove ads and graphics from a website, so that you can concentrate on the text.

If the Reading View is available on a website, you will see a new button next to the address bar:

☞ **Tap**

You see an easy-to-read page with a few relevant pictures. The page looks a bit like a page of an e-book:

To display the Options bar:

☞ **Tap**

On the Options bar:

☞ **Tap** Aa

- Continue on the next page -

You see different options to
adjust the font size, color,
margins and alignment:

To go back to the website:

 Tap ⊗

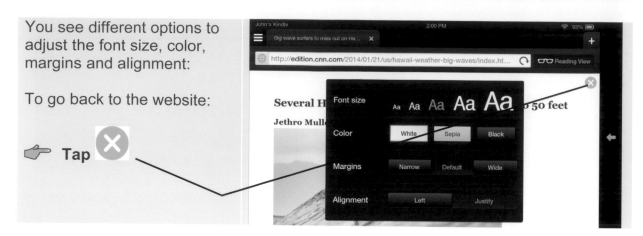

💡 **Tip**

Change the search engine
The *Silk* app uses *Bing* as the default search engine. You can change the search
engine like this:

☞ **Tap** ☰

☞ **Tap** **Settings**

☞ **Tap**
Search engine

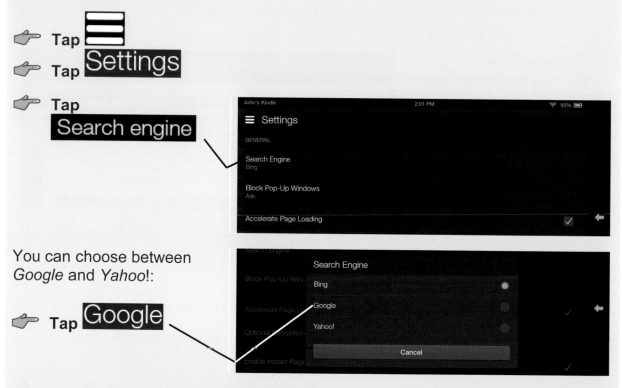

You can choose between
Google and *Yahoo!*:

☞ **Tap** **Google**

The search engine has been set to *Google*.

To go back to the website you were viewing:

☞ **Tap**

4. Using Email with Your Tablet

Your Kindle Fire HDX comes with a built-in app called *Email* that can be used to write, send, and receive email messages just like you do on a regular computer.

In this chapter you will get acquainted with the *Email* app. First, you will need to add an email account in order to start working with the app.

You will find that it is easy to write an email with a Kindle Fire HDX. In this chapter you will write a brief text, then learn how to select, copy, cut, and paste text all on the screen of the Kindle. You will also learn how to use the Next word prediction and Auto-correction functions.

We will also show you how to send, receive, and delete email messages.

In this chapter you will learn how to:

- set up an email account in the *Email* app;
- send an email;
- receive an email;
- move an email to the *Trash*;
- permanently delete an email.

4.1 Adding an Email Account

In this section you will be adding your Internet service provider's account, for instance, an AOL or Verizon account. You will need to have your account information available (username, password, mail server information); this information has been sent to you by your provider. You can also add an email account for *Hotmail*, *Outlook.com*, *Gmail* (from *Google*) or *Yahoo!*.

☞ **Unlock or turn on the Kindle Fire HDX** 𝒪𝒪¹

Open the *Email* app:

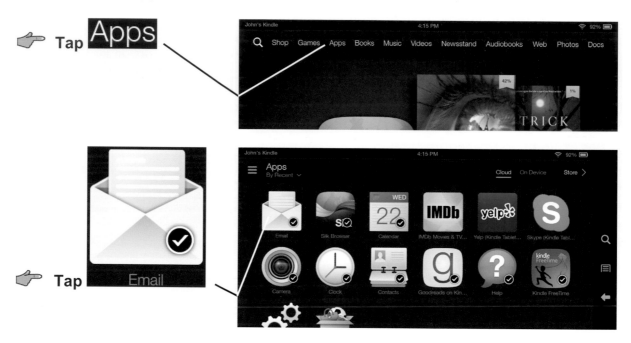

👉 Tap Apps

👉 Tap Email

You will be adding a new email account.

Please note:
If you have an email address ending in *hotmail.com*, *outlook.com*, *gmail.com* or *yahoo.com*, go to *section 4.2 Adding a Hotmail, Outlook, Gmail or Yahoo! Account*.

Please note:
In this section we are holding the Kindle vertically (portrait orientation). This makes it a little easier to see the form fields and to fill in the necessary information.

☞ **If necessary, unlock the screen rotation** 𝒪𝒪¹⁰ **and hold the device upright**

You will see a screen in which you need to enter some basic information regarding your email account. Use the Kindle's onscreen keyboard to enter the information:

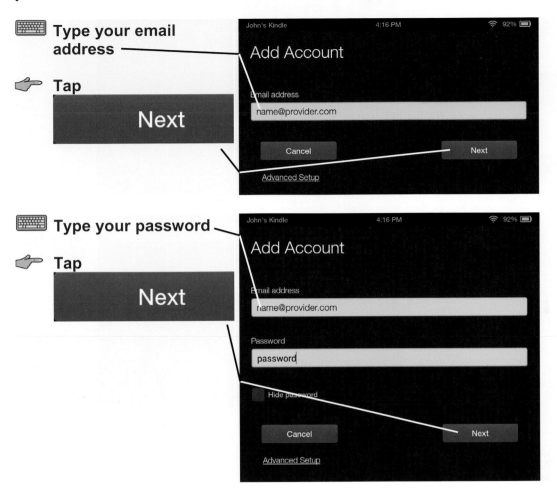

Type your email address

Tap **Next**

Type your password

Tap **Next**

The mail server for your account may be recognized right away. In that case you will see the screen below:

Tap **Go to Inbox**

Continue reading on page 124

If your account has not been recognized, you will need to enter the account data yourself.

☞ **Tap**

Edit Details

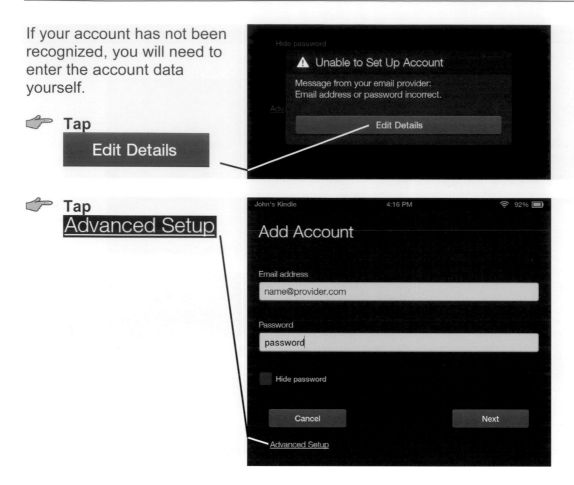

☞ **Tap**

Advanced Setup

You may need to choose whether to set up your email account as an *IMAP* or as a *POP* account:

• IMAP stands for *Internet Message Access Protocol*. This means that you will manage your email messages on the mail server. After a message has been read it will remain stored on the mail server, until you delete it. IMAP is very useful if you want to manage your email messages on multiple computers or devices. Your mailbox will look the same on each of these devices. If you have created folders to arrange your email messages, these folders will be available on each computer you use and on your Kindle as well. If you want to use IMAP you will need to set up all the email accounts on other devices as IMAP accounts.
Please note: not every email provider provides IMAP accounts.

• POP stands for *Post Office Protocol*, which is the traditional way of managing email messages. After you have retrieved your mail, the messages will immediately be removed from the server. However, the default setting on your Kindle for POP accounts is for saving a copy on the server, even after the messages have been retrieved. This means you will still be able to receive these messages on your computer later on.

Now you can enter the information provided by your Internet service provider:

☞ Tap **IMAP** or **POP3**

⌨ By **POP3 server**, type the name of the server for incoming mail

⌨ By **Username**, type your username

⌨ By **Password**, type your password

☞ Drag the page upwards

⌨ By **SMTP server**, type the name of the server for outgoing mail

☞ Tap

Next

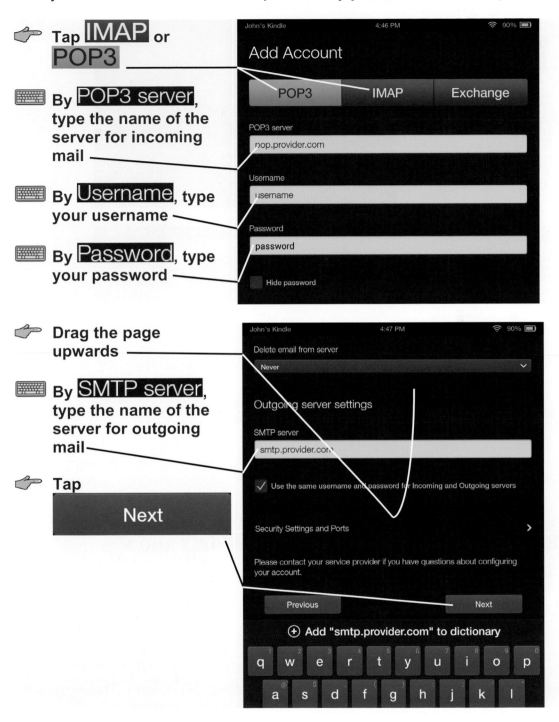

Your email will be synchronized with the *Email* app:

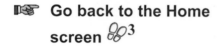 **Tap**

You will see your *Inbox*:

In this example there are no messages:

You may see other messages on your own screen.

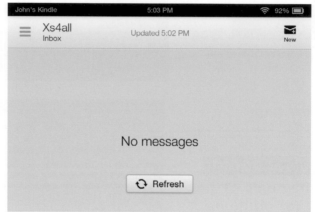

☞ **Go back to the Home screen** 🐾³

If you would like to add a *Hotmail*, *Outlook*, *Gmail* or *Yahoo!* account, you can do that in the following section. Otherwise, skip to *section 4.3 Sending an Email Message*.

4.2 Adding a Hotmail, Outlook, Gmail or Yahoo! Account

Adding a *Hotmail*, *Outlook.com*, *Gmail* (from *Google*) or *Yahoo!* account follows the same procedure. In this example an *Outlook* account will be added.

🦢 **Please note:**

In this section we are holding the Kindle vertically (portrait orientation). This makes it a little easier to see the form fields and to fill in the necessary information.

☞ **If necessary, unlock the screen rotation** 🐾¹⁰ **and hold the device upright**

You will see a screen in which you need to enter some basic information regarding your email account. Use the Kindle Fire HDX's onscreen keyboard to enter the information:

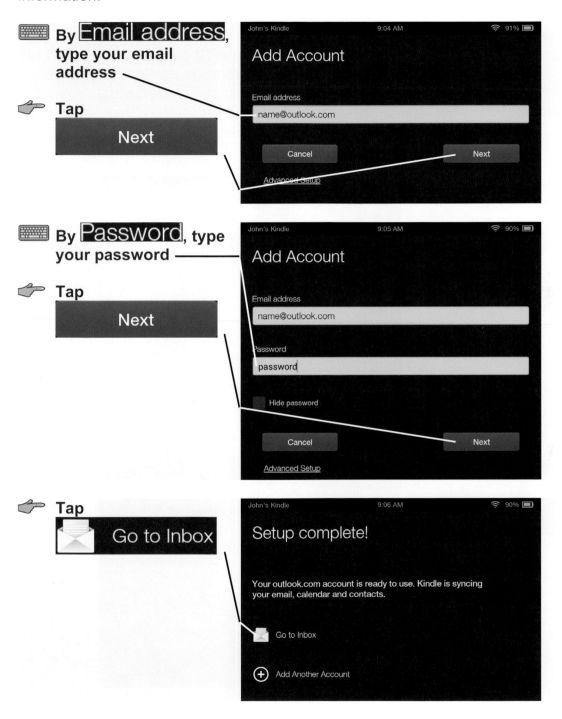

By **Email address**, type your email address

Tap **Next**

By **Password**, type your password

Tap **Next**

Tap **Go to Inbox**

The *Email* app will synchronzie you contacts and calendars automatically. You can decide whether you want to do this with the Kindle or not. By default both options have been selected.

 Please note:

If you want your screen to look the same as the images in *Chapter 5 Managing Your Calendar and Contacts*, then do not synchronize your contacts and/or calendar yet. In *Chapter 5 Managing Your Calendar and Contacts* you can read how to adjust the synchronization settings to include your contacts and calendar.

In this example only the email will be synchronized with the Kindle Fire HDX:

To open the settings for the *Email* app:

☞ **Tap** ≣

☞ **Tap** Settings

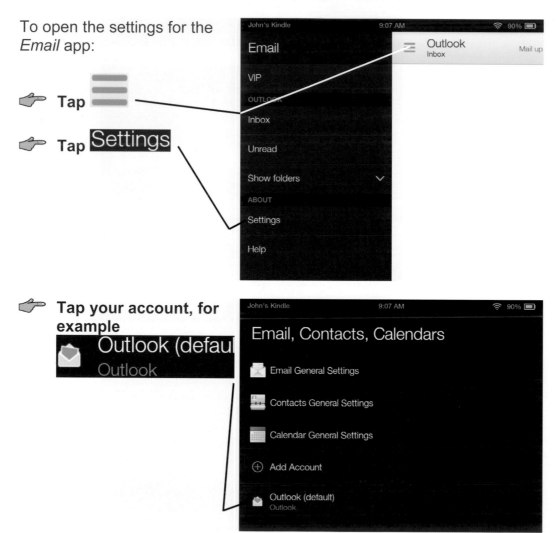

☞ **Tap your account, for example** Outlook (default)

☞ **By** Sync Calendar, tap Off

☞ **By** Sync Contacts, tap Off

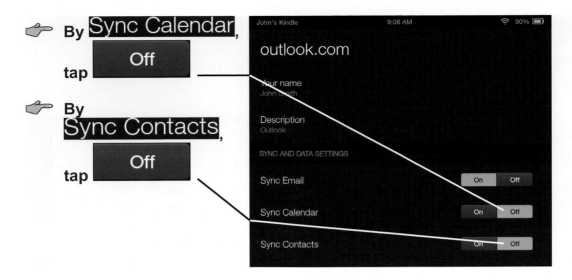

☞ **Go back to the Home screen** 👣³

💡 **Tip**

Multiple email accounts
Do you have multiple email accounts? You can add all of them to your Kindle Fire HDX. Tap ☰, ⊕ Add Account and follow the steps in this or the previous section for each email account.

4.3 Sending an Email Message

You can now practice writing an email message by sending one to yourself. First, you open the *Email* app:

☞ **Open the *Email* app** 👣¹¹

You will see the *Inbox*:

In this example there are no messages.

The screen will look different if you hold the Kindle sideways:

☞ **If necessary, unlock the screen rotation** 👣**10** **and hold the device sideways**

The message list and messages will be displayed on the right-hand side of the screen:

☞ **Tap** ▬▬

You see some of the folders on the left-hand side:

☞ **Tap an empty spot of the screen**

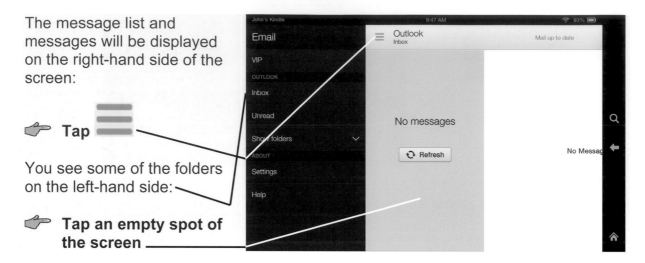

☞ **If you wish, lock the page rotation** 👣**10**

Open a new, blank message:

In the top right-hand corner of the screen:

☞ **Tap New**

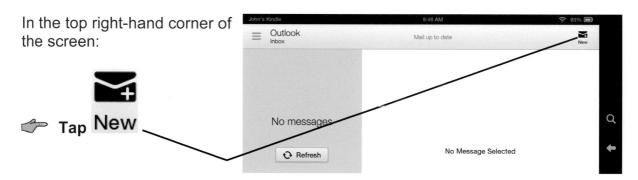

A new message will be opened.

⌨ **By** To:**, type your email address**

Tip

Contacts

If you have added any contacts in the *Contacts* app, you will see a list of names and corresponding email addresses, as soon as you type the first two letters of a name. This way, you can quickly add the email address by tapping the name of the recipient. In *Chapter 5 Managing Your Calendar and Contacts* you will learn more about the *Contacts* app.

By Subject:**, type:**
Test

While you are typing you will see a bar above the keyboard, with all sorts of suggestions for the word you are currently typing:

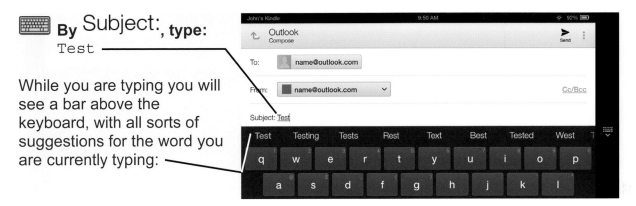

These suggestions are part of two functions called *Next word prediction* and *Auto-correction*. By default, both functions are enabled on the Kindle Fire HDX. While you are typing, you will see suggestions for the entire word, based on the few letters you have already typed. This may save you all lot of typing work. Just try this with the first part of the word 'continuing'.

☞ **Drag the email up**

☞ **Tap the white text box**

⌨ **Type:** Conti

Here you see the Suggestion bar:

Here you see the text you typed:

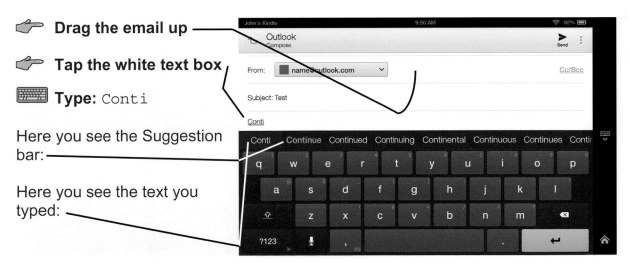

The suggestion displayed in orange  will be accepted automatically when you tap the space bar. To enter the word 'continuing':

☞ **Tap** Continuing

The letters you typed will be replaced by Continuing.

Auto-correction automatically corrects quite a lot of typing errors and spelling mistakes. Just see what happens if you intentionally make a mistake:

☞ **Tap**

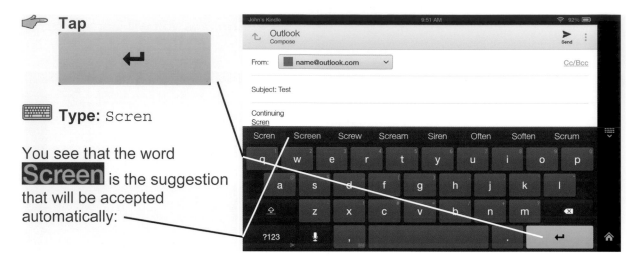

⌨ **Type:** Scren

You see that the word **Screen** is the suggestion that will be accepted automatically:

If you do not notice your mistake and tap the space bar or the key, your text will be corrected automatically.

☞ **Tap** **(space bar)**

 Tip
Accept correction
A suggested (orange) correction will also be accepted when you type a period, a comma or any other punctuation mark.

 Tip
Overrule the suggestions, or select a different suggestion
If the system suggests a word that is wrong, you can also select your own text by tapping it. You can do the same thing with the suggestions that are not orange.

 Tip
Turn off Next word prediction and Auto-correction
In the *Tips* at the end of this chapter you can read how to turn off the Next word prediction and Auto-correction functions.

If you are not satisfied with the text you have typed, you can quickly delete the text with the Delete key:

☞ **Place your finger on the**  **key and press long enough so that both lines are deleted**

⌨ **Type:** `The screen of the Kindle Fire HDX is touch-sensitive.`

In the *Email* app you can also copy, cut, and paste text. You can do this with a single word, multiple words, or with the entire text at once. In this example we will be using a single word. This is how you select a word:

☞ **Place your finger on the word** Fire

The word will be selected and blue handles will appear below the word:

☞ **Release the screen**

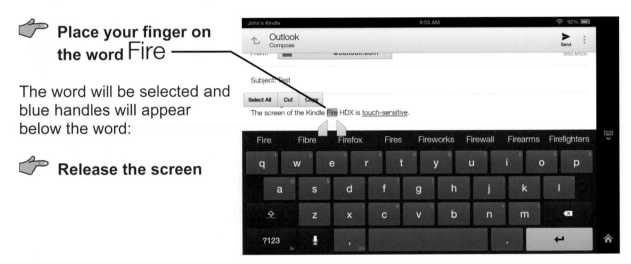

By using the handles you can adjust the selection. Practice selecting the text 'Kindle Fire HDX':

☞ **Drag the left handle**

across Kindle

☞ **Drag the right handle**

across HDX

Now the entire name has been selected:

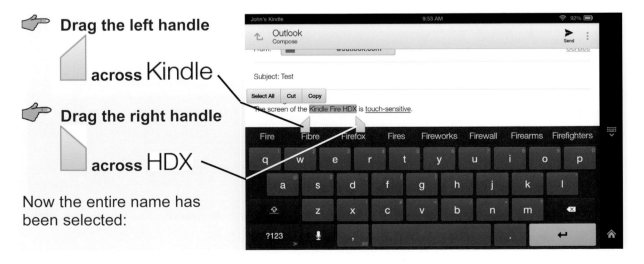

You can cut, copy, or replace the selected words. Practice copying the words:

☞ Tap **Copy**

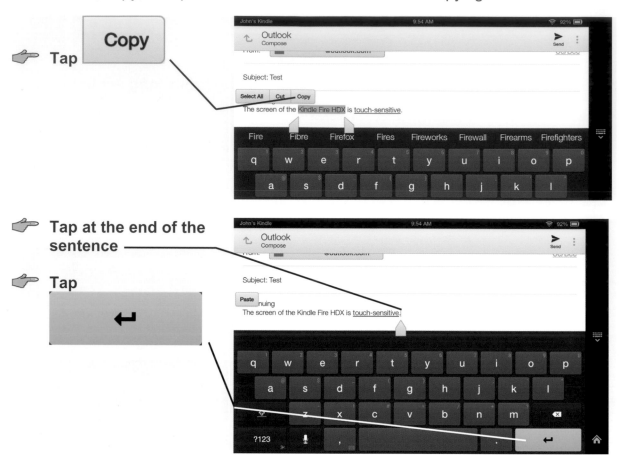

☞ **Tap at the end of the sentence**

☞ **Tap** ←

The words have been copied to the clipboard. This is how you paste them into the text:

☞ **If necessary, place your finger on the blinking cursor**

☞ **Release the screen**

☞ **Tap Paste**

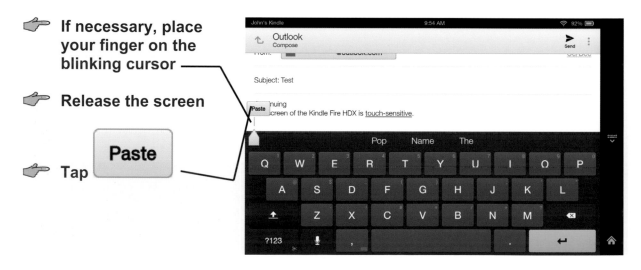

The copied line has been pasted below the first line. Now you can send your test email:

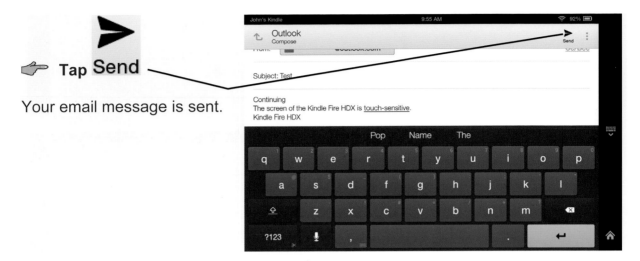

☞ **Tap Send**

Your email message is sent.

You will return to your *Inbox*.

4.4 Receiving an Email Message

Once the message has been sent, it will be received shortly afterwards. The message appears at the top of your *Inbox*. If you do not receive the message right away, you can refresh your *Inbox* like this:

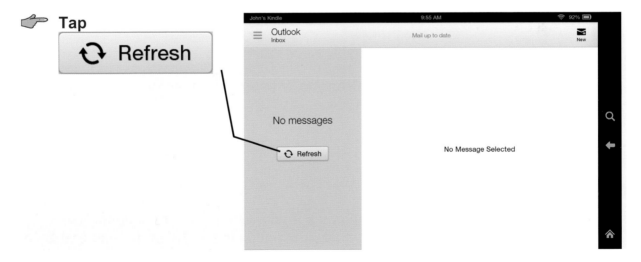

☞ **Tap**

↻ Refresh

You will see the new message:

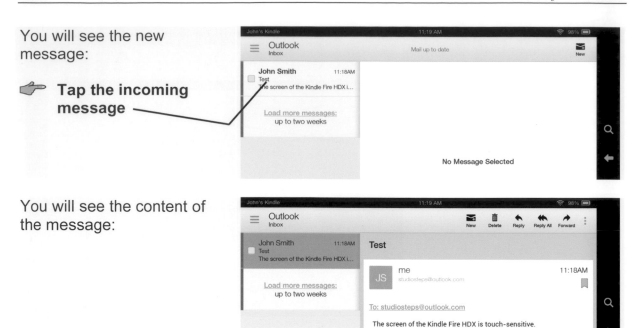

☞ **Tap the incoming message**

You will see the content of the message:

In the bar on the top right-hand side you can see additional buttons. Here is what these buttons do:

🗑 **Delete**   Move a message to the *Trash*.

↩ **Reply**   ↩↩ **Reply All**   ↪ **Forward**   Reply to or forward a message.

✉ **New**   Open a new email message.

⋮   Open a menu with additional options. See more information in the *Tip* at the end of this chapter.

Tip

Search
On the Options bar on the right-hand side you see the familiar buttons that appear in

every app and library. Use the 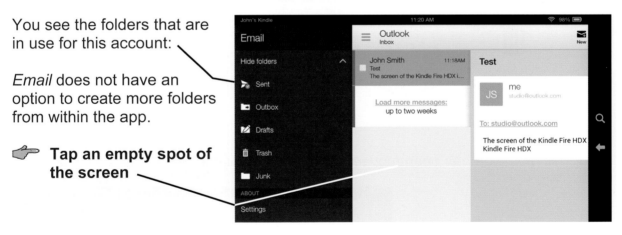 button to search your messages for a name or
keyword. You can select where you want to search, in subjects, from, to or all.

This is how you display the
complete folder list:

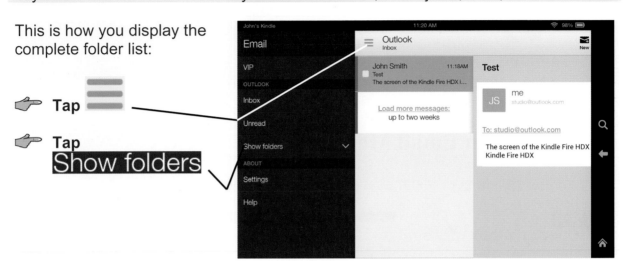

☞ **Tap** ▬

☞ **Tap**
Show folders

You see the folders that are
in use for this account:

Email does not have an
option to create more folders
from within the app.

☞ **Tap an empty spot of
the screen**

 HELP! Where are my folders?
Did you organize your *Inbox* on your computer in tidy folders? Those folders are only
visible in the *Email* app when:
- you use IMAP on all devices where you use this email account. With IMAP all
  messages and folders are stored on the mail server. Your mailbox will look the
  same on all devices.
- you use a *Hotmail*, *Outlook.com* or Yahoo! account.

- Continue on the next page -

Folders you create on a computer for a POP3 account are not imported with your account.
Gmail does not allow you to create new folders at all. But the labels you can use instead are visible in the *Email* app.

You can move emails from one folder to another like this:

☞ **Check the box** 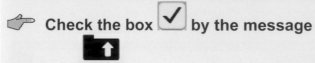 **by the message**

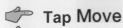

☞ **Tap Move**
☞ **Tap the name of the folder you want to move the email to**

4.5 Deleting an Email Message

You can now delete your test message:

☞ **Check the box** ✓ **by the message**

☞ **Tap Delete**

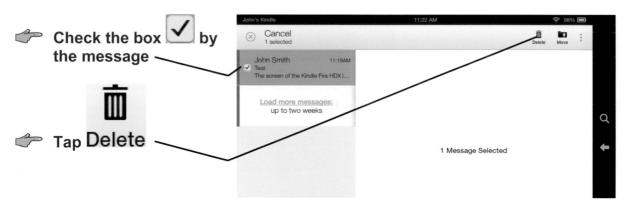

The email message has been moved to the *Trash*. You can verify this:

☞ **Tap** ≡

☞ **Tap** 🗑 **Trash**

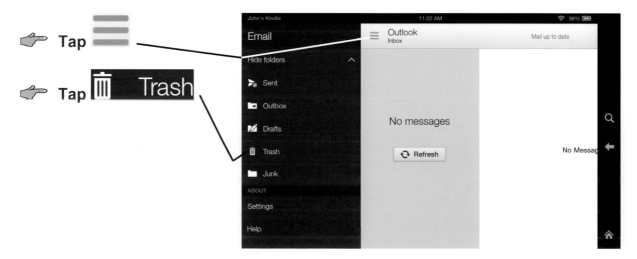

The deleted message has been placed in the *Trash*:

If you wish you can
permanently delete the email
message from the *Trash* as
well:

☞ **Check the box** ☑ **by
the message**

☞ **Tap** 🗑 **Delete**

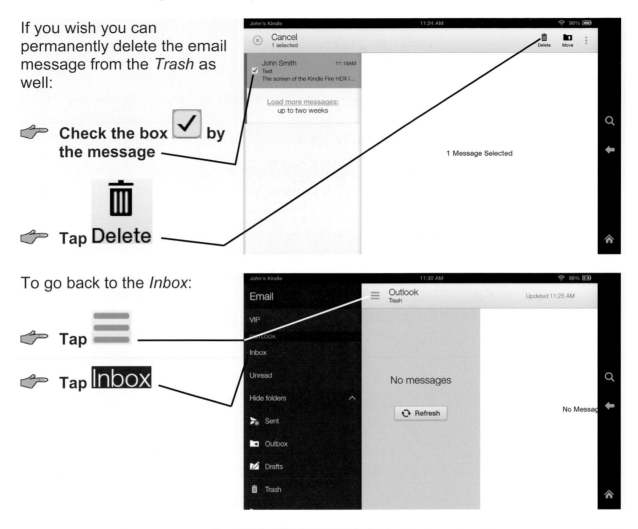

To go back to the *Inbox*:

☞ **Tap** ≣

☞ **Tap Inbox**

▐☞ **Go back to the Home screen** 🐾³

▐☞ **If you wish, lock or turn off the Kindle Fire HDX** 🐾⁵

In this chapter you have learned to use the *Email* app on the Kindle Fire HDX. You
have practiced sending, receiving, and deleting an email message.

4.6 Background Information

Dictionary

Account	A combination of a username and a password, which provides access to a specific, private service. A subscription with an Internet service provider is also called an account.
Auto-correction	A function that automatically corrects typing and spelling errors, based on suggestions from the Next word prediction function.
Contacts	A standard app on the Kindle Fire HDX that lets you view and edit your contacts information.
Email	A standard app on the Kindle Fire HDX that lets you send and receive email messages.
Fetch	The traditional method of retrieving new email messages: you open your email program and connect to the mail server. You can set the program up to automatically check for new messages at regular intervals, as long as the email program is opened.
Gmail	A free email service provided by the manufacturers of the well-known *Google* search engine. The app with which you can send and receive emails through *Gmail* is also called *Gmail*.
Inbox	A folder in which you can view your received messages.
Next word prediction	A function that displays suggestions for a word while you are typing.
Push	When the *push* method is set and supported by your Internet service provider, new email messages will be sent to your email program by the mail server right away. Even if your email program has not been opened and your Kindle Fire HDX is locked.
Signature	A default salutation that is inserted at the end of your outgoing email messages.
Trash	A folder in which your deleted messages are stored. Only after deleting them from the *Trash*, the messages are permanently deleted.
Yahoo! Mail	A free email service provided by the manufacturers of the well-known *Yahoo!* search engine.

Source: Kindle Fire HDX User Guide and Wikipedia

4.7 Tips

 Tip

Add a signature to your messages

Below every email message you send, you can also add a default signature. For instance, a standard salutation, or your name and address. This text is called your *signature*. This is how you add a signature:

☞ **Tap** ≡

☞ **Tap Settings**

☞ **Tap your email account**

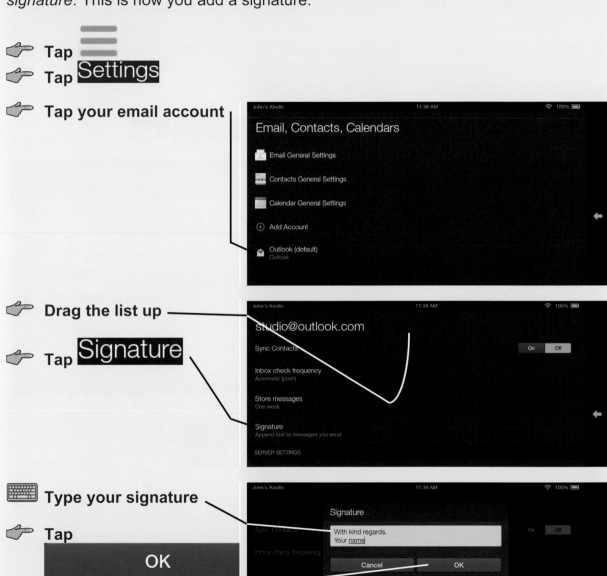

☞ **Drag the list up**

☞ **Tap Signature**

⌨ **Type your signature**

☞ **Tap**
OK

To go back to the *Inbox*:

☞ **Tap**

Tip

Disable Next word prediction and Auto-correction
The Next word prediction and Auto-correction functions may become annoying, as the Suggestion bar takes up additional space on your screen. The Auto-correction function may lead to unwanted text corrections. The dictionary will not recognize every single word you type but will still try to suggest alternative words. This can result in strange corrections, especially if you have made some spelling errors and did not notice these. Without knowing it, you may have accepted these corrections by typing a period, a comma, or a blank space. This is how you disable both of these functions:

☞ **Open the *Settings* screen** ✂️^{12}
☞ **Drag the list up**
☞ **Tap** Language & Keyboard, Keyboard Settings

You will see various keyboard settings:

To turn off both functions:

☞ **By** Auto-correction, tap **Off**

The switch will turn to On | Off .

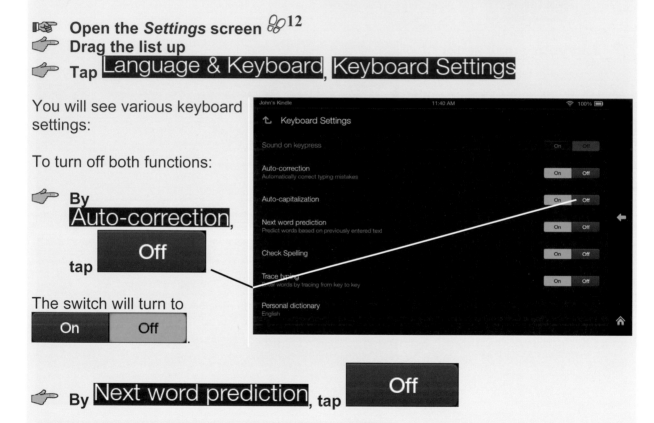

☞ **By** Next word prediction, tap **Off**

With this setting, you will no longer see any suggestions while you are typing. Typing errors are no longer corrected.
If you turn Auto-Correction on and Next word prediction off, nothing changes. You will still see suggestions, and typing errors will be corrected.
If you turn Auto-Correction off and Next word prediction on, you will still see suggestions, but typing errors are no longer corrected automatically. The text you typed will be the orange text in the suggestions bar.

Tip: when you are using the onscreen keyboard, you can quickly display the keyboard by placing your finger on the space bar and press Keyboard Settings .

Tip

Push or fetch

If you also use your computer to manage your emails, you will already be familiar with the *fetch* function: you open your email program and connect to the mail server, in order to retrieve new messages. You can set the mail program to automatically check for new messages at regular intervals, while the program is open.

By default, the *Email* app automatically checks for new email. This is called the *push* function: with this setting new email messages will be sent to the *Email* app right after they have been received by the mail server. This happens even when the *Email* app is not open or your Kindle Fire HDX is locked. The only situation in which you will not receive email messages is when the Kindle Fire HDX has been completely turned off.

Please note: if you are connected to the Internet through the mobile data network and you do not have a subscription for unlimited data traffic at a fixed price, it is better to turn off the automatic synchronization (push) function of the *Email* app. If you do not have such a subscription you will need to pay for the data traffic. If messages with large attachments are pushed to your Kindle Fire HDX this can cost you quite a bit of money. It is better (and less expensive) to manually synchronize your email account every once in a while, after you have connected to the Internet through Wi-Fi.

In the next *Tip* you can find out how to change the synchronization settings on your Kindle Fire HDX.

Tip

Adjusting the Inbox Check Frequency

This is how you can view the Inbox Check Frequency for email. From the *Email* app:

☞ Tap

☞ Tap Settings

☞ **Tap your account**

By default, *Email* automatically checks for new email:

☞ **Tap**
Inbox check frequen

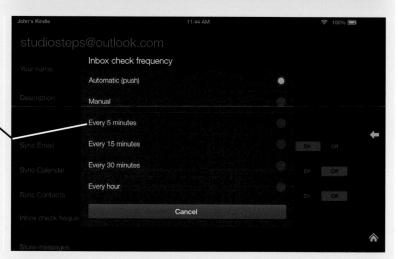

☞ **Tap the desired frequency**

You can also select Manual. In that case you check for new email by tapping the

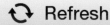 button or dragging the left side of the screen downwards.

💡 **Tip**

Email General settings

There are a few more settings that you may want to take a look at:

👉 **Tap** ☰

👉 **Tap** Settings

👉 **Tap** ✉ Email General Sett

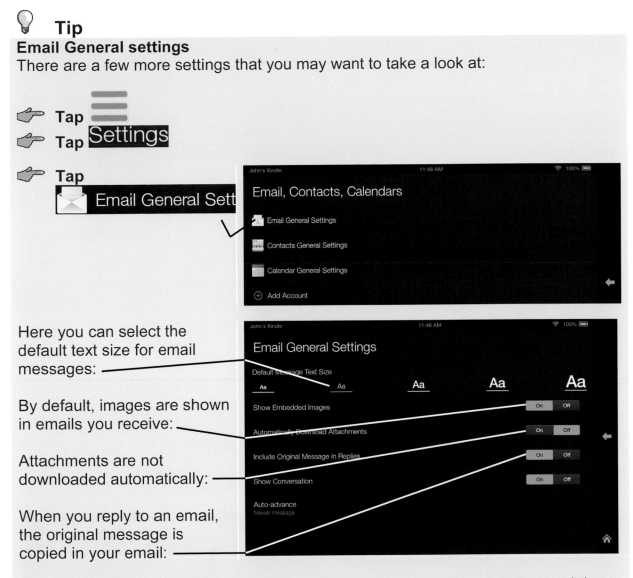

Here you can select the default text size for email messages:

By default, images are shown in emails you receive:

Attachments are not downloaded automatically:

When you reply to an email, the original message is copied in your email:

You can adjust these settings to your personal preferences. To return to your *Inbox*:

👉 **Tap**

Tip

CC and BCC
You can send a copy of an email to another recipient. There are two possibilities: a carbon copy (CC) or a blind carbon copy (BCC). In a copy, all recipients see the addresses of the other recipients. In a blind copy, the recipients of the blind copy are not visible to the other recipients. To send a copy you tap the Cc/Bcc option in the new message screen. You can add the recipients to the field Cc: or Bcc: .

 Tip

Select a sender
If you have added multiple email accounts to your Kindle, you can select from which email account an email has to be sent:

 By From:, **tap**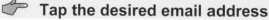

☞ **Tap the desired email address**

 Tip

More options for a new email
There are some more things you can do with the *Email* app. You can send a photo or a document with an email as an attachment. You can also modify the layout of an email by adjusting the font size, font color and other elements.
You can even save a draft of an email that you are not ready to send. Later you can open it, work on it some more, save it again or actually send it.

☞ **Tap** ⋮

You see the various options:

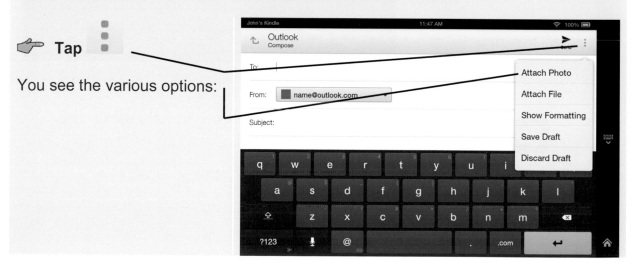

5. Managing Your Calendar and Contacts

Your Kindle Fire HDX also contains an address book and a calendar. The *Contacts* app enables you to manage your contacts. You can manually enter contact information. Once you have added a contact, you can edit or delete the information. If you have set up a *Hotmail*, *Outlook*, *Gmail* or *Yahoo!* account on your Kindle Fire HDX, you can synchronize your contacts with your computer or other devices so that you have the same list of contacts on all these devices.

The *Calendar* app enables you to keep a calendar and manage your activities. It is compatible with the most popular online calendar systems. You need a *Hotmail*, *Outlook.com*, *Gmail, Yahoo!* or *Microsoft Exchange* account to be able to use the *Calendar* app. When you add, edit, and delete events on your tablet, the Kindle Fire will sync the *Calendar* app with your account. That way you have the same calendar on your computer and all your devices. You can also sync multiple calendars from multiple accounts.

In this chapter you will learn how to:

- add, edit and delete contacts in the *Contacts* app;
- add, edit and delete events in the *Calendar* app.

Please note:

You need a *Hotmail*, *Outlook.com*, *Google*, *Yahoo!* or *Microsoft Exchange* account to:
- be able to store your contacts in a different account than your *Amazon* account;
- be able to use the *Calendar* app.
If you do not have one these accounts, you can just read through this chapter, or you can create a free *Hotmail*, *Outlook.com*, *Google* or *Yahoo!* account.

☞ **For a *Hotmail* or *Outlook.com* account, go to www.outlook.com**
☞ **For a *Google* account, go to accounts.google.com**
☞ **For a *Yahoo!* account, go to www.yahoo.com**
☞ **Follow the instructions onscreen**

For your email of your work you may be able to get a *Microsoft Exchange* account, contact your network administrator for assistance.

5.1 Adding a Contact

Open the *Contacts* app from the *Apps* library:

☞ **Unlock or turn on the Kindle Fire HDX** ✋¹

👉 **Tap** Apps

👉 **Tap** Contacts

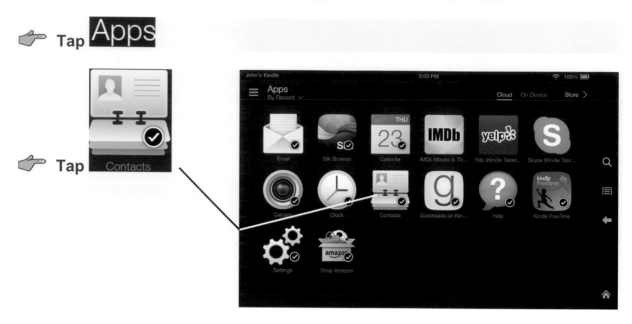

In this example there are no contacts stored on the Kindle Fire HDX:

Here you can add your own profile. You do not need to do that now:

To add a new contact:

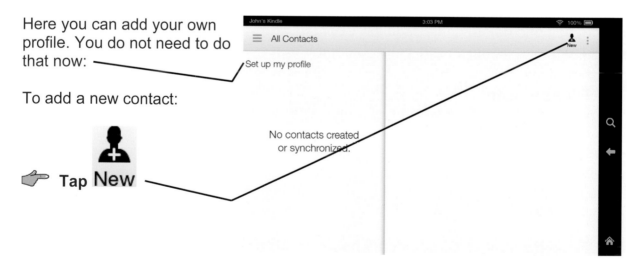

👉 **Tap** New

You will be asked which account you want to use to synchronize. Depending on the type of email account you added in the previous chapter, you can choose between your *Amazon* account, or your *Hotmail*, *Outlook.com*, *Gmail* or *Yahoo!* account.

If you do not use any of these email accounts, you can select your *Amazon* account. This way you can automatically back up your contact data to the Cloud Drive, the free online storage that comes with your *Amazon* account.

You can select the account you want to use:

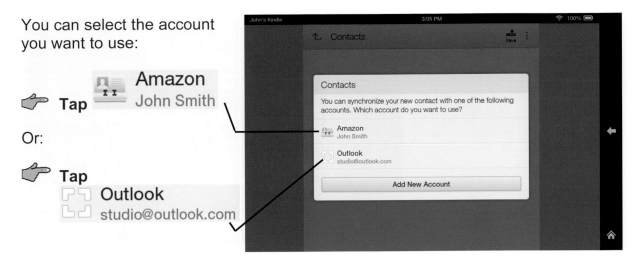

☞ **Tap**   **Amazon** John Smith

Or:

☞ **Tap**   **Outlook** studio@outlook.com

In this example the *Amazon* account was selected. You will see a confirmation that your Amazon contacts will be backed up to the Cloud Drive:

☞ **Tap**

OK

You will see the window in which you can add a new contact. In this example we will add a fictitious contact. But of course you can enter the information for one of your own contacts, if you prefer. You will be using the onscreen keyboard:

To show the keyboard and fill in the information into the fields:

☞ **Tap** First name

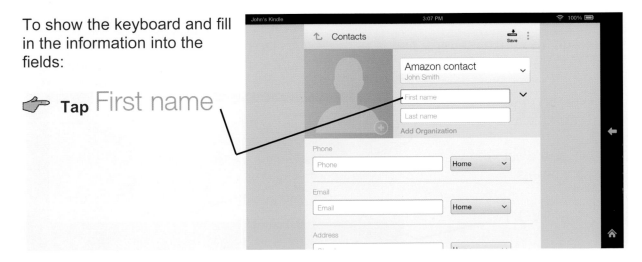

The onscreen keyboard appears:

Type your contact's first name

This is how you jump to the next line:

☞ Tap **Next**

Type your contact's last name

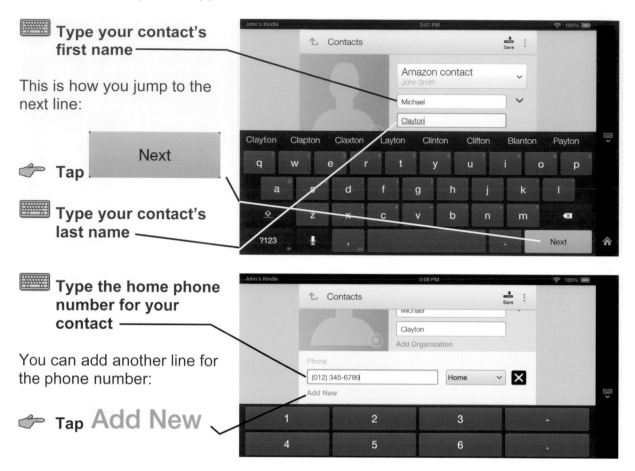

Type the home phone number for your contact

You can add another line for the phone number:

☞ Tap **Add New**

✏ Please note:
When you enter a phone number, the punctuation (parentheses, dashes and spaces) will be added automatically.

By default, the next line for a phone number will display the **Mobile** ∨ label. You can change this label yourself, and turn it into a work phone number:

☞ Tap **Mobile** ∨

You will see a list with various available labels:

☞ Tap **Work**

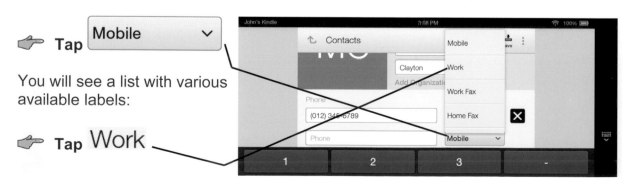

Type the work phone number for your contact

☞ **Tap**

> Next

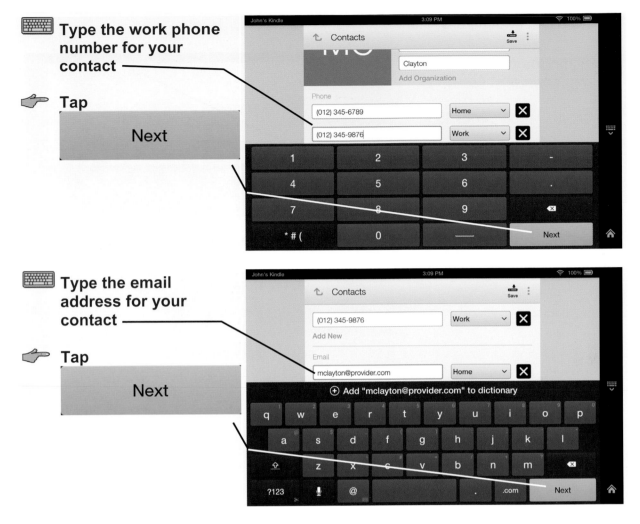

Type the email address for your contact

☞ **Tap**

> Next

💡 Tip

Change a label

You can also change the label of the email address from home to work, if you prefer.

You can add your contact's home address:

Type the street name and number

At the bottom of the screen:

☞ **Tap**

> Next

Next, you can add the city, state, zip or postal code and country:

⌨ **Type the city, state, zip code and country**

You can save the contact:

☞ **Tap Save**

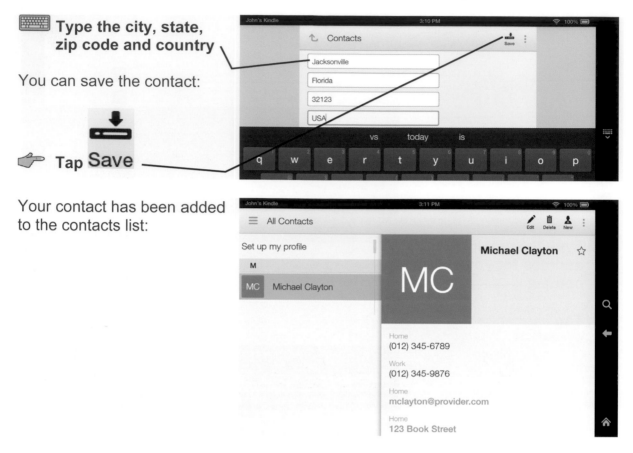

Your contact has been added to the contacts list:

☞ **Add four more contacts** 📖¹³

5.2 Editing a Contact

Every now and then, you will need to edit a person's contact information. For example, you may need to add a new phone number or change an address. This is how you open a contact to edit the contact information:

☞ **Tap the desired contact**

☞ **Tap Edit**

This is how you edit the phone number, for example:

☞ **Place your finger on the phone number**

The phone number is selected:

You can type the new phone number right away:

⌨ **Type the new phone number**

☞ **Tap Save**

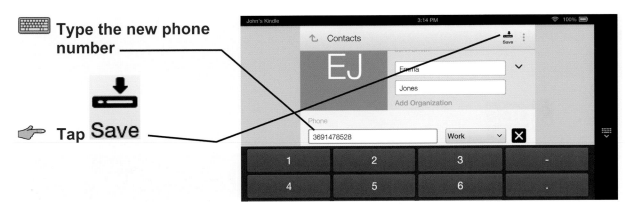

☞ **Go back to the Home screen** 👣³

5.3 Calendar App

The *Calendar* app lets you maintain a calendar on your Kindle Fire HDX. You need to set up synchronization with an online email account such as *Hotmail*, *Outlook.com*, *Google, Yahoo!*, or *Microsoft Exchange* in order to be able to use the *Calendar* app. Also, calendar synchronization has to be turned on for this account. You can check to make sure that calendar synchronization has been turned on like this:

☞ **Open the *Email* app** 👣¹¹

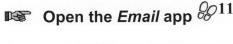
☞ **Tap** ≡, **Settings**

☞ **Tap your account**

☞ **If necessary, by** Sync Calendar **tap**

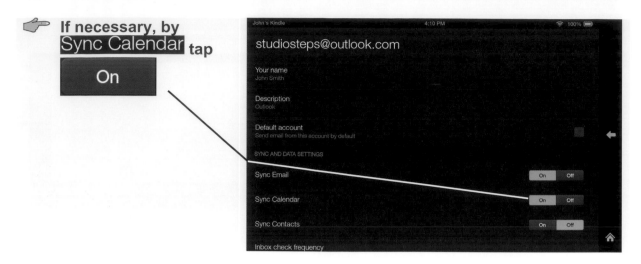

☞ **Go back to the Home screen** ⚓³

Here is how to open the app:

☞ **Tap**

☞ **Tap**

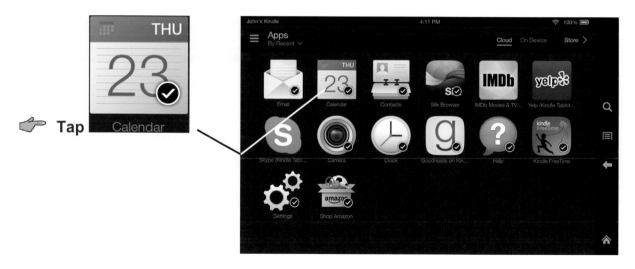

The calendar is opened and the current view displays one week.

At the top you can select a different view:

If you select a date other than the current day, you can use

the **Today** button to quickly return to your appointments today:

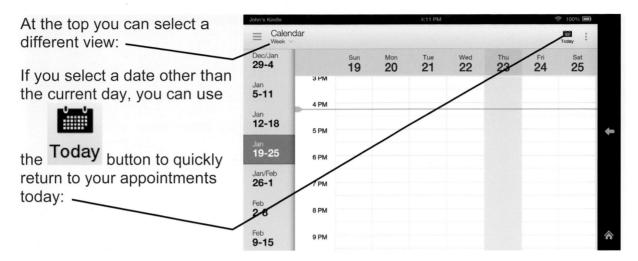

You can change the view to display a full week, month or year. Here is how to view the full month:

☞ Tap Week ∨

☞ Tap Month

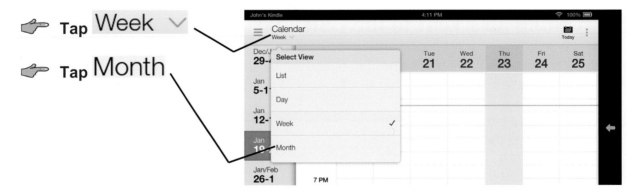

The current month will be displayed. You can go back to the weekly display:

☞ Tap Month ∨

☞ Tap Week

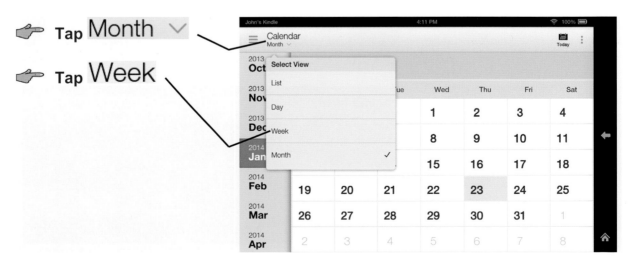

You can skip quickly to the next week like this:

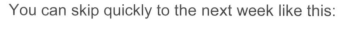 **Swipe the screen from right to left**

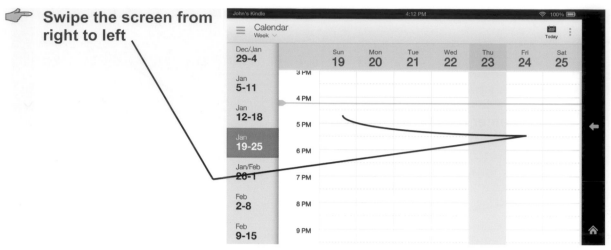

Now you see the next week.

5.4 Adding an Event to the Calendar

In the *Calendar* app, an appointment is called an event. You can practice adding an event to your calendar:

☞ **Tap the day of the event for a moment, for instance, Wednesday**

☞ **Release the screen**

☞ **Tap New event**

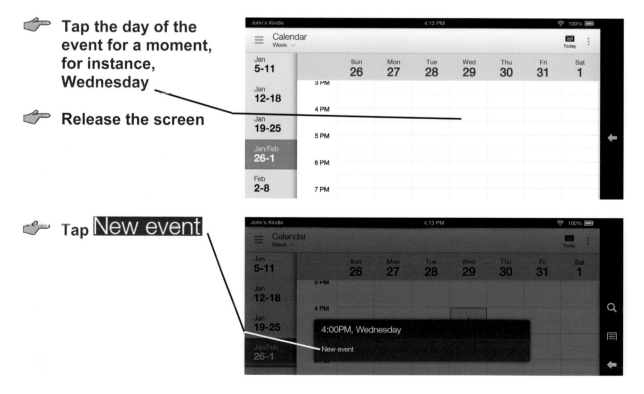

Now, you can enter a name for the event:

⌨️ **Type a name, for example:** Tennis lesson

You can change the start and end time of the event:

👉 **Tap** | 04:00 pm |

You can adjust the hours and minutes by gently dragging the numbers up and down:

👉 **Drag the hour upwards until it indicates**
7 : 00 PM

If the start time is correct:

👉 **Tap**
| OK |

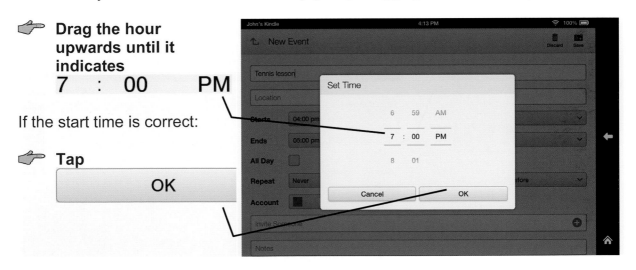

The end time has now been
reset to 8:00 pm:

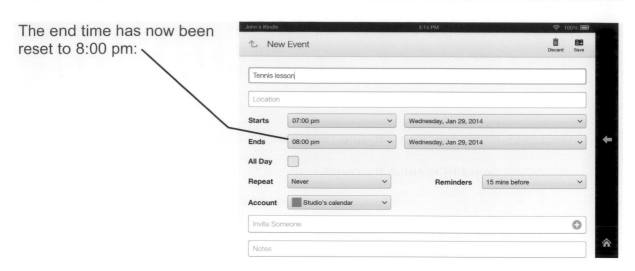

Tip

Correct start time
If you add an event by clicking the correct time shown in the day or week view, the start time is immediately set to the correct time.

Tip

All day
If an event takes up the entire day:

 Check the box ☑ **by All Day**

You can also enter a location for the event:

 Tap by Location

 Type a location, for example: Tennis court

There are more options possible in the screen where you add the event:

Repeat

Here you can set a repeat frequency for the event. For instance, every week or every month. By default, the **Never** option is selected.

Reminders

Here you can set up a reminder for the event. The reminder is a notification sound on the Kindle. You can choose whether you want to receive this notification a few minutes, a few hours, a few days or a week before the event. By default, the **15 mins before** option is already selected.

If you use multiple calendars in your account(s), you can select which calendar the event should be added to:

☞ **Drag the page upwards**

☞ **Tap**

       Studio's calendar

☞ **Tap the calendar you want to use**

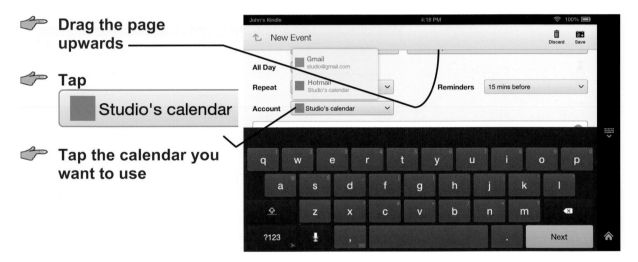

After you have entered all the information concerning the event:

☞ **Tap Save**

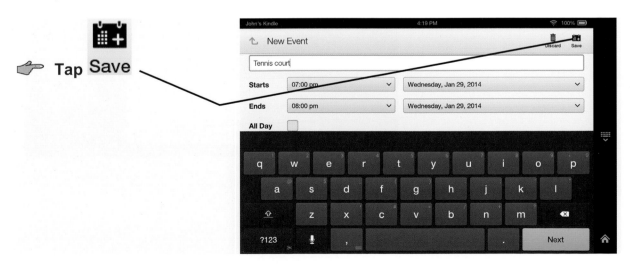

☞ **If necessary, swipe the page upwards**

You will see the event appear in the calendar:

If an event is changed or cancelled, you can edit or delete the event like this:

☞ **Tap the event**

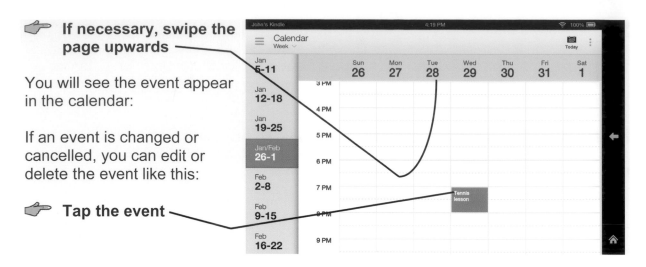

You will see the details of the event:

If you wish to edit the event,

you can tap ⋮, **Edit**:

To delete the event:

🗑

☞ **Tap Delete**

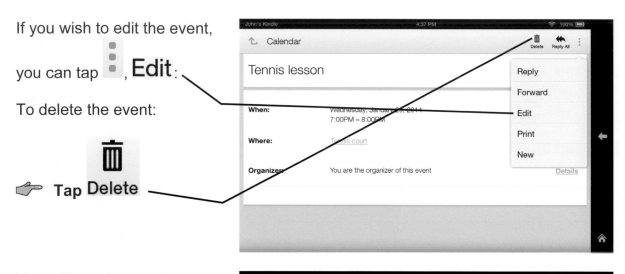

You will need to confirm this:

☞ **Tap**

⎿ **OK** ⏌

☞ **Go back to the Home screen** 👣³

5.5 Background Information

Dictionary

Calendar	An app that helps you plan activities and events.
Contacts	An app for managing your contacts.
Event	An appointment in the *Calendar* app.
Favorites	In the *Contacts* app, a contact can be added to your favorites by tapping the star next to the name.
Field	An element used to enter contact information. For example, *First name* and *Zip code* are fields.
Google Calendar	A service by *Google* that lets you keep a calendar. You need to use your *Google* account in order to do this.
Label	Field name.
Outlook Calendar	A service by *Microsoft* that lets you keep a calendar. You need to use your *Hotmail* or *Outlook.com* account in order to do this.
Synchronize	Literally, it means to equalize content. You can also synchronize contact and calendar data with your *Hotmail*, *Outlook.com*, *Gmail*, *Yahoo!* or *Microsoft Exchange* account.

Source: Kindle Fire HDX User Guide, Wikipedia

5.12 Tips

 Tip

Delete or add a field

If you want to completely delete a contact field you never use, you do not need to delete the information shown in this field first.

☞ **Tap the desired contact**

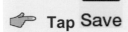

☞ **Tap Edit**

☞ **By the field you want to delete, tap**

☞ **Tap Save**

If you want to restore a field you deleted or add an extra field, just follow these steps:

☞ **Drag the page upwards** ——————

☞ **Tap**

Add More Fields

New fields have been added to the contact data:

Now you can continue editing the data and save the information like you did before.

Tip

Delete a contact

If you ever need to remove a person from your contacts list, just follow these steps:

☞ **Tap the desired contact**

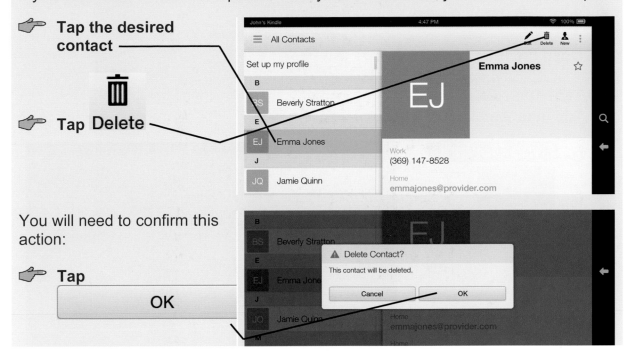

☞ **Tap Delete**

You will need to confirm this action:

☞ **Tap**

OK

 Tip

Searching for contacts

If you have stored lots of contacts in the *Contacts* app it may be difficult to quickly find the contact you need. Fortunately, the Kindle search function also works in this app:

☞ **Open the *Contacts* app** 14

☞ **Tap** Q

⌨ **Type the first two letters of the first or last name**

In this example one contact is found: —

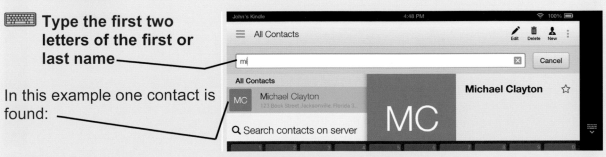

Please note: the search function also searches other fields, such as address, city, state and country.

Tip

Adjusting the synchronization settings for contacts

If you want to sync all contacts with for example your *Hotmail* or *Outlook* account, you do that like this:

☞ **Open the *Email* app** ✂11

👉 **Tap** ☰ , `Settings`

👉 **Tap your account**

👉 **By** `Sync Contacts`,

tap `On`

From now on, your contacts will be synchronized with your email account.

 Tip

Using favorites

You can mark a contact as a favorite like this:

👉 **Tap the star** ☆

The star turns yellow ★ :

- Continue on the next page -

To quickly display all contacts with a blue star:

👉 **Tap** ☰

👉 **Tap** VIPs

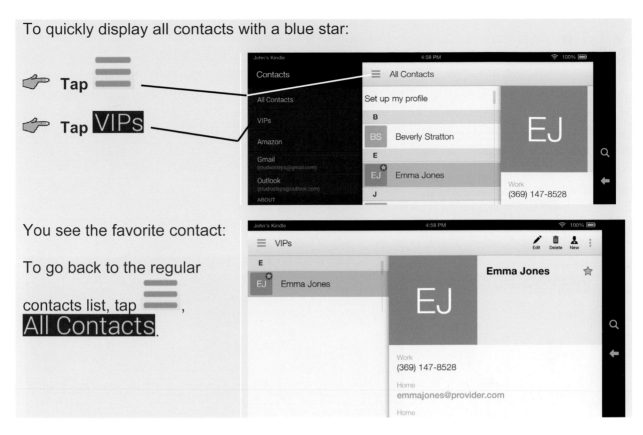

You see the favorite contact:

To go back to the regular

contacts list, tap ☰ ,
All Contacts.

💡 **Tip**

Multiple calendars
On the Kindle you can use multiple calendars. If you use multiple calendars in your account(s), you can select which calendar(s) should be displayed in the *Calendar* app:

👉 **Tap** ☰

If you do not want to display a calendar:

👉 **Tap the desired calendar**

The checkmark ✓ is deleted.

Tip

Start the weekly calendar on another day

By default, the weekly calendar is displayed with Sunday as the first day. If you would rather have the week start on Saturday or Monday, you can adjust the setting like this:

☞ **Open the *Email* app** ✌️ 11

👉 **Tap**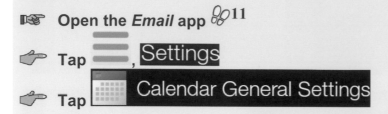

👉 **Tap** Calendar General Settings

👉 **Tap** Week Starts On

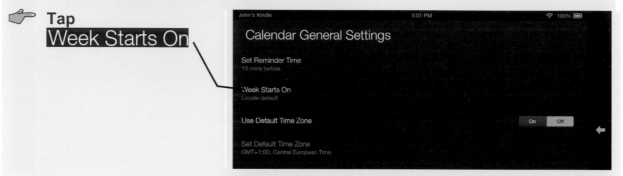

👉 **Tap the desired start day**

The start day will be changed.

To return to the calendar:

👉 **Tap**  **twice**

6. Transferring Files to the Kindle Fire HDX

There are two ways to transfer files from your computer to your Kindle Fire HDX. The first one is USB transfer. The second method is involves the use of a free program called *Amazon Cloud Drive*. This program lets you upload and download documents, photos and video clips to your Cloud Drive, the free 5 GB online storage space that comes with your *Amazon* account.

In this chapter you will try out both methods using the free practice files that you can download from the website that comes with this book.

In this chapter you will learn how to:

- download the practice files to your computer;
- connect the Kindle Fire HDX to the computer;
- copy files to the Kindle Fire HDX by USB transfer;
- download and install *Amazon Cloud Drive* on your computer;
- upload files to your Cloud Drive;
- access your Cloud Drive online.

 Please note:
The instructions in this chapter have been made for a computer running *Windows*. Mac users can install the free *Android File Transfer* app that will enable a USB transfer.

☞ **Go to kindle.com/support/downloads on your Mac**
☞ **Follow the instructions in the windows**

6.1 Two Transfer Methods

There are two methods to transfer files from your computer to your Kindle Fire HDX:

- *USB transfer*: you connect your Kindle Fire HDX to your computer using a USB cable. When the device has been recognized, you can use the *File Explorer* to copy files to the correct folder on the Kindle Fire HDX. This method is also called *sideloading*.
- *Amazon Cloud Drive*: a free program you can use to upload files to your Cloud Drive, the free 5 GB online storage space that comes with your *Amazon* account. The program creates a folder on your computer that is synchronized automatically with your Kindle Fire HDX. Once the files are on your Cloud Drive, you can download them to your Kindle Fire HDX using a Wi-Fi connection.

Both methods are easy to use. USB transfer is the best choice if you want to transfer a large amount of files to your Kindle Fire HDX, and you want them there right away. For example when you want to transfer 150 photos from your vacation in Mexico, so you can take them with you on your Kindle Fire to a family gathering. Or if you go on vacation and you want to transfer your complete e-book collection. If there is any doubt about whether Wi-Fi access is available at the place you will be visiting, it is better to have the files stored in advance on your device.

Files that are stored on your Cloud Drive are visible on your Kindle Fire HDX, but do not take up storage space. When you have a Wi-Fi connection, you only need one tap to download the file you want to use on your Kindle Fire HDX.

In this chapter you will be practicing both methods. There are files available for you to practice with on the website that goes with this book.

➥ Please note:

The practice files we use are available online by the website that goes with this book. They will be used in the next chapter as well as this one. It is a good idea to work through this chapter first, to be able to follow the examples in *Chapter 7 Photos, Video, Music and Documents*.

6.2 Downloading the Practice Files

You can download the practice files from the website that comes with this book:

 Go to www.visualsteps.com/kindlefirehdx on your computer $\mathscr{G}$ **15**

☞ **Click**

Practice files

☞ **Click**
Kindle Fire HDX Prac

☞ **Click** ➡ **Save as**

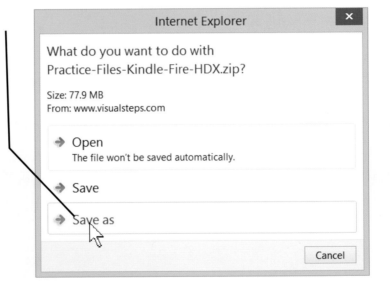

☞ **If necessary, click**
▼ Browse Folders

You store the practice files in the *(My) Documents* folder:

Click 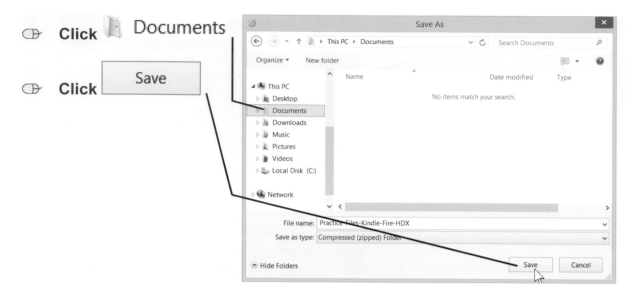 Documents

Click Save

The files are downloaded. This might take a couple of minutes.

As soon as the folder has been received, you see a bar at the bottom of your screen:

Click Open folder

The practice files are stored in a compressed folder. You can unzip (unpack) the folder like this:

Right-click

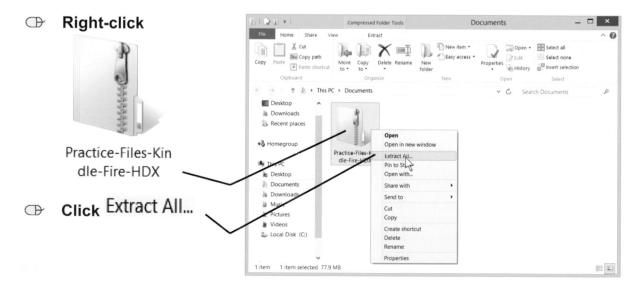

Practice-Files-Kin dle-Fire-HDX

Click Extract All...

☞ **Select the text \Practice-Files-Kindle -Fire-HDX** ⌁¹⁶

⌨ **Press** **Delete**

Now the folder will be saved in the (*My*) *Documents* folder.

☞ **Click** **Extract**

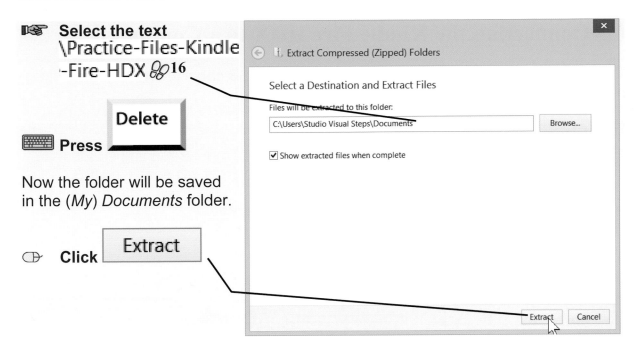

The files will be extracted. After unzipping you will see the folder *Practice Files Kindle Fire HDX*:

The zipped folder can be deleted:

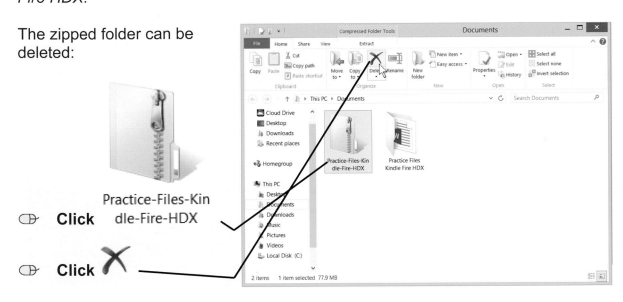

☞ **Click** Practice-Files-Kin dle-Fire-HDX

☞ **Click** ✗

☞ **Close all windows** ⌁¹⁷

6.3 Connecting the Kindle Fire HDX to a Computer

You need to connect the Kindle Fire HDX using the USB cable provided in the packaging of your Kindle Fire HDX with one narrow end.

 Please note:

The instructions in this chapter have been made for a computer running *Windows*. Mac users can install the free *Android File Transfer* app that will enable a USB transfer.

☞ **Go to kindle.com/support/downloads on your Mac**
☞ **Follow the instructions in the windows**

You connect the Kindle Fire HDX like this:

☞ **Connect the narrow end of the USB cable to the Micro-B USB port**

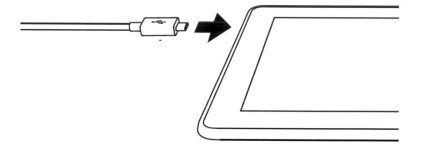

☞ **Connect the other end to a USB port on your computer**

You may see a message on your computer screen, telling you the device driver is being installed. A few seconds later your Kindle Fire HDX is ready to use.

You may also see the *AutoPlay* window:

☞ **If necessary, close the *AutoPlay* window 👣¹⁷**

☞ **In *Windows 8.1*, go to the desktop 👣¹⁸**

You can open *File Explorer* like this:

☞ **Click**

☞ **If necessary, click**
This PC

☞ **Click the device**

Kindle

You may see Kindle in the left Navigation Pane. In that case, click Kindle.

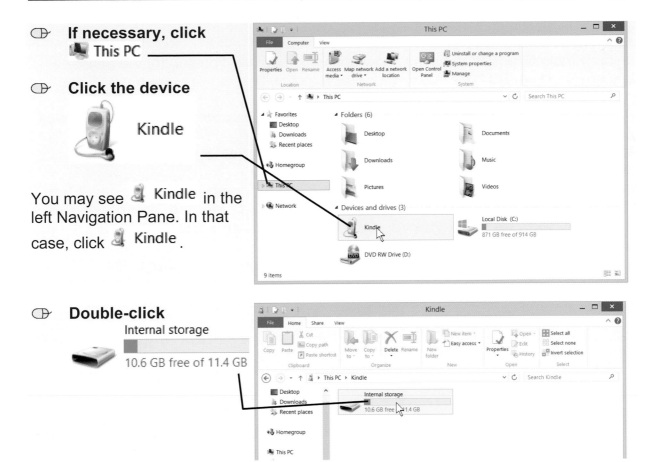

☞ **Double-click**
Internal storage
10.6 GB free of 11.4 GB

You see the folders on the Kindle Fire HDX:

There are different folders for different types of files. For example: books, documents, movies, music and pictures.

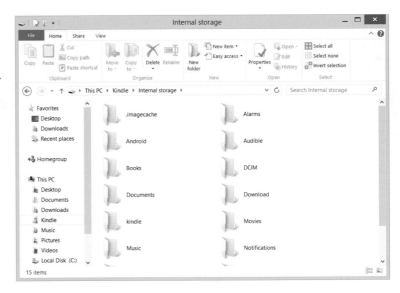

 **HELP! I do not see my Kindle.**

If your Kindle Fire HDX does not show up in *File Explorer* you can try the methods below:

☞ **Check if the plugs of the USB cable have been connected in the right way**

☞ **Charge the Kindle Fire HDX's battery if it is about to run out**

☞ **Disconnect any other USB devices from your computer and connect the Kindle Fire HDX to a different USB port on the computer. Do not use the USB ports on the keyboard, on the monitor, or on a USB hub**

☞ **Unlock the Kindle Fire HDX, in case it has been locked with a PIN**

If *File Explorer* still does not recognize the Kindle Fire HDX:

☞ **Re-start the computer and connect the Kindle Fire HDX to your computer once again**

If this does not work you can re-start the Kindle Fire HDX. Here is how to do that:

☞ **Press and hold the Power button for twenty seconds**

After six to eight seconds, the screen will go blank. This is normal. Continue to hold the power button.

☞ **After twenty seconds, release the Power button**

☞ **Press the Power button again**

If you have successfully restarted your Kindle, you will see the start-up screen.

☞ **Try to connect your Kindle Fire HDX again, preferably to a different USB port**

6.4 Copying Files Using USB Transfer

The easiest way to transfer files from your computer to your Kindle is to drag the files from one *File Explorer* window to another. You can open an extra *File Explorer* window like this:

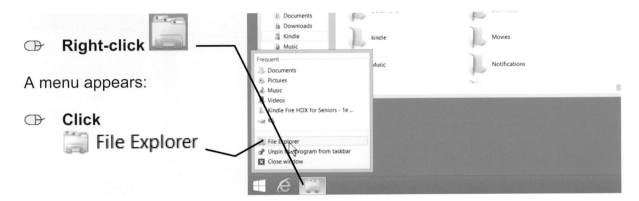

☞ **Right-click**

A menu appears:

☞ **Click**
    File Explorer

A second window has opened
on top of the first window:

In the second window you display the practice files:

☞ **Click** Documents **to open the (*My*) *Documents* folder**

Practice Files

☞ **Double-click** Kindle Fire HDX

In *Windows 8.1* and *Windows 7*, you can display the windows side-by-side by dragging them to the side of the screen. In *Windows Vista* you need to place the windows side-by-side by moving them manually. In *Windows 8.1* and *Windows 7*, you move the window *Practice Files Kindle Fire HDX* first:

☞ **Drag the window against the right-hand side of the screen**

As soon as the mouse pointer hits the edge of the screen, you see a new window outline appear: ————————

☞ **Release the mouse button**

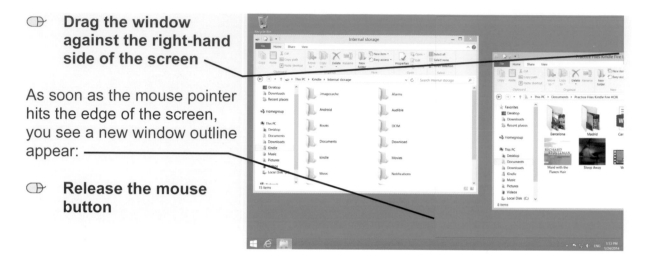

You see that the window now takes up half of the screen. Now you move the other window:

☞ **Drag the window against the left-hand side of the screen**

As soon as you see a new window outline appear:

☞ **Release the mouse button**

Both windows have the same size:

Now you can copy some of the practice files to the correct folder on the Kindle Fire HDX:

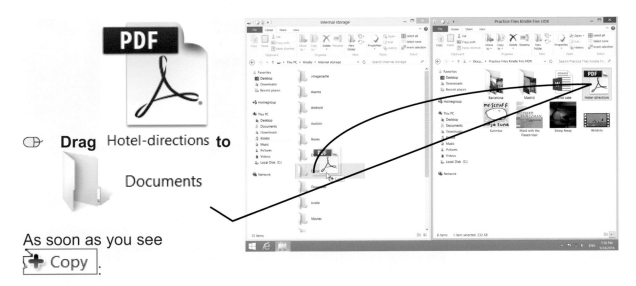

⊕ **Drag** Hotel-directions **to**

Documents

As soon as you see
➕ Copy .

⊕ **Release the mouse button**

You can do the same with a folder containing photos:

⊕ **Drag the scroll bar downwards**

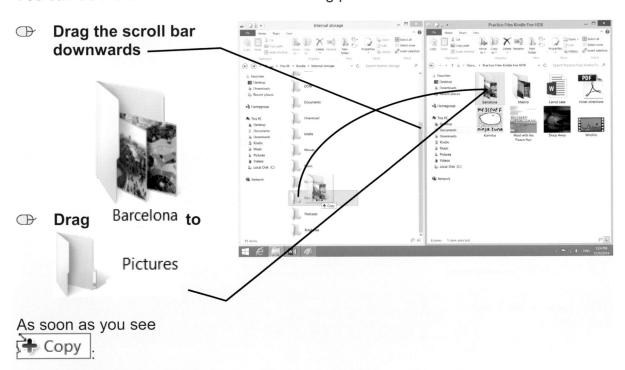

⊕ **Drag** Barcelona **to**

Pictures

As soon as you see
➕ Copy .

⊕ **Release the mouse button**

You see that the files are copied to the Kindle Fire HDX:

The practice files contain three MP3 music files. You can select three consecutive files like this:

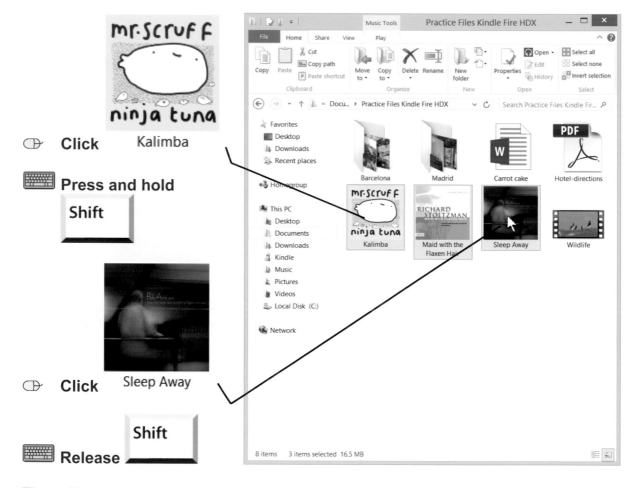

👆 **Click**   Kalimba

⌨ **Press and hold**

    Shift

👆 **Click**   Sleep Away

    Shift
⌨ **Release**

Three files have been selected:

☞ **Drag the selected files**

Music

to

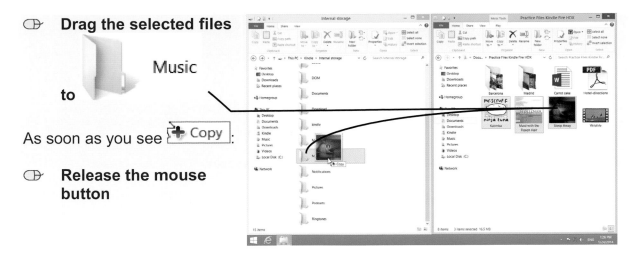

As soon as you see ➕ Copy :

☞ **Release the mouse button**

You may see a warning that you may not be able to play the files you copy. The Kindle Fire HDX can play MP3 files, so go ahead and copy them:

☞ **Check the box** ✔️ **by** Do this for all files

☞ **Click** ➡️ Yes

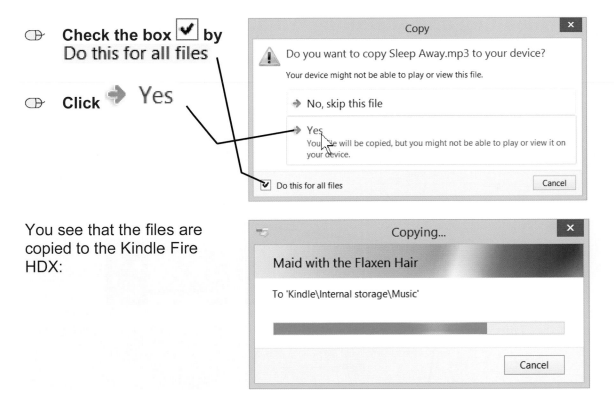

You see that the files are copied to the Kindle Fire HDX:

You can also copy the video clip to the Kindle Fire HDX:

☞ **Copy** Wildlife **to** 📁 Movies 🦶19

You might see the warning again:

☞ **If necessary, click** ➡ Yes

You have copied files to your Kindle Fire HDX using USB transfer. Now you can disconnect the device:

☞ **Disconnect the Kindle Fire HDX from the computer**

☞ **Close all windows** &&¹⁷

You have tried the first method to transfer files to your Kindle Fire HDX. In the next section you will download and install *Amazon Cloud Drive* to your computer.

6.5 Downloading and Installing Amazon Cloud Drive

You can download the free program *Amazon Cloud Drive* from the Amazon website:

☞ **Go to www.amazon.com/clouddrive on your computer** &&¹⁵

☞ **Click**
❯ Continue to your Clo

☞ **Click ❯ Learn more**

☞ **Click**

 HELP! I cannot find this option.
Amazon changes their web pages very frequently. If you cannot find the *Cloud Drive* web page, it may have been moved. You can find the correct hyperlink on the website for this book: **www.visualsteps.com/kindlehdx/news.php**

☞ **Click**   Run

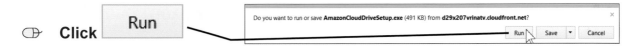

You may see a security warning:

☞ **Click**   Install

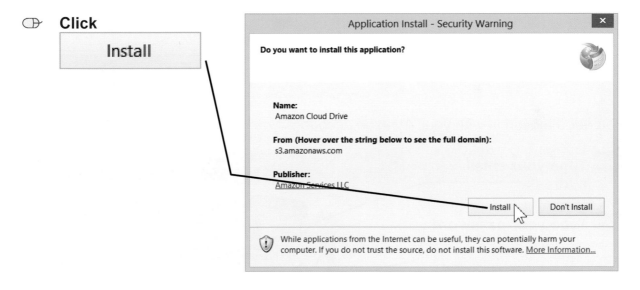

The green progress bar
indicates the percentage of
completion:

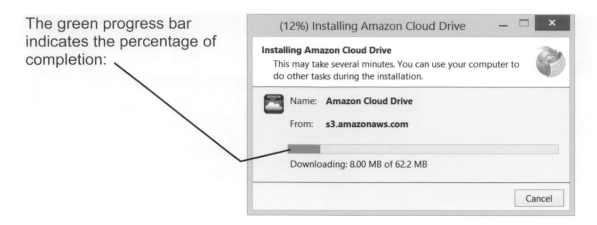

You see the first setup screen:

⊂ **Click** | Next |

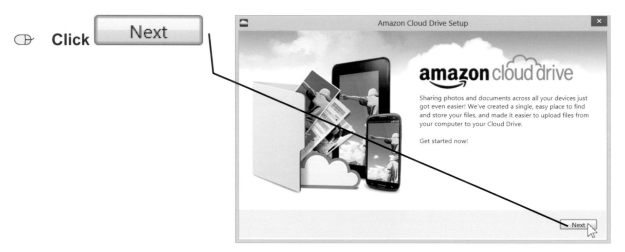

You need to sign in with your *Amazon* account:

⌨ **Type your email
address**

⌨ **Type your password**

⊂ **Click** | Sign in |

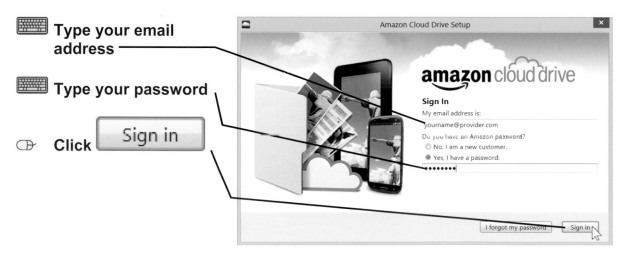

☞ **Click**

Create my Cloud Drive

Amazon will now create a folder called *Cloud Drive* on your computer. This folder will synchronize automatically with your online Cloud Drive. If you add a file to the folder, it is automatically uploaded to your Cloud Drive, and vice versa.

You see this message:

The *Cloud Drive* folder contains default folders for documents, pictures and videos:

These folders can be accessed from the apps *Docs*, *Photos* and *Videos* on the Kindle Fire HDX.

New folders you create with

New

folder can only be accessed via the Amazon website using the *Silk* app. This means you cannot create a new folder for example, with your e-books and view them on your Kindle.

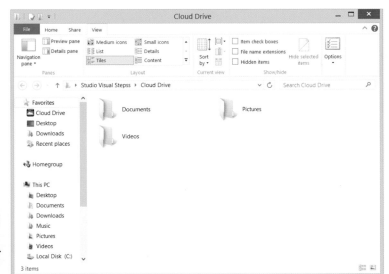

☞ **Close** *Internet Explorer* ✂¹⁷

HELP! I do not see the Cloud Drive folder.

If you do not see the *Cloud Drive* folder, you can open it like this using *File Explorer*:

☞ **Click**

6.6 Uploading Files to the Cloud Drive

Files you add to the *Cloud Drive* folder will be uploaded automatically to your Cloud Drive. You can use the same method to add files as you did in *section 6.4 Copying Files Using USB Transfer*. First you open an extra *File Explorer* window like this:

☞ **Right-click**

A menu appears:

☞ **Click**
   File Explorer

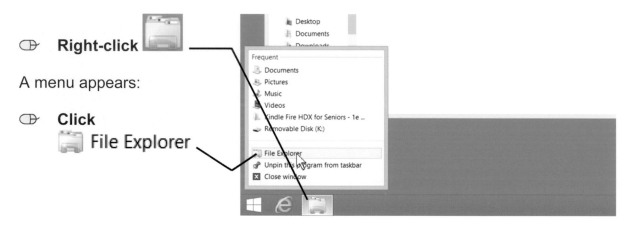

A second window has opened on top of the first window. In the second window you display the practice files:

☞ **Click** Documents **to open the (*My*) *Documents* folder**

Practice Files
☞ **Double-click** Kindle Fire HD

You display the windows side-by-side:

☞ **Let the *Practice Files Kindle Fire HDX* window fill the right-hand side of the screen** 👣²⁰

☞ **Let the *Cloud Drive* window fill the left-hand side of the screen** 👣²⁰

You see both windows. Now you can copy the practice files:

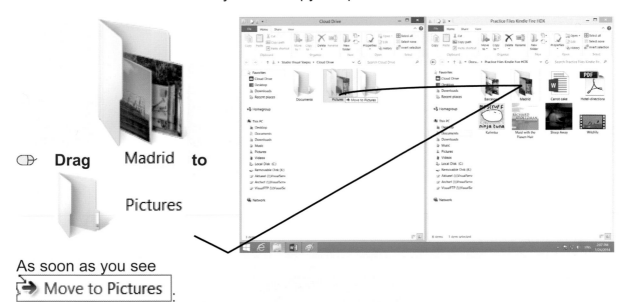

☞ **Drag**   Madrid   **to**

   Pictures

As soon as you see
📑➡ Move to Pictures .

☞ **Release the mouse button**

Since the *Cloud Drive* folder is on the same hard drive as the folder containing the practice files, the folder is moved instead of copied. You do the same with a document:

☞ **Move**   Carrot cake   **to**   Documents   👣²¹

The documents, the photos and the video have now been copied to the Cloud Drive.

Please note:

You cannot upload music files to your *Cloud Drive* folder. If you want to upload your music files, you can use *Amazon Cloud Player*.

This is a service that allows you to stream music to your Kindle Fire HDX.

Streaming means that the music is sent to your Kindle Fire HDX as you are listening to it, over a Wi-Fi connection. The music is stored online, not on your Kindle Fire HDX.

Music you purchase from the *Amazon MP3 Store* is stored on your Cloud Drive for free. If you want to upload your own music collection, you can import the first 250 songs for free. Importing up to 250,000 songs costs $24.99/year.

You can read more about *Amazon Cloud Player* in the *Tips* at the end of this chapter.

You can check the remaining storage space like this:

☞ **Click** ◢

☞ **Place the mouse pointer on** ☁

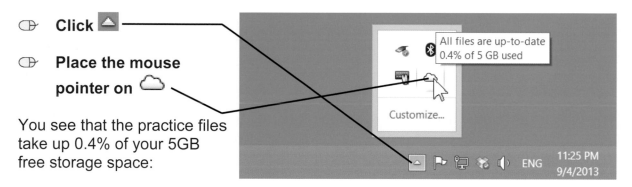

You see that the practice files take up 0.4% of your 5GB free storage space:

All practice files have been copied, some directly to the Kindle Fire HDX and the others to the Cloud Drive.

☞ **Close all windows** 👣17

6.7 Accessing the Cloud Drive Online

You can access the contents of your Cloud Drive from any computer with an Internet connection. You can check if the files have been uploaded to the Cloud Drive like this:

☞ **Open the web page www.amazon.com** ✂ 15

👆 **Place the mouse pointer on Your Account ▾**

Hello. Sign in

👆 **Click** Sign in

⌨ **Type your email address and password**

👆 **Click** Sign in using our secure server ▶

👆 **Click**
Hello, John
Your Account ▾

👆 **Click** Your Cloud Drive
5 GB of free storage

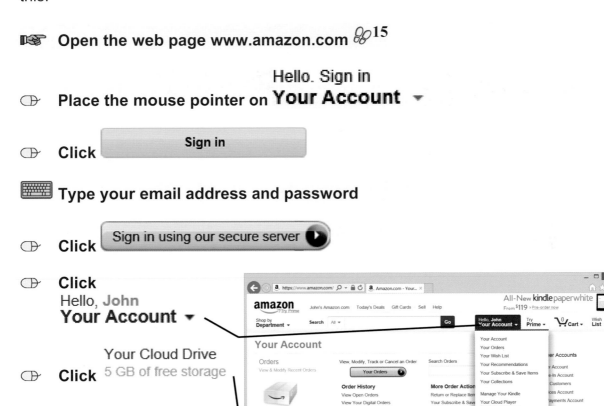

👆 **If necessary, click** ❯ Continue to your Cloud Drive

You see the three default folders:

👆 **Click** Documents

You see the document you uploaded:

On the left hand-side you see the folder list:

☞ By Pictures, click ➕

☞ Click Madrid

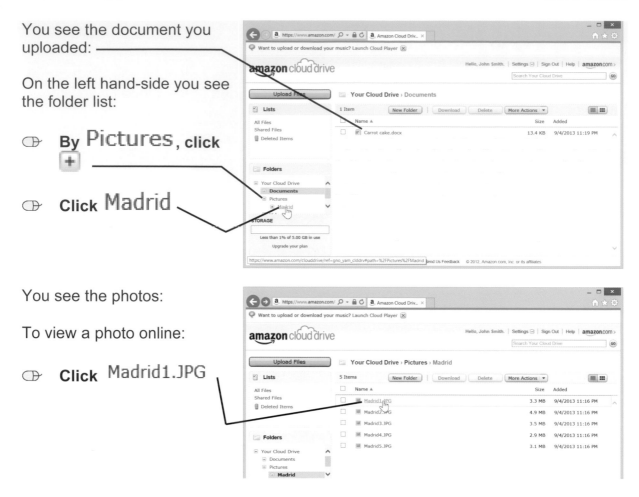

You see the photos:

To view a photo online:

☞ Click Madrid1.JPG

You see the photo and you can even watch a slideshow:

☞ **Move the mouse pointer to the top of the window**

A bar appears:

☞ Click ▶ Slideshow

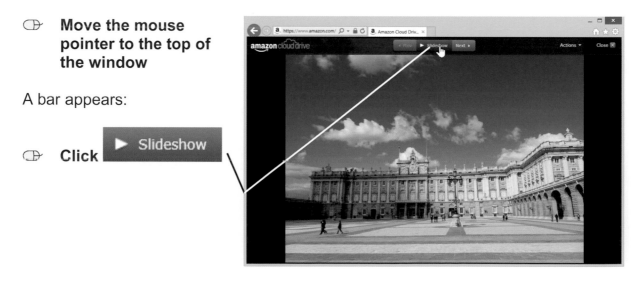

The photos from the selected folder appear one-by-one. To go back to the Cloud Drive website:

👆 **Move the mouse pointer to the top of the window**

👆 **Click** Close

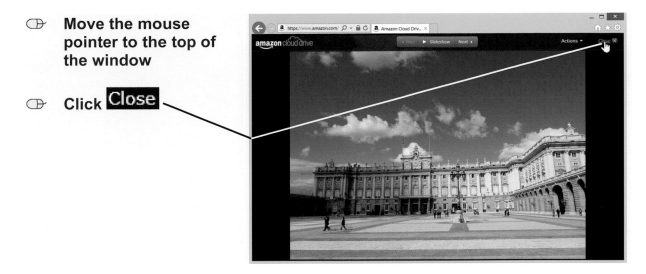

If you use a public computer, it is best to sign out before you close the browser window. That way no one will have access to your files:

👆 **Click** Sign Out

You will see the sign in window again.

In the next chapter you will learn how to work with photos, movies, documents and music.

👉 **Close all windows** 👣 [17]

6.8 Background Information

Dictionary

Amazon Cloud Drive	Program that assists in transferring files from your computer to your Cloud Drive. It creates a folder called *Cloud Drive* on your computer. This folder will synchronize automatically with your online Cloud Drive. If you add a file to the folder, it is automatically uploaded to your Cloud Drive and vice versa.
Cloud Drive folder	The folder that is created on your computer by the *Amazon Cloud Drive* program.
Compressed folder	A compressed folder contains one or more files that have been compressed to reduce file size. Compressed files and folders take up less storage space and can be transferred to other computers more quickly than uncompressed files and folders.
Desktop	The main working space on your computer screen.
Driver, device drive	A driver is a small piece of software that tells the operating system and other software how to communicate with a piece of hardware.
File Explorer	*File Explorer*, previously known as *Windows Explorer*, is a tool for file management and navigation.
Micro-B USB cable	This cable has a regular USB connector on one end that you can plug into your PC or Mac, and a small (micro-B) connector on the other that fits into the slot on your Kindle Fire HDX.
MP3	Short for *MPEG-2 Audio Layer 3*. MP3 is the most common kind of digital music file.
MP4	Short for *MPEG-4 Part 14*. MP4 is a digital multimedia format most commonly used to store video and audio.
Sideloading	Transfer files from the Kindle Fire HDX using a USB cable. Also called *USB Transfer*.
Streaming	Playing a media file that is sent to your Kindle Fire HDX as you are listening to it or watching it, over a Wi-Fi connection. The music or video is stored online, not on your Kindle Fire HDX.
Unzip	Decompress or unpack a compressed folder.

- Continue on the next page -

USB	Short for *Universal Serial Bus*, an industry standard for short-distance digital data communications. USB allows data to be transferred between devices.
USB Cable	Popular cable type, used mostly to connect computers to peripheral devices such as tablets, cameras, printers, scanners, and more.
USB Port	Standard cable connection interface on personal computers and consumer electronics.
USB Transfer	Transfer files from the Kindle Fire HDX using a USB cable. Also called *sideloading*.
Zipped folder	See *Compressed folder*.

Source: Kindle Fire HDX User Guide, Wikipedia

Storage space on your Kindle Fire HDX
The Kindle Fire HDX has 16 or 32 GB storage space.
A regular e-book takes up less than 1 MB storage space, so it is not likely that you will run out of space because of your book collection. But if you store high quality photos, music and (HD) video on you Kindle Fire HDX you will run out of space faster.

Storage space on the Cloud Drive
Files you store online on the Cloud Drive do not take up storage space on the Kindle Fire HDX. Your *Amazon* account comes with 5 GB free online storage space. Digital items you buy in the Amazon stores are stored on the Cloud Drive without using your free 5 GB storage space. This means you can use 5 GB storage space for files you transfer from your computer to your Kindle Fire HDX. If 5 GB is not enough, you can purchase more space (prices as of February 2014):

- 20 GB $ 10.00 / year
- 50 GB $ 20.00 / year
- 100 GB $ 50.00 / year

- 200 GB $ 100.00 / year
- 500 GB $ 250.00 / year
- 1,000 GB $ 500.00 / year

To purchase more space:

☞ **Open the web page www.amazon.com** 👣8, 👣15

☞ **Sign in with your *Amazon* account on www.amazon.com** 👣22

☞ **Click Your Account ▼** , Your Cloud Drive 5 GB of free storage , Upgrade your plan

Hello, John

6.9 Tips

 Tip

Requirements for videos
The Kindle Fire HDX only plays MP4 video files. MP4 is the format of the videos you record with a smartphone and many other devices.
Videos or home movies you upload to the *Videos* folder on your Cloud Drive, to stream them to your Kindle Fire HDX, cannot exceed twenty minutes in length.

 Tip

Amazon Cloud Drive tile
The *Amazon Cloud Drive* program automatically creates a tile on the *Windows 8.1*

start screen: . This tile gives quick access to the *Cloud Drive* folder. In *Windows 7* and *Vista*, the program icon is placed in the Start menu.

 Tip

Download file from Cloud Drive
Need a file from your Cloud Drive? You can download it like this:

☞   **Check the box ☑ by the file, for example** Madrid1.JPG

☞   **Click** ⎣ Download (1) ⎦

Now you can open or save the file:

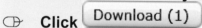

Do you want to open or save **Madrid1.JPG** (3.25 MB) from **zcd-00.s3-external-1.amazonaws.com**?   ×

                                                                    Open   Save ▾   Cancel

Tip

Transfer your book collection to the Kindle Fire HDX
If you have e-books on your computer, you can transfer them to your Kindle Fire HDX by USB transfer. The only problem is that the books you transfer like this, will appear in the *Docs* library, not in the *Books* library.

☞ **Drag the selected file(s) to**

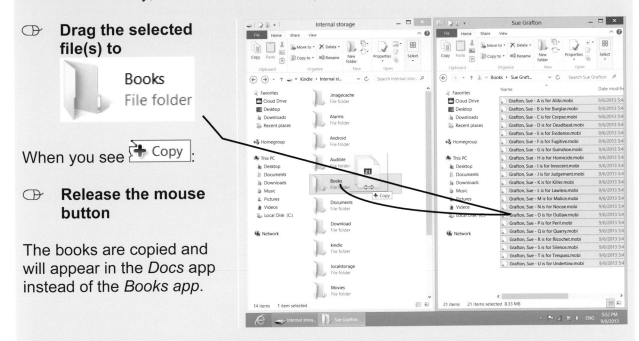

When you see ⊞ Copy :

☞ **Release the mouse button**

The books are copied and will appear in the *Docs* app instead of the *Books app*.

Please note: this only works for .mobi files and PDF files. The Kindle Fire HDX does not support the .epub file format. But you can convert .epub files to .mobi files with the *Calibre* program, for example.

Please note: this does not work when the books are stored in folders. Make sure you only copy the .mobi files to the *Books* folder.

Tip

Amazon Cloud Player

Amazon Music Importer is a free program you can use to upload music files to *Amazon Cloud Player*. *Amazon Cloud Player* is a service that allows you to stream music to your Kindle Fire HDX. Music you purchase from the *Amazon MP3 Store* is stored online for free. You can import your own music files as well. The first 250 songs can be imported for free. If you want to add more music, you can import up to 250,000 songs for $24.99/year. You can download *Amazon Music Importer* like this:

☞ **Open the web page www.amazon.com on your computer** ⬿15

👆 **Place the mouse pointer on** Hello. **Sign in** **Your Account** ▾

👆 **Click** Sign in

⌨ **Type your email address and password**

👆 **Click** Sign in using our secure server ▶

👆 **Place the mouse pointer on** Hello, John **Your Account** ▾

👆 **Click** Your Cloud Player / Play from any browser

👆 **Click** Get started --- it's free

👆 **Click** Import now

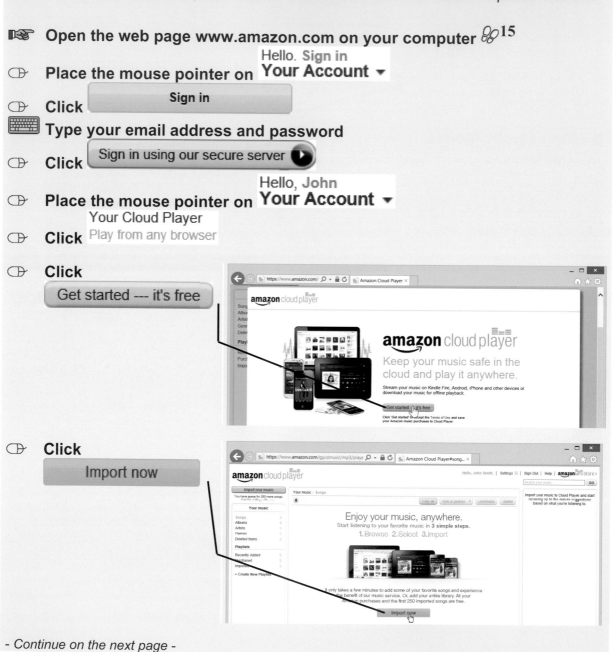

- Continue on the next page -

You will see the download instructions:

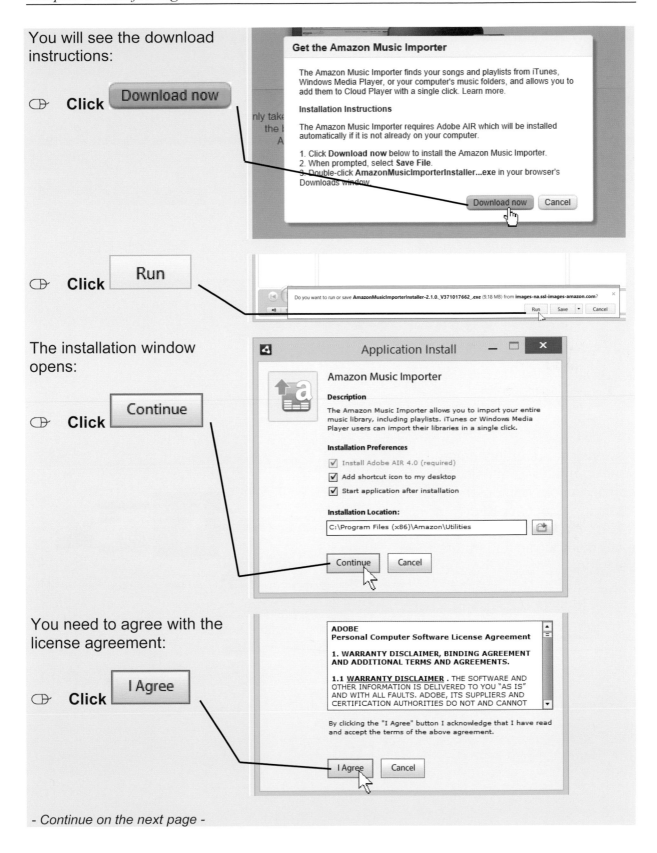

☞ **Click** Download now

☞ **Click** Run

The installation window opens:

☞ **Click** Continue

You need to agree with the license agreement:

☞ **Click** I Agree

- Continue on the next page -

You may see a window about your firewall. You need to give permission to continue:

👉 **Click** [🛡 Allow access]

☞ **Give permission to continue**

Now you need to authorize your device to import music to your *Cloud Player*. A total of ten devices can be authorized with your *Cloud Player*.

👉 **Click** [Authorize Device]

Now you can start scanning your computer for music. You can scan your computer totally or select specific folders to scan. In this example specific folders are selected:

👉 **Click**

- Continue on the next page -

In this example the music files are stored in the *Music* folder:

☞ **Click** 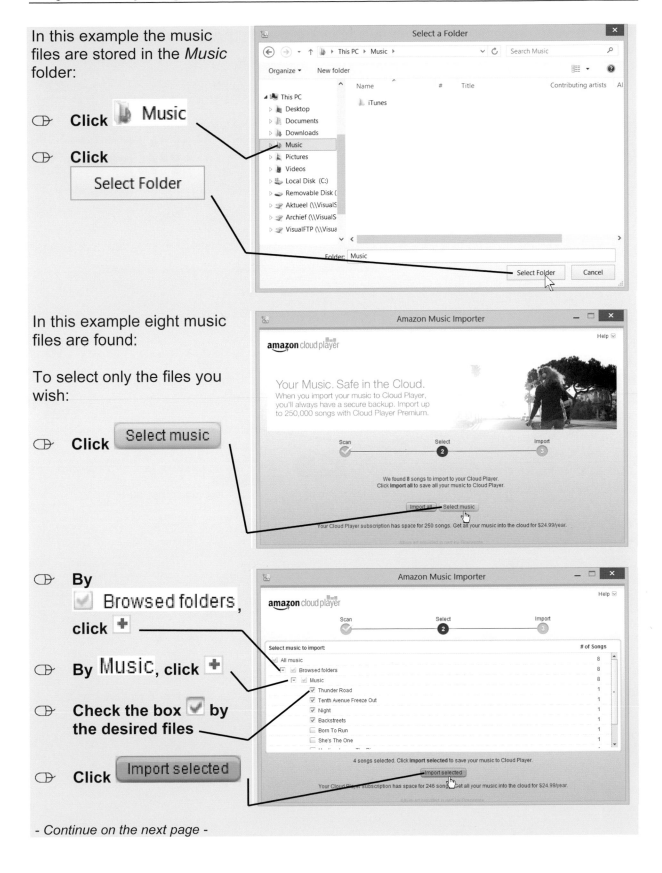 **Music**

☞ **Click**

Select Folder

In this example eight music files are found:

To select only the files you wish:

☞ **Click** Select music

☞ **By** ☑ Browsed folders, **click** ➕

☞ **By** Music, **click** ➕

☞ **Check the box** ☑ **by the desired files**

☞ **Click** Import selected

- Continue on the next page -

The importing process will start and you can follow the progress in the window. When the songs have been imported:

⊕ **Click** Close

Now you can go back to the browser window:

☞ **Open the browser window**

⊕ **If necessary, click** ↻

You see the imported files in the *Cloud Player* window:

You can play the music files on your Kindle as described in the next chapter.

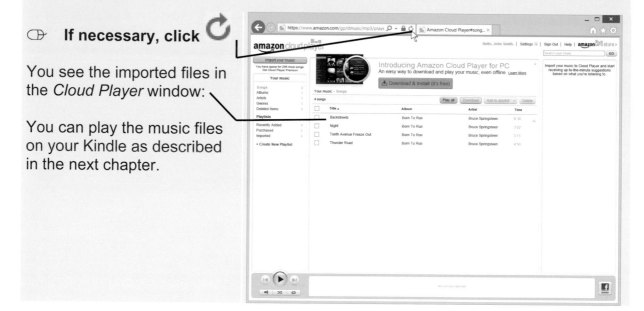

7. Photos, Video, Music and Documents

You can do more with your Kindle Fire HDX than just read books, send emails and surf the web. The *Photos* library lets you view the photos that are stored on your device and on your Cloud Drive. You can download the photos from the Cloud Drive to the Kindle Fire HDX and send them by email. You can even take pictures with the camera on the front of the Kindle Fire HDX.

If you want to watch your videos you can use the video player in the *Photos* library. Just like pictures, you can also shoot video with the camera on the front.

Your Kindle Fire HDX also contains a *Music* library and a music player. You can play the music files stored on your Kindle Fire HDX and create playlists of your favorite songs.

The *Docs* library contains the documents that you have stored on your Kindle Fire HDX. You can view these documents with the *OfficeSuite* viewer. Editing documents is only possible with a paid app.

In this chapter you will learn how to:

- view photos;
- download photos from the Cloud Drive;
- send a photo by email;
- take pictures with your Kindle Fire HDX;
- play a video;
- shoot a video;
- play music;
- create a playlist;
- view documents.

 Please note:

To be able to follow all the examples in this chapter, the practice files should be copied to the Kindle Fire HDX and to the Cloud Drive. If you have not done that yet, please work through *Chapter 6 Transferring Files to The Kindle Fire HDX* first.

7.1 Viewing Photos in the Photos library

Photos on the Kindle and the Cloud Drive can be viewed in the *Photos* library. Here is how you open the *Photos* library:

👉 Tap

If this is the first time you use the *Photos* app, you will see a couple of setup screens that offer to help you add photos to your Kindle. The setup screens are all displayed in portrait mode:

☞ **If necessary, unlock the screen rotation** $\mathscr{O}^{10}$ **and hold the Kindle upright**

👉 **Tap**

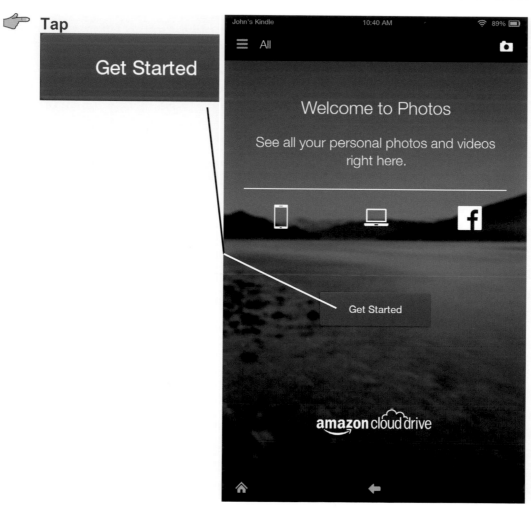

For now, you do not need to add photos from your smartphone or other mobile device:

 Tap

 I don't use these

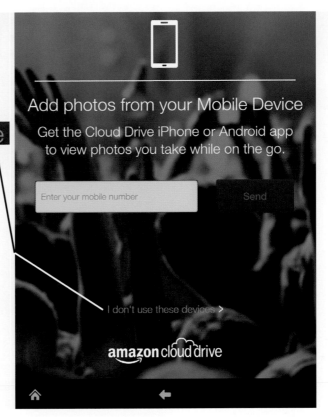

The 'photo uploader' mentioned in this screen is *Amazon Cloud Drive*.
You have already added photos from your computer using *Amazon Cloud Drive*, so you can skip this step:

☞ **Tap**

I don't use a PC or

You do not need to add your
Facebook photos now:

☞ **Tap**

I don't use Faceboo

In *Chapter 9 Using Skype,
Facebook and Twitter* you
can read more about using
Facebook on your Kindle Fire
HDX.

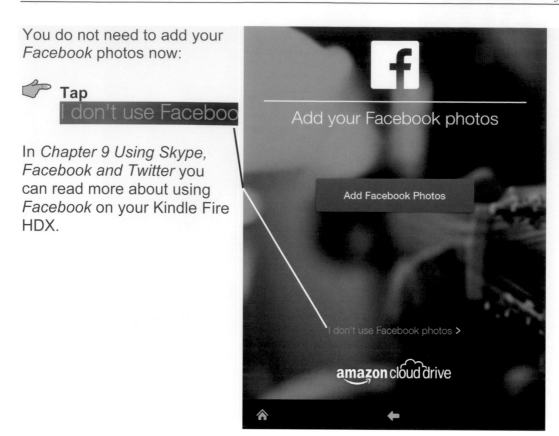

Now you can turn the Kindle again:

☞ **Turn the Kindle Fire HDX horizontally**

You will see the folder with practice photos that you copied to your Cloud Drive and
stored on your device. To see only the photos stored on the Kindle Fire HDX:

☞ **Tap**

☞ **Tap** Device

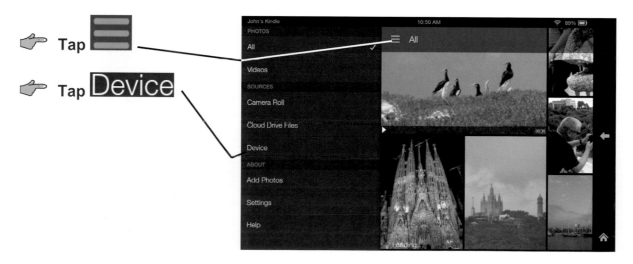

Now you will see two folders: the practice photos and the video you copied to the Kindle Fire HDX via USB transfer:

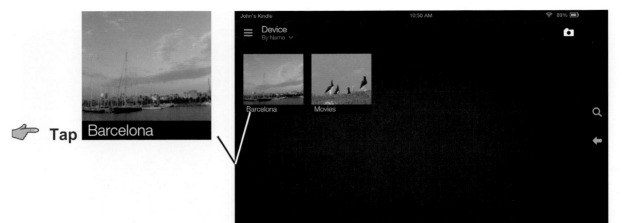

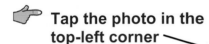
☞ **Tap** Barcelona

The photos in the folder are displayed in different sizes:

☞ **Tap the photo in the top-left corner**

 Tip

Different display
If you hold the Kindle Fire HDX upright, you will see the photos arranged in square shaped tiles:

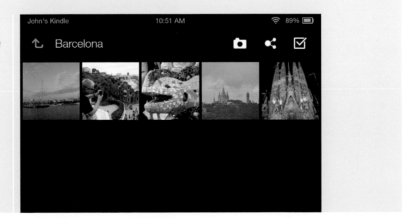

The photo will be displayed on a full screen with the Options bar on the right-hand side and the menu bar at the top. This is how you make the Options bar and Menu bar disappear:

☞ **Tap the photo**

The bars disappear and you see the photo full screen. You can quickly go to the next photo:

☞ **Swipe the photo from right to left**

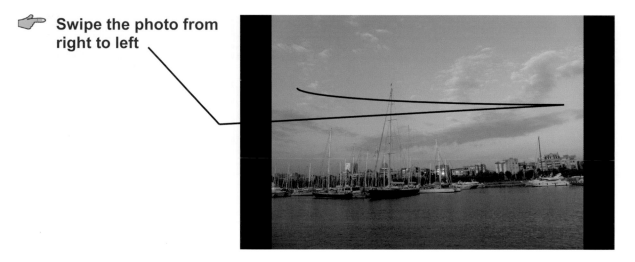

You will see the next photo.

☞ **Swipe the photo from right to left**

You will see the third photo. You can also zoom in on a photo. To do this, you need to use the same touchscreen gestures you previously used while surfing the Internet:

 Tap the photo

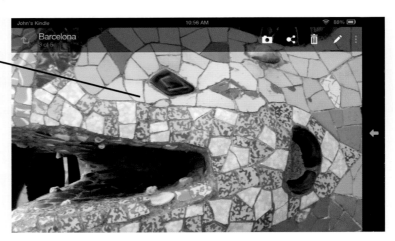

You see the bars again:

 Double-tap the photo

You will zoom in on the photo:

You can zoom in even further:

 Place your thumb and index finger on the screen and spread

them apart

You will zoom in further:

 Tip

Move
You can move the photo you have zoomed in on by gently dragging it with your finger in the desired direction (up, down, left or right).

This is how you zoom out again:

 Place your thumb and index finger on the screen and move them towards

each other (pinching inwards)

Tip

Double-tap
You can also double-tap to quickly zoom out to the regular view of the photo.

Now you will again see the regular view of the photo. You can go back to the first photo like this:

☞ **Swipe the screen twice from left to right**

You will see the first photo again. To go back to the *Photos* library:

☞ **Tap**

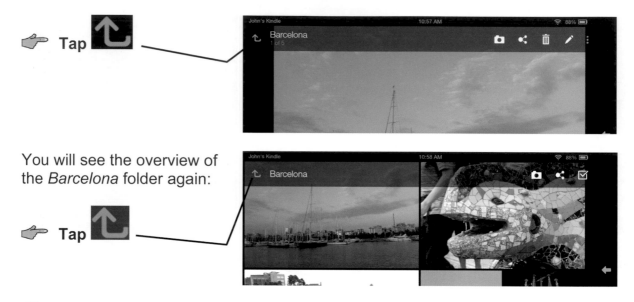

You will see the overview of the *Barcelona* folder again:

☞ **Tap**

 Tip

Delete a photo
There are two ways to delete a picture from the Kindle Fire HDX. The first method uses the Options bar:

☞ **Tap** 🗑

☞ **Tap** OK

The second method uses a pop-up menu on the photo itself:

☞ **Tap and hold the photo**
☞ **Tap** Delete
☞ **Tap** OK

7.2 Viewing Photos on the Cloud Drive

You can view photos stored on the Cloud Drive the same way. You open the *Cloud Drive Files* library:

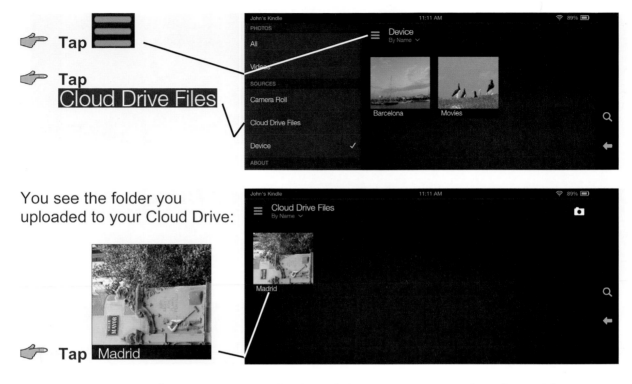

☞ **Tap**

☞ **Tap**
Cloud Drive Files

You see the folder you uploaded to your Cloud Drive:

☞ **Tap** Madrid

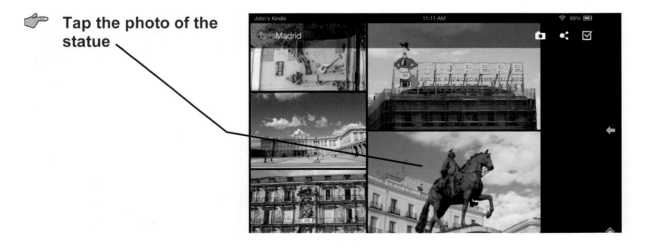

The photos on the Cloud Drive are displayed the same way as the photos that are stored on the Kindle Fire HDX:

☞ **Tap the photo of the statue**

You can also zoom in on photos that are stored on the Cloud Drive. You do not need to do that now.

7.3 Downloading Photos From the Cloud Drive

Photos that are on the Cloud Drive can only be viewed when you have a Wi-Fi connection. If you want to store a photo from the Cloud Drive on your Kindle Fire HDX so you can view it offline, you need to download it. You can do that like this:

 **Place your finger on the photo and hold it**

 **Tap**  Download

You will briefly see this message: **Now downloading to your device...**. You can check to see if the photo has been downloaded:

 **Tap** ⤴ **twice**

 **Tap** ☰, Device

The *Device Photos* library now contains a folder named *Madrid*:

☞ **Tap** Madrid

The folder only contains one photo:

☞ **Tap the photo**

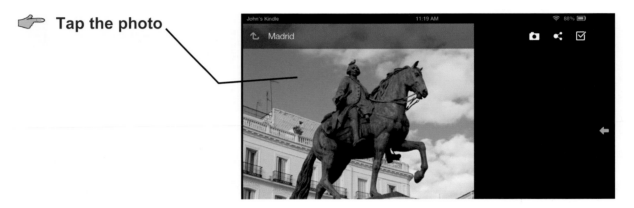

You will see the photo full screen.

7.4 Sending a Photo by Email

If you have a nice picture on your Kindle Fire HDX, you can share it with someone by sending it as an attachment in an email. You can do that right from the *Photos* app:

☞ **Tap** [icon]

☞ **Tap** ✉ **E-mail**

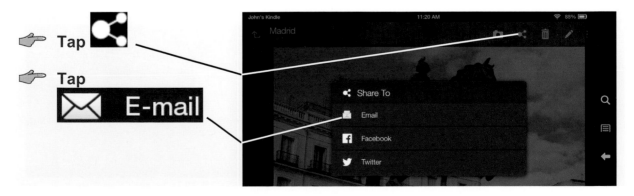

HELP! I do not see the Menu bar.
The Menu bar will appear when you tap the photo.

A new message will be
opened with the photo added
as an attachment: ——

You can send the message
the same way as you learned
in *Chapter 4 Using Email with
Your Tablet.* For now, this will
not be necessary:

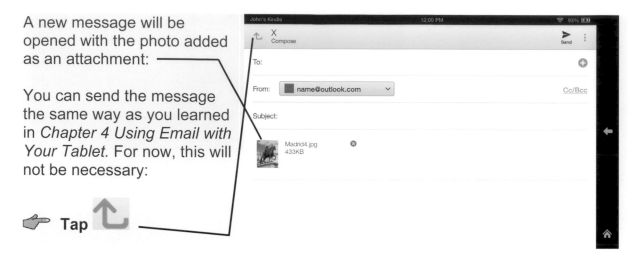

☞ **Tap**

You will see the photo again.

7.5 Taking Pictures

You can use the camera on the front of the screen to take pictures.

➥ **Please note:**
Make sure there is enough light. The Kindle Fire HDX does not have a flash. If you
take pictures in poor lighting conditions, the photos will look grainy.

You can go back to the *Photos* library:

☞ **Tap** 🔙 **twice**

☞ **Tap** 📷

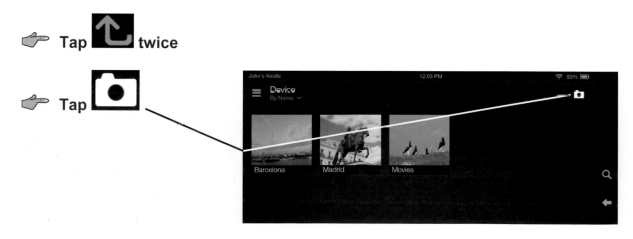

The photos and videos you take with your Kindle can be saved automatically on the Cloud Drive. Automatic photo uploads count against your total Cloud Drive storage, and are enabled by default when you are connected to a Wi-Fi network. In this example we have chosen not to save the photos and videos on the Cloud Drive:

☞ **Tap**
No thanks, turn it o

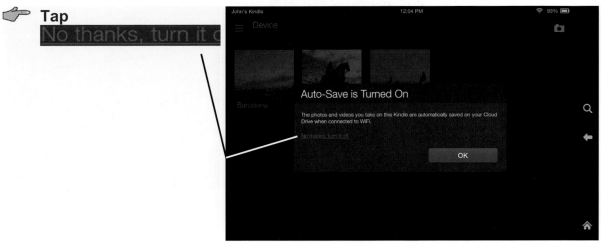

💡 **Tip**

Enable automatic uploads
If you decide later to allow your photos to be saved automatically to the Cloud Drive, you can turn automatic photo uploads on like this:

☞ **Open the *Settings* screen** 👣12

☞ **Tap** Applications, Photos

☞ **Tap** On

Here you see the amount of space you are currently using in your total Cloud Drive storage:

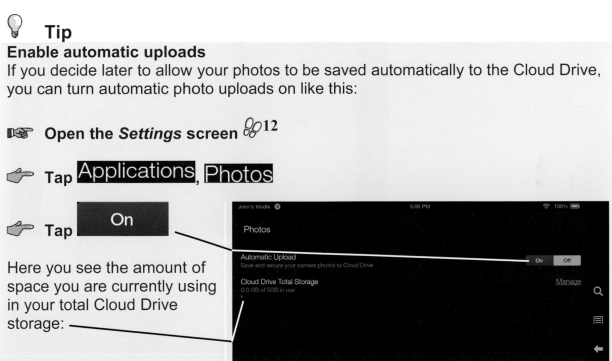

Since the camera faces you when you look at the screen, you can use it to quickly make a 'selfie' (self-portrait):

☞ **Hold the Kindle Fire HDX in front of you**

This is how you take the picture:

👉 Tap

You hear the sound of a camera shutter.

The photo will be stored on your Kindle Fire HDX.

The picture you took appears as a thumbnail image at the bottom of your screen:

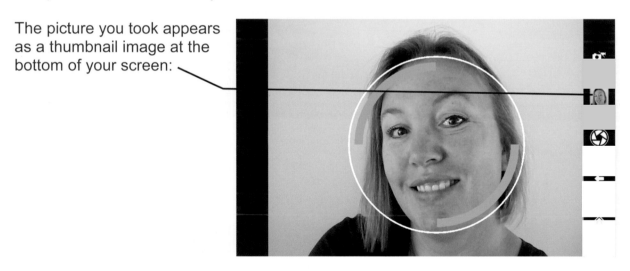

Taking a picture of an object in front of you is a bit harder, since you cannot see the screen when you turn the Kindle Fire HDX around:

👉 **Hold your finger near the** 🔘 **button and point the camera towards the object you want to photograph**

👉 Tap 🔘

You will hear the sound of the camera shutter again.

Tip

Zoom and focus

You can digitally zoom in and out using the volume control buttons on the back of the Kindle Fire HDX or pinch the screen with two fingers. You can also tap the screen to focus on a specific location.

To go back to the *Photos* library:

👉 **Tap**

You will see that the pictures you took with the Kindle Fire HDX are stored in the default folder called *Camera Roll*:

👉 **Tap** Camera Roll

➥ Please note:

If you have chosen to upload the photos to the Cloud Drive automatically, the checkmark ✅ by the folder indicates that the photos in the folder have been uploaded:

The folder contains the photos you just took:

👉 **Tap** ⬅️

You will see the *Photos* library again.

7.6 Playing a Video

The practice files you transferred to the Kindle Fire HDX also contain a video. You can view this video like this:

☞ **Tap** Movies

You will see a thumbnail of the practice video:

☞ **Tap the video**

The video will be played right away on a full screen:

☞ **Tap the image**

Here is the volume button:

With this button you can rewind the video:

With the slider ▭ you can fast forward or rewind the video:

This is the pause/play button:

To go back:

☞ **Tap**

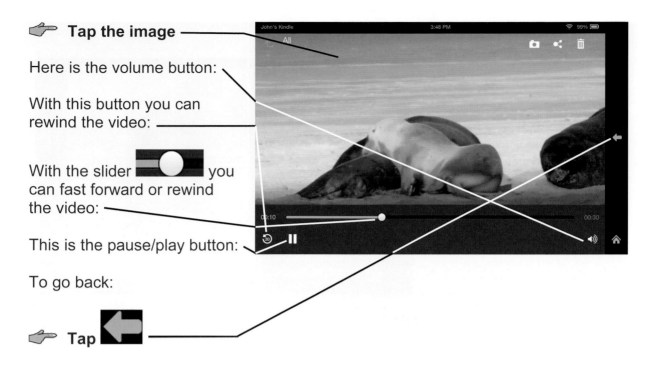

7.7 Shoot a Video

You can also record videos with the camera on the front of your Kindle. To do that:

☞ **Tap** 📷

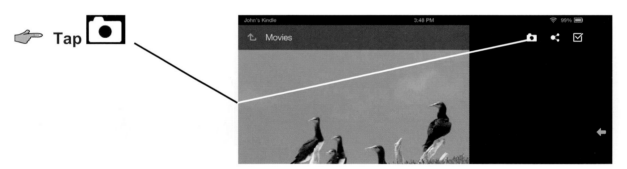

The camera mode will switch to video mode:

☞ **Tap** 📷🎥

To start recording:

👉 **Tap**

The camera is recording. The ⬤ button changes to ⬛. You use the same
button to stop recording:

👉 **Tap**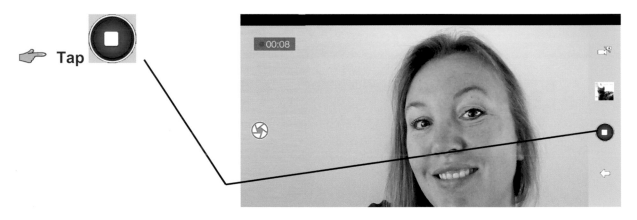

🢂 **Please note:**

When you record a video, you can use the same options for zooming in and out and
focusing on a certain point as you do with picture taking. See the *Tip* on page 211.

Your video recordings are also stored in the *Camera Roll* folder. This is the same
folder that contains the pictures you took with the Kindle camera. You can view your
recorded videos in the same way you learned with the practice video in the previous
section. For now you can go back to the Home screen:

👉 **Tap**  **twice**

7.8 Playing Music

The Kindle Fire HDX also contains a good music player. To open the player, you first need to open the *Music* library:

☞ Tap Music

If you open the *Music* app for the first time, you might see the Cloud Drive. To open the songs on the device:

☞ Tap On Device

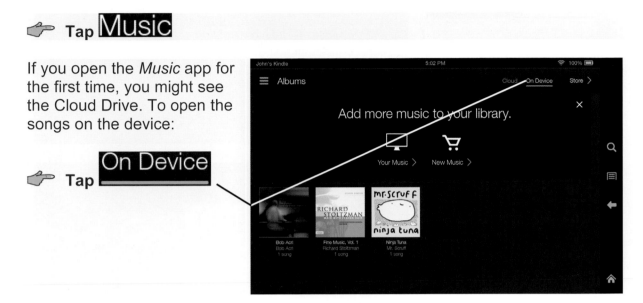

The *Music* library contains three practice files:

The practice files are taken from three different albums. To display the individual songs:

☞ Tap ▬

☞ Tap Songs

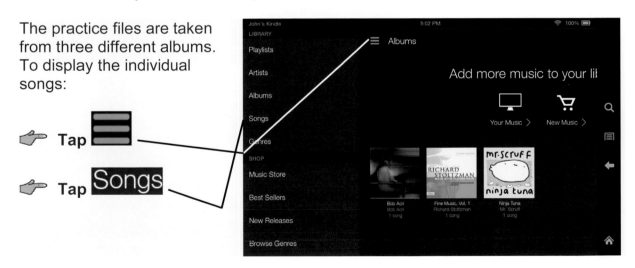

👉 **Tap a song, for example**

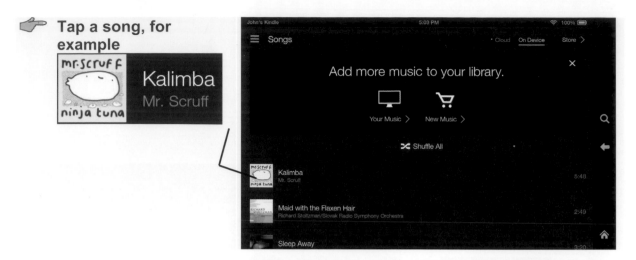

You hear the song and the music player will be displayed full screen:

You will see various buttons which give you control over how the music is played:

Here are the functions for these buttons:

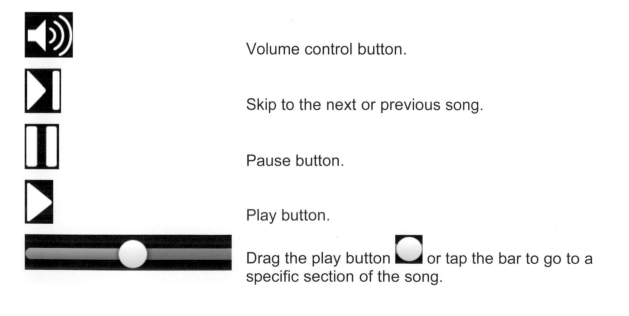

Volume control button.

Skip to the next or previous song.

Pause button.

Play button.

Drag the play button ⬤ or tap the bar to go to a specific section of the song.

Random play (also called shuffle).

Repeat:
- tap once: all songs will be repeated. The button turns into .
- tap twice: the current song will be repeated. The button turns into .

You can hide the music player and go back to the song list. In the top-left corner of the screen:

 **Tap**

You see the song list again:

The music player has moved to the bottom of the screen:

To display the full music player again:

 **Tap an empty part of the music player**

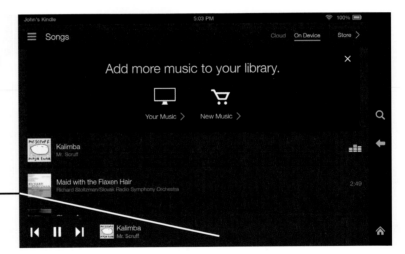

You see the music player full-screen. In the top-left corner of the screen:

Tap

While the music is playing, you can quit the app and do something else:

☞ **Go back to the Home screen** ⌘³

The music will keep playing. You can display the control buttons of the *Music* app in any other app, by opening the *Quick settings* menu:

☞ **Open the *Quick settings* menu** 🐾²

You will see the control buttons for the *Music* app in the notification area: To pause the music:

☞ **Tap**

☞ **Swipe upwards**

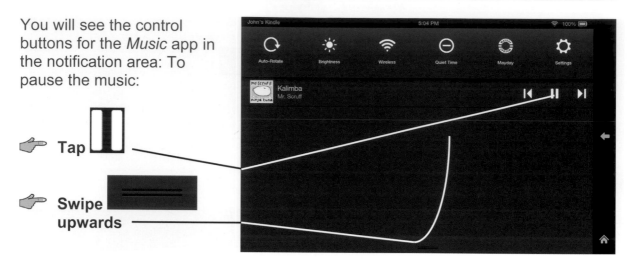

Now you will see the Home screen again. You can open the *Music* app again:

☞ **Tap** Music

7.9 Create a Playlist

A useful option in the *Music* library is the possibility of creating playlists. A playlist contains your favorite songs in the order you prefer. Once you have created such a list you can play it over and over again. This is how you create a new playlist in the *Music* library:

☞ **Tap**

☞ **Tap** Playlists

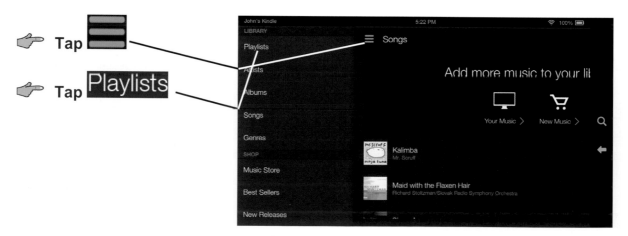

You will see that there already is one default playlist, the Recently Added playlist:

To create a new playlist:

☞ **Tap** ➕

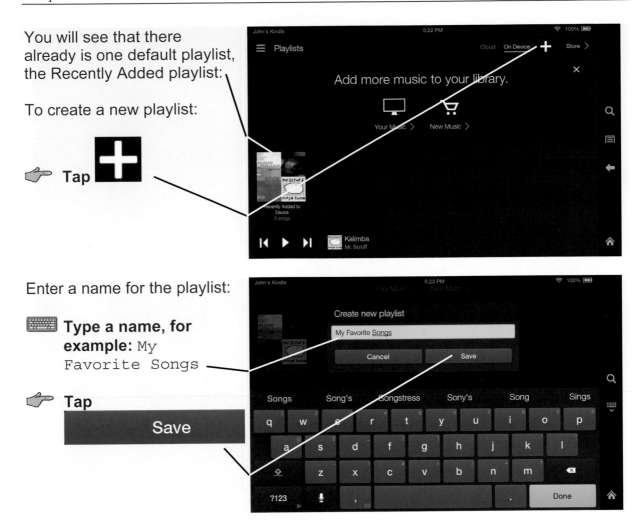

Enter a name for the playlist:

⌨ **Type a name, for example:** My Favorite Songs

☞ **Tap**

Save

Now you can add your songs to the playlist:

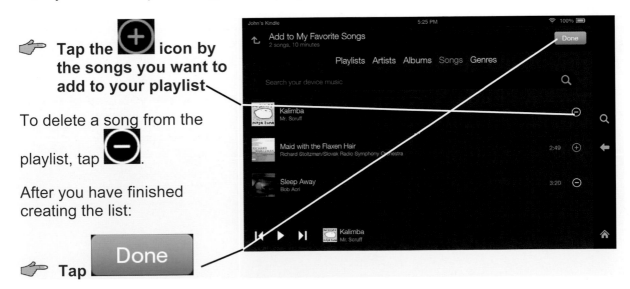

☞ **Tap the ⊕ icon by the songs you want to add to your playlist**

To delete a song from the playlist, tap ⊖.

After you have finished creating the list:

☞ **Tap** **Done**

You see the new playlist:

If you want to add or remove songs, tap .

If you want to play the playlist in random order, tap ⚡ Shuffle All.

☞ Tap ↰

You see the new playlists:

☞ **Go back to the Home screen** 👣³

7.10 Viewing Documents

The *Docs* library contains a handy document viewer. Unfortunately you cannot edit documents. This is how you open the *Docs* library:

☞ Tap

☞ Tap ⊠

First take a look at a document on your device:

☞ Tap **On Device**

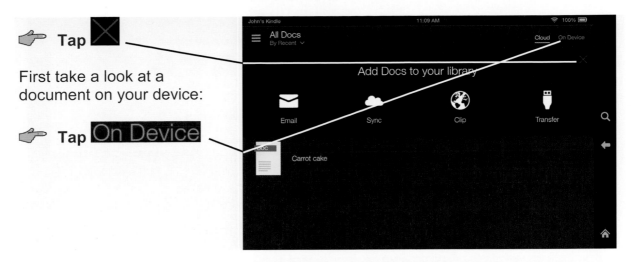

You will see the PDF file you copied to the Kindle Fire HDX:

☞ **Tap**

You see a part of the PDF file:

To see the rest of the page:

☞ **Swipe the page up**

☞ **Swipe the page down**

Tap the page

Thumbnails of the pages will be displayed at the bottom of the screen:

The practice file only has one page:

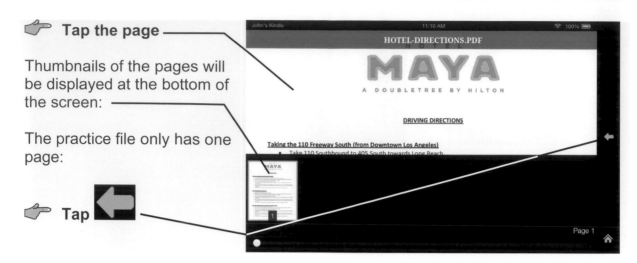

 **Tap**

💡 **Tip**

Navigate with thumbnails
If you want to go to a different page in a document with multiple pages:

👉 **Tap the thumbnail**

You can check the contents of the *Cloud Docs* library:

👉 **Tap Cloud**

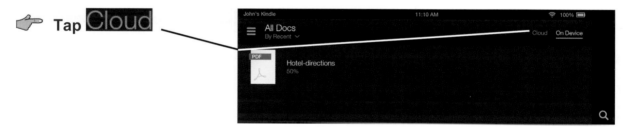

You will see the *Microsoft Word* document that you uploaded to the Cloud Drive:

At the top of the screen you see different options to sort the documents on your Cloud Drive:

👉 **Tap**

DOC

Carrot cake

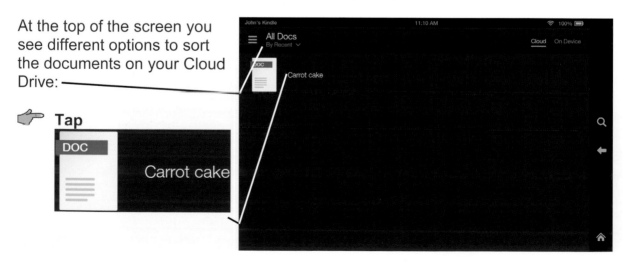

Since the document is on your Cloud Drive, it has to be downloaded to your Kindle Fire HDX before you can open it:

The download starts:

As soon as the download has finished, you can open the file:

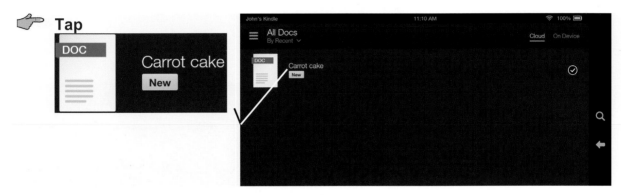

All *Microsoft Office* files will be opened in the *OfficeSuite Viewer* app:

The Menu bar shows various things you can do with the document:

Tap the ⠿ icon to see additonal options:

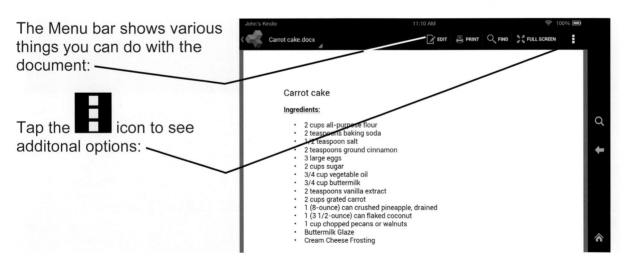

The practice file only has one page. Swipe the page upwards to see the bottom of the page.

You can go back to the *Docs* library like this:

Tap

To check if the downloaded document has been stored on the device:

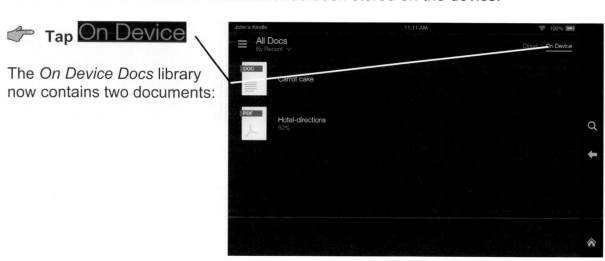

Tap **On Device**

The *On Device Docs* library now contains two documents:

☞ **Go back to the Home screen** 👣³

☞ **Lock or turn off the Kindle Fire HDX, if you wish** 👣⁵

In this chapter you have learned how to work with photos, videos, music and documents both on your device and on the Cloud Drive.

7.11 Background Information

Dictionary

Camera Roll	The name of the folder that contains the pictures and videos you have taken with your Kindle Fire HDX.
Docs library	The section of the Kindle Fire HDX where you store and view your documents.
IMDb	Short for *Internet Movie Database*. The Kindle Fire HDX contains an app with the same name. It allows you to look up information about movies, actors, TV series and more.
Music library	The section of the Kindle where you store and play your music files. You can also create playlists here.
OfficeSuite	App you can use to browse, organize and view files on the Kindle Fire HDX. By default, the free *OfficeSuite Viewer* is installed on your Kindle. To edit files you will need a paid app.
Photos library	The section of the Kindle Fire HDX where you store your photos. You can also take pictures with the camera on the front of the Kindle Fire HDX.
Playlist	A collection of songs arranged in a certain order.
Send-to-Kindle	Service that allows you and people on your Approved Personal Document Email list to email documents, photos and Kindle books to your Kindle. For that you use the email address ending with @kindle.com that is connected with your device.
Shuffle	Play in random order.
Videos	App on the Kindle with which you can rent or buy movies and TV shows.
Zooming	Take a closer look or view from a distance.

Source: Kindle Fire HDX User Guide, Wikipedia

7.12 Tips

 Tip

Add a photo to a contact
You can add a photo of a contact to your contact's data. You can use a photo that was taken with the camera on the Kindle or one that has been transferred to the Kindle through USB. The photo can be found in the *Photos* app.

☞ **Open the *Contacts* app** 🐾14
☞ **Tap the desired contact**

☞ **Tap** *Edit*

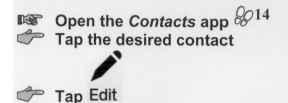

☞ **Tap**

☞ **Tap** Add Photo

Select the album that contains the photo:

☞ **Tap** Photos

☞ **Tap** Just once

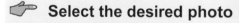

☞ **Select the desired photo**

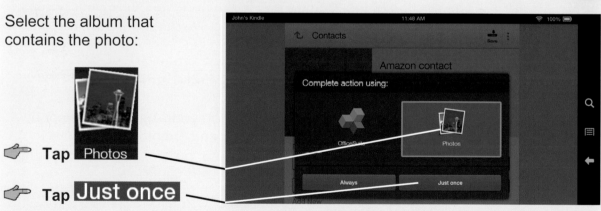

The photo has been added to the contact information:

☞ **Tap** Save

🔆 Tip

Adding an attachment to an email

In this chapter you have learned how to email a photo from the *Photos* library. Using *OfficeSuite*, you can attach any file on your Kindle Fire HDX to an email:

☞ **Open the *Email* app** 🐾¹¹

👉 **Tap New**

👉 **Tap** ⋮

You can choose between a photo or a file:

👉 **Tap Attach File**

👉 **Tap OfficeSuite**

👉 **Tap**
   Internal storage
   Files saved on internal st...

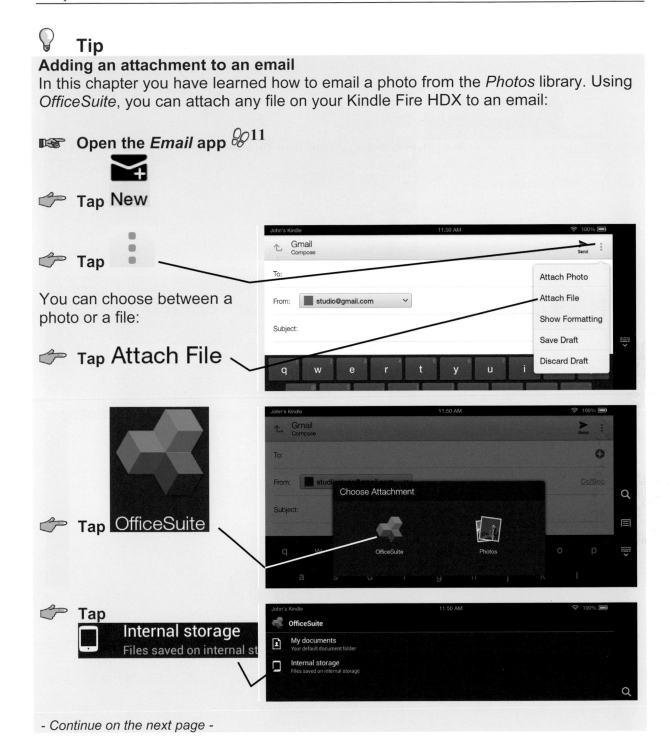

- Continue on the next page -

You see all of the folders on
the Kindle Fire HDX:

☞ **Tap**

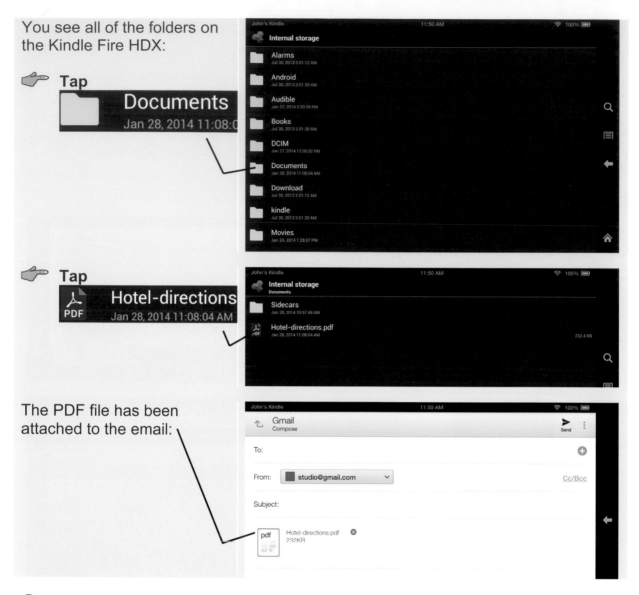

☞ **Tap**

The PDF file has been
attached to the email:

💡 **Tip**

OfficeSuite app
The *OfficeSuite* app comes in handy when you want to browse the files on your
Kindle Fire HDX. This app is automatically opened when a *Word* or *Excel* file is
opened via the *Docs* library.

OfficeSuite Pro is a paid app offering many more options than this viewer. It allows
you to create, view, and edit *Microsoft Word* and *Excel* files. In *Chapter 8
Downloading and Managing Apps* you can read how to download and install paid
and free apps.

Tip

Copying photos to your computer

In *Chapter 6 Transferring Files to the Kindle Fire HDX* you learned how to copy files from your computer to your Kindle using USB transfer. You can use the same method to do things in reverse and transfer files from your Kindle Fire HDX to your computer.

For example the pictures you took with the Kindle Fire HDX. These pictures can be found in the folder named *DCIM*:

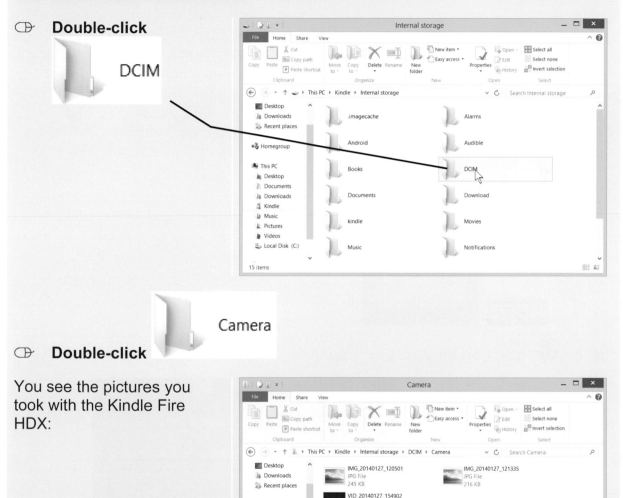

Double-click DCIM

Double-click Camera

You see the pictures you took with the Kindle Fire HDX:

If you have turned on the option that allows automatic upload to the Cloud Drive, you can also download the photos from there. But if you have the automatic upload option turned off, you can copy them to your computer through USB transfer, as described in *Chapter 6 Transferring Files to the Kindle Fire HDX*.

Tip

Printing from the Kindle Fire HDX
The Kindle does not come with a default app that enables printing. There are various paid apps available that fill that gap, and offer a way to print from your Kindle to your wireless printer.
If your printer is installed in a network environment, the Kindle can look for apps to use this printer.

 Tip

IMDb app
IMDb is short for *Internet Movie Database. IMDb* started in 1990 as a hobby project by an international group of movie and TV fans. *IMDb* is now the world's most popular source for movie and TV information. It offers a searchable database of more than 100 million data items including more than 2 million movies, TV and entertainment programs and more than 4 million cast and crew members. *IMDb* was acquired by Amazon. The *IMDb* app is one of default apps on your Kindle Fire HDX.

You can open the *IMDb* app like this:

 Tap Apps, IMDb Movies & TV...

The first time you start the app, you need to decide how you are going to use it.

You will see the start page:

If you do not have an IMDb account yet, you can log in with your *Amazon* account:

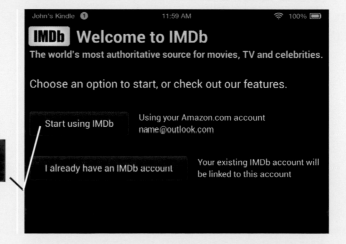

 Tap

 Start using IMDb

- Continue on the next page -

☞ **Tap**

Start using IMDb

Here you can watch the latest trailers:

With 🔍 you can search for information on a movie or TV series:

Tip

Videos app
The *Videos* app allows you to rent or buy popular movies and TV series. If you choose to rent, the item can be watched for a specific time. If you buy a movie or TV series, you can view it as often as you like.
Some TV series allow you to watch the first episode for free and then give you the option of purchasing the remaining episodes.

☞ **Tap**

Tap 🔍 to search for the desired movie or TV show:

You can also tap ▤ to search per category.

☞ **Tap an item** ——

You will see various options for renting and buying:

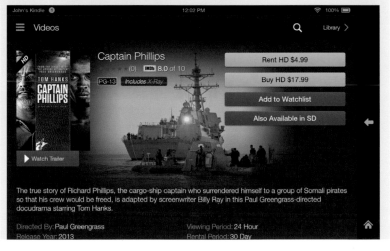

Tip

Send-to-Kindle

You and your approved contacts can send documents to your registered Kindle devices and your Kindle library by emailing them to your *Send-to-Kindle* email address. You can find your *Send-to-Kindle* email address here:

☞ **Open the *Settings* screen** 🐾¹²

👉 **Tap**

Here you see your Send-to-Kindle email address:

To send a document to your Kindle device, simply attach it to an email addressed to your *Send-to-Kindle* email address. It is not necessary to include a subject in the email.

Supported file types are:
Microsoft Word (.DOC, .DOCX), RTF (.RTF), HTML (.HTML, .HTM), JPEG (.JPEG, .JPG), PNG (.PNG), BMP (.BMP), GIF (.GIF), PDF (.PDF) and Kindle Format (.MOBI, .AZW).

Documents can only be sent to your Kindle devices or apps from email accounts that you added to your Approved Personal Document Email List. To edit this list:

☞ **Go to www.amazon.com/manageyourkindle** 🐾¹⁵

☞ **Sign in with you *Amazon* account** 🐾²²

- Continue on the next page -

You see your Kindle library, with the books you downloaded from the *Bookstore*:

☞ **Click**
   Personal Document Sett

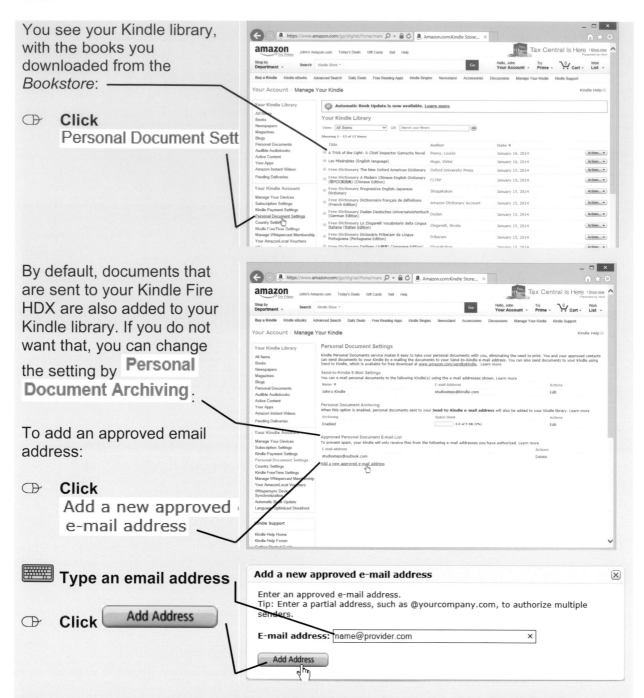

By default, documents that are sent to your Kindle Fire HDX are also added to your Kindle library. If you do not want that, you can change the setting by Personal Document Archiving.

To add an approved email address:

☞ **Click**
   Add a new approved
   e-mail address

⌨ **Type an email address**

☞ **Click** Add Address

The email address will be added to your Approved Personal Document Email list. From now on, documents, photos and Kindle books mailed from that email address to your *Send-to-Kindle* email address will be delivered to the appropriate library on your Kindle device and your Kindle library online.

8. Downloading and Managing Apps

In the previous chapters you have become acquainted with most of the standard apps that are already installed on the Kindle Fire HDX. But there are lots of other things you can do with your Kindle Fire HDX. In the *Amazon Appstore* you will find thousands of other apps. There are many available for free and lots of others that can be purchased for as little as a few dollars.

The collection of apps is enormous. You can find apps for reading the daily news, consulting the weather forecast, playing games, searching for recipes, and viewing sports results. You will surely find an app that interests you.

In this chapter you will learn how to download a free and a paid app from the *Appstore*. If you no longer want to use an app you can delete it from your device. Since the apps you bought are also stored on your Cloud Drive, you can download it again when you want it back.

In this chapter you will learn how to:

- download and install a free app;
- purchase and install an app;
- use the Carousel;
- switch between recent apps and content;
- delete an app from the device;
- use collections.

8.1 The Standard Apps on the Kindle Fire HDX

In the previous chapters you have become acquainted with most of the standard apps that are already installed on the Kindle Fire HDX.

☞ **Unlock the Kindle Fire HDX or turn it on** 👣¹

You can open the *Apps* library like this:

👉 Tap

You see the standard apps that come with the Kindle Fire HDX:

The apps on your screen may be displayed in a different order. The app that you used last, is moved to the first spot on the page:

Here is an overview of the standard apps on the Kindle Fire HDX that have not been discussed in the previous chapters and what you can do with them:

Look up information about movies, TV series and actors in the Internet Movie Database.

App that helps you to find places to eat, shop, drink and relax.

This app opens the online Amazon webshop.

Make free voice and video calls to other *Skype* users.

- Continue on the next page -

App to find and share books you like and see what your friends are reading.

Link to online user guide and customer service. Only the *Getting Started* section can be used offline.

Set alarms, use the stopwatch or timer.

Control which apps, videos and books your child (or grandchild) can use and set time limits for Kindle use.

8.2 Downloading a Free App

In the *Appstore* you will find thousands of free apps. You can open the *Amazon Appstore* like this:

 If necessary, tap

In the top-right corner:

 Tap

The *Amazon Appstore* will be opened.

You will see the start page with featured apps and games:

You can browse categories:

👉 Tap ▬

👉 Tap **Browse Categories**

You will see a list of available app categories:

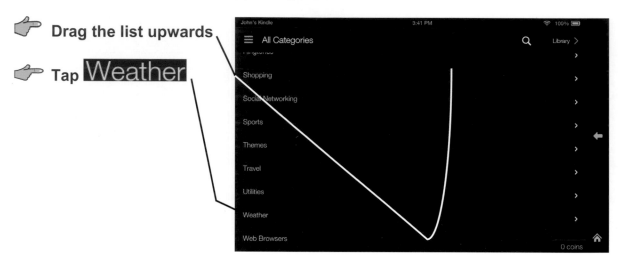

👉 **Drag the list upwards**

👉 Tap **Weather**

Now you will see a long list of the most popular free and paid apps that have something to do with the weather. You can refine the list and show the free apps only:

👉 By **Top Free**, tap **See more**

Take a look at one of the most popular free apps:

Tap

If you do not see this app, you can download another free app.

Now you will see a page with more information about this app. This is how you download the app:

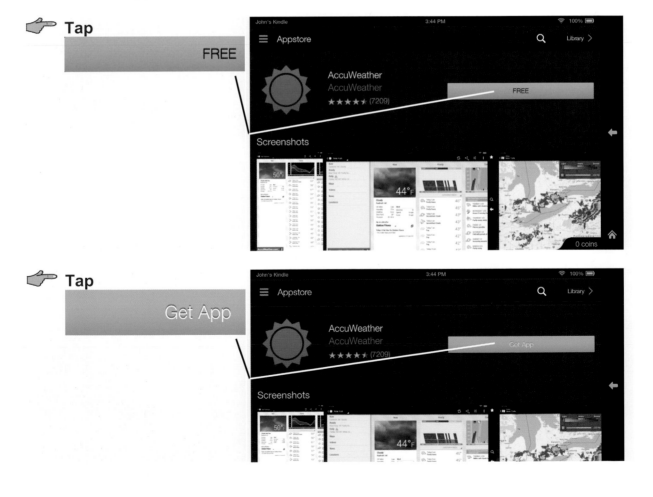

Tap FREE

Tap Get App

The app will be installed:

You can see the percentage remaining for the app to be downloaded and installed:

The app is now installed:

You can open the app from this page:

☞ **Tap**

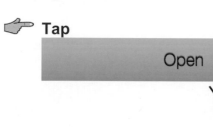

When you use the *AccuWeather* app for the first time, a few introductory screens are shown. You will need to agree to the Terms of Use in order to use the app:

☞ **Tap**

You will see a tip for using the app:

☞ **Tap**

You do not have to enable the alerts and notifications:

☞ **Tap**

You can add a location:

 Tap

The onscreen keyboard appears:

Type the first letters of your location

A list appears:

Tap your location

You will see the *AccuWeather* app with the current weather at your selected location:

Go back to the Home screen

Tap **Apps**

The new app has been placed on the first spot:

☞ **Go back to the Home screen** 🦶³

In the next section you will learn how to purchase an app.

8.3 Downloading a Paid App

If you want to download an app that is not free, you pay for it with the credit or debit card associated with your *Amazon* account.

☞ **Open the *Appstore*** 🦶²³

Previously, you have searched for an app by browsing the categories. You can also enter the name of the app you want to download directly:

👉 **Tap** 🔍

Here is an example of a fun app that challenges you to apply the laws of physics and figure out the best moment to cut a rope, in order to feed candy to a hungry little monster:

⌨ **Type:** cut the rope

👉 **Tap** 🔍

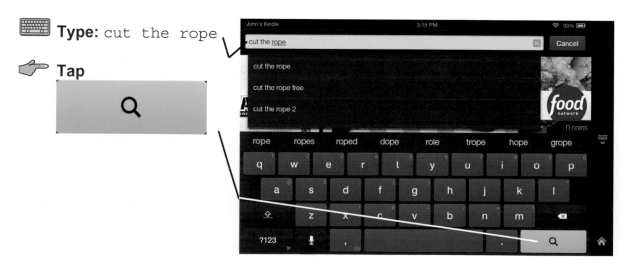

You see the relevant apps:

 Tap

Please note:

In the next section we will be purchasing the app. You can decide for yourself if you want to continue with the steps to purchase this app. Of course, you do not need to buy the exact same app as in this example. You can also just read further to understand how the purchasing and downloading works.

Please note:

All app purchases are final. You cannot return an app or other digital content for a refund the way you can return with an e-book.

You see the page with a description of the app. This is how you buy the app:

 Tap

$0.99 or 99 coins

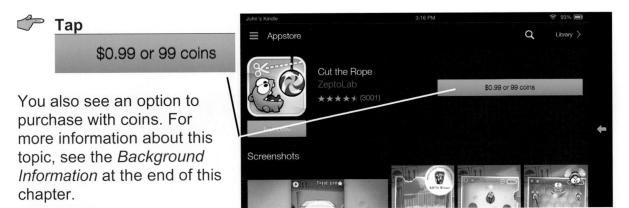

You also see an option to purchase with coins. For more information about this topic, see the *Background Information* at the end of this chapter.

Tip

Test drive

Some apps allow you to test the app for a couple of minutes before you purchase it.

In that case you will see the **Test Drive** option.

In this example, the app is purchased using the *Mobile 1-Click* payment method. The option is already selected:

☞ **Tap**

Get App

The app will be downloaded and installed.

You see the percentage remaining for the app to be downloaded and installed:

The app is installed when you see **Open**:

You can try this app later. Now go back to the *Apps* library:

☞ **Tap** Library >

The app you just purchased
has been added to the *Apps*
library:

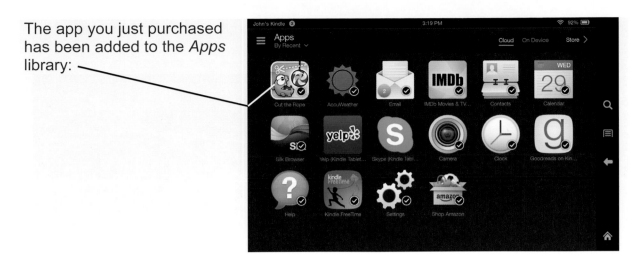

8.4 The Games Library

The game you just downloaded has been added to the *Apps* library. Your Kindle Fire
HDX also contains a *Games* library:

☞ **Go back to the Home screen** ${\wp}{\wp}^3$

☞ Tap

You will be asked if you want to create an *Amazon GameCircle Profile* to compare
high scores with your friends. You do not need to do that now:

☞ Tap **No thank you**

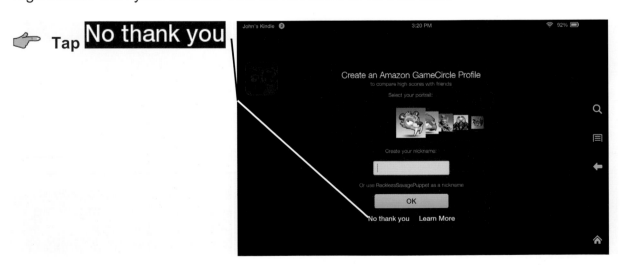

The *Games* library lists all the game apps you have purchased and downloaded to your Kindle Fire HDX.

Next to the game icon you see your personal statistics for the game:

You can start the game by tapping the game icon. To open the *Games Store*:

 **Tap** Store >

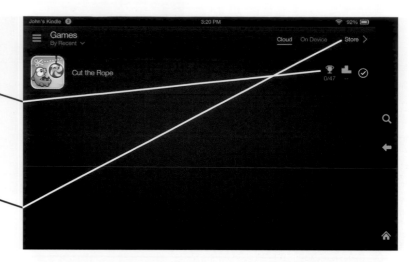

You see the Games section of the *Appstore*:

Here you can download free and paid games in the same way you did in previous sections.

 Go back to the Home screen ♾️3

💡 Tip

Prevent unauthorized purchases

You will have noticed that it is very easy to quickly purchase apps and books with the credit or debit card that is connected to your account. Amazon calls this payment method *Mobile 1-Click*. However convenient this is, it may become a problem if your Kindle Fire HDX is used by someone who is not allowed to make purchases. For example if you let your child (or grandchild) borrow your Kindle Fire HDX to play a game. Some games will require you to buy (fake) money to use for bartering, while playing the game. Other games offer extra levels. These are called *in-app purchases*. They are paid for through your credit card. If you have enabled *Mobile 1-Click*, anyone playing the game will be able to buy things without you noticing it.

- Continue on the next page -

For those occasions you can set limitations. There are different ways to do that:

- use Parental Controls that are not connected to a profile: set a password for purchases and block or unblock certain apps and content;
- create a profile for your child that only gives access to a secure environment with apps, books and videos that you select in the *Kindle FreeTime* app;
- disable in-app purchases;
- disable *Mobile 1-Click* payment altogether.

In the *Tips* at the end of this chapter you can read how to set these limitations.

8.5 Using the Carousel

The Carousel on the Home screen displays your most recently viewed books, videos, music and apps. With the Carousel, you can quickly switch between the apps and other items you are working on at the same time.

The Carousel will display different icons on your own screen.

This is how you move the icons:

 Swipe the Carousel gently from right to left

You see more icons:

 Swipe the Carousel from right to left

You will see the last icon of the Carousel.

☞ **Tap the e-book** ———

The e-book may not be the last icon in your Carousel. In that case:

☞ **Slowly drag the Carousel from left to right**

☞ **Tap the e-book**

You can switch to another app:

☞ **If necessary, tap the middle of the page**

☞ **Tap** 🏠

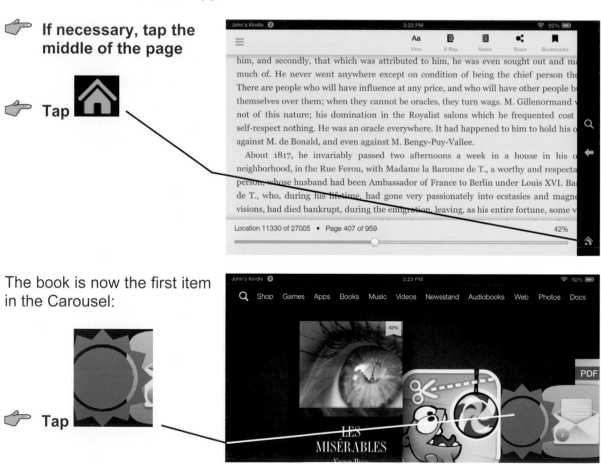

The book is now the first item in the Carousel:

☞ **Tap**

You will see *the AccuWeather* app.

8.6 Switching Between Recent Apps and Content

While you are using the app, you can use the Options bar to quickly switch to another recently used app. You view the Options bar like this:

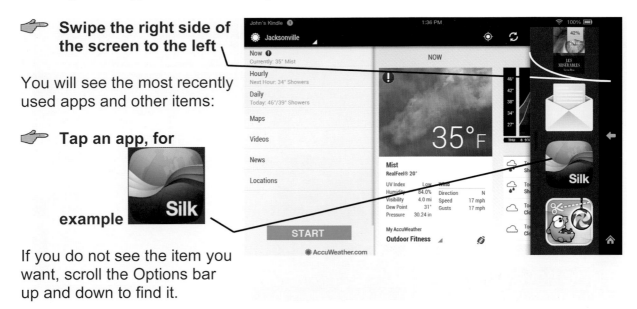

☞ **Swipe the right side of the screen to the left**

You will see the most recently used apps and other items:

☞ **Tap an app, for**

example

If you do not see the item you want, scroll the Options bar up and down to find it.

The app is opened:

If you want to go back to the Home screen:

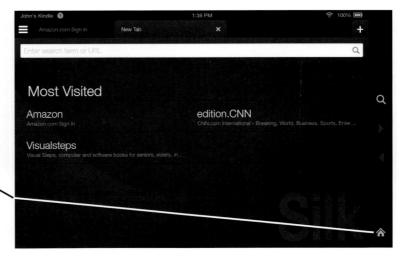

☞ **Tap**

8.7 Deleting an App

If you have downloaded an app that, on second thought, is a bit disappointing, you can easily delete from your device. Try that with the free app you downloaded earlier:

☞ Tap **Apps**, On Device

☞ **Tap and hold**

A menu appears:

☞ **Tap**
   Remove from Devic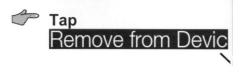

The app is removed from the device:

☞ **Tap** Cloud

The app no longer takes up space on your device.

As you see, the app is still available in the *Cloud Apps* library:

The app does not have a checkmark ✓, indicating it is not stored on your device:

Please note:

An app that is stored on your Cloud Drive, does not use any of your free 5 GB online storage space. All apps and other digital content you purchase in the *Amazon Appstore*, are stored for free on their servers.

If you want to use the app again, you have to download it to your device:

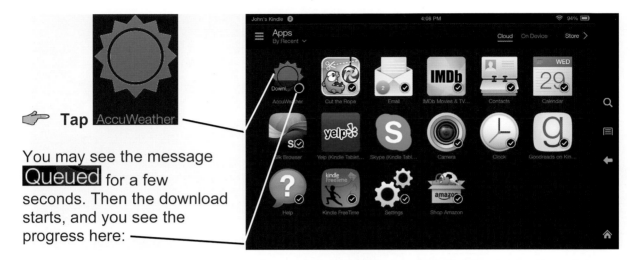

☞ **Tap** AccuWeather

You may see the message Queued for a few seconds. Then the download starts, and you see the progress here: ————

Now the app is stored on the device again, as indicated by the checkmark :

☞ **Tap** On Device

You see that the app has been added to the *On Device Apps* library again:

 Tip

Permanently remove an app from the Cloud Drive

Even though the app does not use up your 5 GB free storage space on your Cloud Drive, you may want to permanently remove an app from the *Cloud Apps* library on the Cloud Drive. In the *Tips* at the end of this chapter you can read how to do that.

8.8 Using Collections

You also have the option of saving apps into folders, on the Kindle these are called *collections*. You can make a folder containing you favorite apps or create folders per subject or topic. You do that like this:

☞ **Press an app, for**

example

☞ **Tap**
Add to Collection

☞ **Tap**
⊕ New Collection

Type the name for your collection:

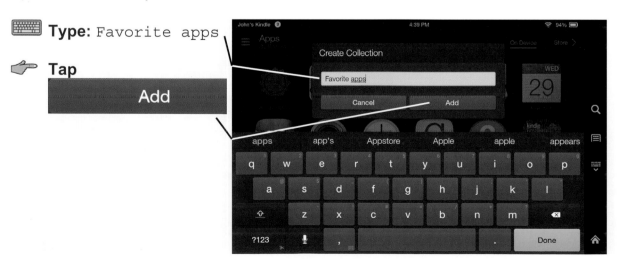

⌨ **Type:** Favorite apps

☞ **Tap**
Add

The collection is created. You can view the collection like this:

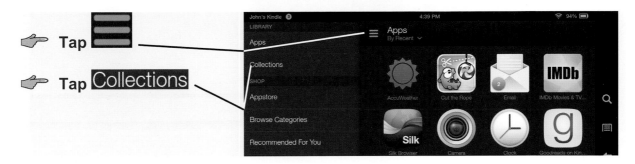

👉 **Tap**

👉 **Tap** Collections

On this page, you will see a summary of all your app collections:

If you would like to add
another app to the collection:

👉 **Tap the collection**

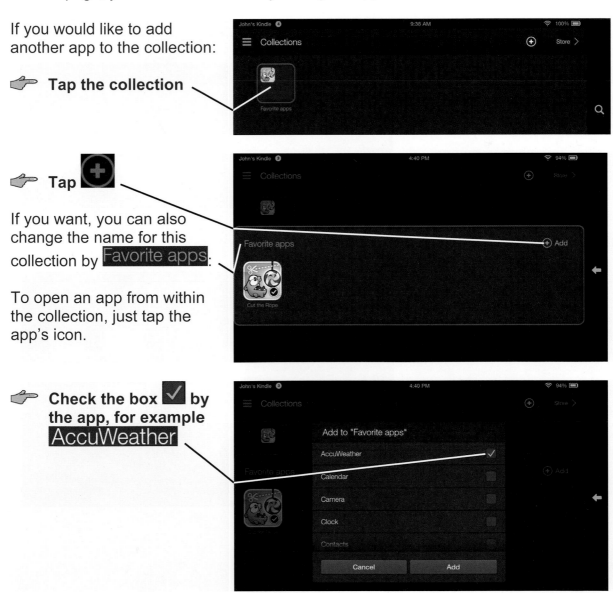

👉 **Tap** ➕

If you want, you can also
change the name for this
collection by Favorite apps.

To open an app from within
the collection, just tap the
app's icon.

👉 **Check the box** ✅ **by
the app, for example**
AccuWeather

Now this app has been added:

☞ **Tap an empty spot outside of the frame**

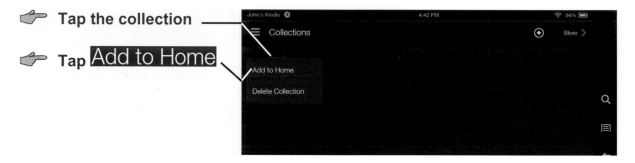

You can reach your app collections through the Collections page. You will need to open this page first in order to access an app that has been added to a collection. But you can also add the collection to your Home screen:

☞ **Tap the collection**

☞ **Tap Add to Home**

🖐☞ **Go back to the Home screen** 👣³

☞ **Swipe the screen upwards**

You see all the apps on the Home screen:

The collection has been added at the bottom:

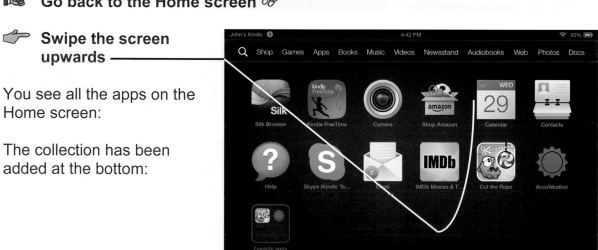

You can arrange the apps or collections on the Home screen in the order you prefer. You do that like this:

☞ **Press your finger on the collection**

You can move the collection:

☞ **Drag the collection upwards to the first row**

Now when you view the Carousel on the Home screen, the collection is just visible:

☞ **Swipe the screen downwards a bit**

You see the collection:

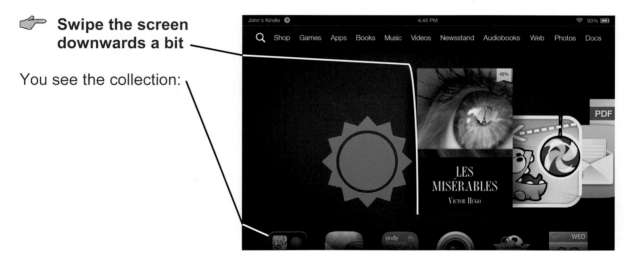

If you hold the Kindle upright, you will see the collection easier:

☞ **If necessary, unlock the screen rotation** $\mathcal{QQ}^{10}$ **and hold the device upright**

You see the collection:

Creating collections is not limited to apps alone, you can also create collections for books, audiobooks and docs. You do this in the same way you did when you created a collection of apps.

However, it is not possible to collect items of different types into a collection.

 Tip

Deleting a collection

If you would like to remove a collection from the Home screen, do the following:

 Press the collection

 Tap Remove

To remove the entire collection from the Collections page:

 Press the collection

 Tap Delete Collection

☞ **If you want, you can lock the Kindle Fire HDX, or turn it off** 🐾⁵

In this chapter you have learned how to download free and paid apps from the *Amazon Appstore*.

8.9 Background information

Dictionary

Amazon Appstore   An online store where you can download free and paid apps.

Amazon Coins   Amazon Coins is a virtual currency for U.S. customers to purchase apps, games and in-app items.

Games library   Section of your Kindle Fire HDX where your game apps are stored. The *Games* library also gives access to the *Amazon GameCircle* where you can compare scores with your friends and to the *Games Store*, the games section of the *Appstore*.

Kindle FreeTime   Create a profile for your child that gives access to a secure environment with apps, books and videos that you select.

Mobile 1-Click   Type of payment method from Amazon, where you can pay for content with only one click through the credit or debit card associated with your *Amazon* Account.

Parental Controls   Set a password for purchases and block or unblock certain apps and content.

Source: Kindle Fire HDX User Guide

Amazon coins
You can use Amazon Coins to purchase Kindle Fire HDX compatible apps, games and digital in-app items. This payment option is only available for U.S. customers. You can buy an Amazon Coins bundle at a discount from the *Appstore* on your Kindle, from the *Amazon Appstore* on Amazon.com, or from the How do I use coins? link on the detail page of any eligible item. You can also earn promotional Amazon Coins when you purchase selected apps and in-app items.
For more information, visit the Amazon.com website.

8.10 Tips

  Tip

Amazon Gift Cards

Amazon.com Gift Cards in different denominations are sold by grocery, drug and convenience stores throughout the U.S. and have no purchase fees. In the UK and Canada, gift cards in local currency are only available online from the Amazon website. If you have received a gift card, you can add it to your account like this:

☞ **Open the *Settings* screen** 🦶*12*

👉 **Tap** My Account, Gift Cards & Promotional Codes Redeem a gift card and view your current balance

☞ **Sign in with your *Amazon* account** 🦶*22*

Here you see your gift card account balance:

👉 **Tap the box below** Enter Your Code

⌨ **Type the claim code found on your gift card**

Please note: you do not need to type capital letters or dashes (-).

👉 **Tap** Go

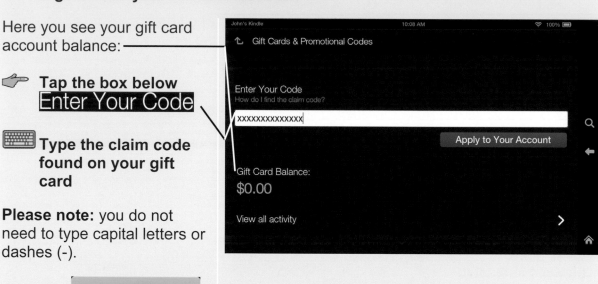

You will briefly see a message that the Gift Card is succesfully redeemed.

Your new Gift Card balance may not appear right away. But if you open this screen a few minutes later, the amount has been added. Your Gift Card balance will automatically be applied towards your next eligible purchase.
If the Gift Card balance is not enough for that purchase, the remaining amount will be charged to the credit or debit card associated with your *Amazon* account.

Tip

Updating apps

The apps that have been installed on your Kindle will need to undergo updates from time to time. These updates are usually free and are often essential for solving various problems. An update can also contain some new features or functions, such as a new game level. By default, automatic updates are enabled on your Kindle Fire HDX. This means an update is installed as soon as it becomes available. Most of the time, you will not even notice that the update takes place.

Please note: if you are using a mobile Internet connection via 3G/4G, these automatic updates may result in high costs. It is better to have the apps updated only when there is a Wi-Fi connection available.

If you want to change these settings:

☞ **Open the *Settings* screen** 👣**12**

👉 **Tap** 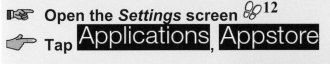 **Applications, Appstore**

👉 **Tap** **Automatic Updates** Enabled

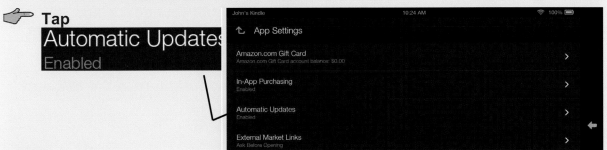

You will see the settings for automatic updates:

If you want to disable automatic updates:

👉 **By** **Enable Automatic Upd**

tap **Off**

By default you are notified by email when updates are installed.

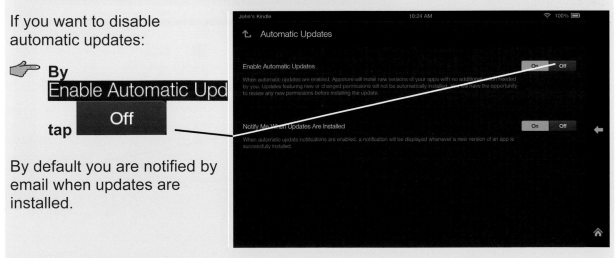

- Continue on the next page -

Once you have disabled automatic updates, you can check for updates like this:

☞ Tap  **Apps, Store** >

☞ Tap ▤, **App Updates**

☞ **Follow the instructions**

 Tip
Remove app or other item from the Carousel
It is very easy to remove a recently used app, book, or other item from the Carousel:

☞ **Tap and hold the desired icon**

☞ **Tap** Remove from Carousel

 Tip
Removing an app from the Cloud Drive
In this chapter you have learned how to delete an app from your device and how to download it again from your Cloud Drive. It is also possible to remove an app from the Cloud Drive.

☞ **Open the web page www.amazon.com/manageyourkindle in the *Silk* app** 🐾8

☞ **Sign in with you *Amazon* account** 🐾22

You see all items in your *Kindle* library:

☞ **By an app, tap**
Actions... ▼

☞ **Tap**
> Manage Your Apps

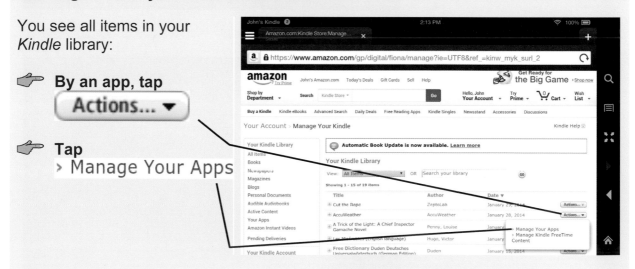

- Continue on the next page -

Next to the app you want to delete:

👉 **Tap** Actions... ▼

👉 **Tap** > Delete this app

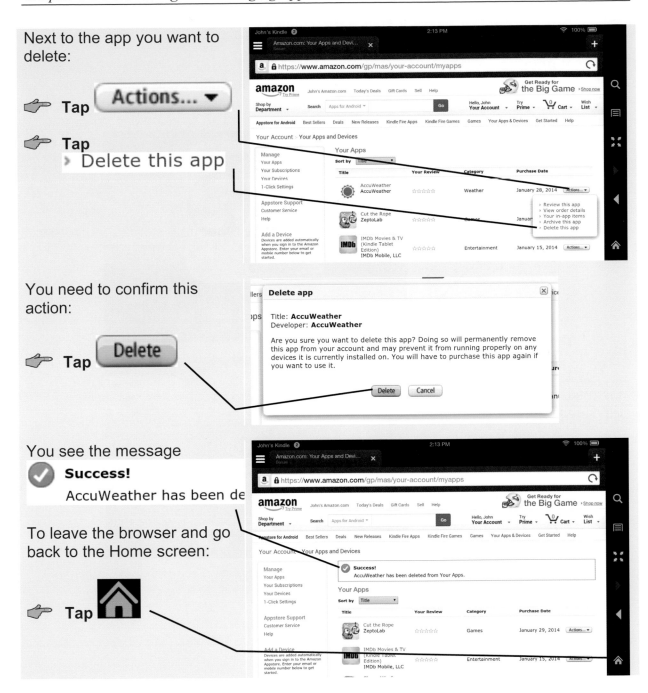

You need to confirm this action:

👉 **Tap** Delete

You see the message

✅ **Success!**
AccuWeather has been de...

To leave the browser and go back to the Home screen:

👉 **Tap** 🏠

Tip

Carousel options

When you hold the Kindle Fire HDX upright, you will see different icons below the Carousel:

You see recommendations from Amazon below the apps or other content you purchased:

Below icons of other apps you see icons with which you can quickly access specific parts of the app:

For example a new tab, the search option or bookmarks in the *Silk* app.

Tip

Setting up Parental Controls

You can set up Parental Controls on your Kindle. You can disable a number of options in general so that a user cannot use them at all. Or you can create a child profile with the free *Kindle FreeTime* app. This option allows you to add the specific content you want for each child profile you create.

☞ **Open the *Settings* screen** 🐾**12**
👉 **Tap**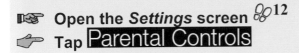

Make sure the Parental Controls option has been turned on:

You see two options: the *Kindle FreeTime* app and the Parental Control option on the Kindle.

To enable Parental Controls:

👉 **Tap** On

Now you need to create a Parental Controls password:

⌨ **Type a password**

⌨ **Type the password again**

👉 **Tap**

Done

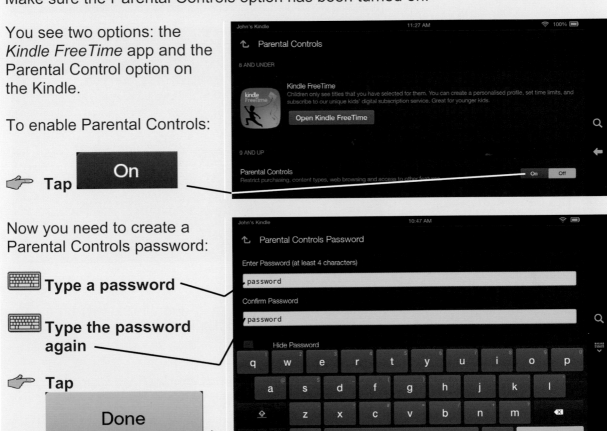

- *Continue on the next page -*

In the following Parental Controls screen, you will see various settings that you can block or unblock, or turn on or off:

☞ **Drag the list upwards**

Here you can turn off Parental Controls: ⎯⎯⎯

Block or unblock the web browser, email, sharing on social networks and using the camera: ⎯⎯⎯

☞ **Drag the list upwards**

(De)activate password protection for purchases: ⎯⎯

Block or unblock different types of content: ⎯⎯⎯

Change the Parental Controls password: ⎯⎯

You can also require a password to turn on Wi-Fi and location based services: ↙

When an app or other content is blocked you cannot use it, even if you have the Parental Controls password. You have to go back to Parental Control settings and unblock the app or content to be able to use it again.

Another option is using the *Kindle FreeTime* app. With the *Kindle FreeTime* app you can set a profile for each child (or grandchild) and select:
- which apps your child (or grandchild) can use;
- which books he can read;
- which videos he can watch;
- the total screen time or the maximum time for each activity.

Web browsing and store purchasing from within apps are not accessible when the apps are used in *Kindle FreeTime*. You can only select the apps, books and videos that have been purchased on the Kindle Fire HDX. Most of the standard apps are off-limits. *Kindle FreeTime* allows you to set up to six profiles. It is also possible to upgrade to *Kindle FreeTime Unlimited,* a monthly subscription that offers thousands of books, apps, movies, and TV shows for children ages three to eight years old.

Tip

Disable in-app purchases

Some games will require you to buy (fake) money to use for bartering while playing the game. Other games offer to remove advertisements or add extra levels for a price. These are called *in-app purchases*. They are paid for through your credit card. With *Mobile 1-Click* payment, anyone playing the game will be able to buy things without you noticing it. You can disable in-app payments like this:

☞ **Open the *Settings* screen** 👣¹²

👉 **Tap** `Applications`, `Appstore`

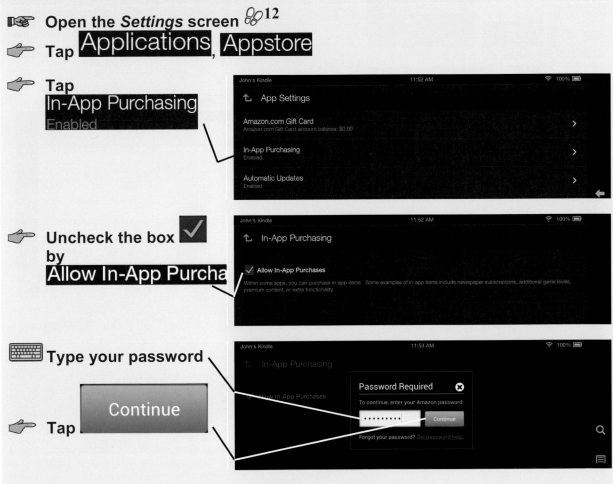

👉 **Tap**
`In-App Purchasing`
`Enabled`

👉 **Uncheck the box** ✅
by
`Allow In-App Purcha`

⌨ **Type your password**

👉 **Tap** `Continue`

In-app purchases are no longer allowed.

☞ **Go back to the Home screen** 👣³

💡 **Tip**

Turn off Mobile 1-Click payments
If you would like to turn off *Mobile 1-Click*:

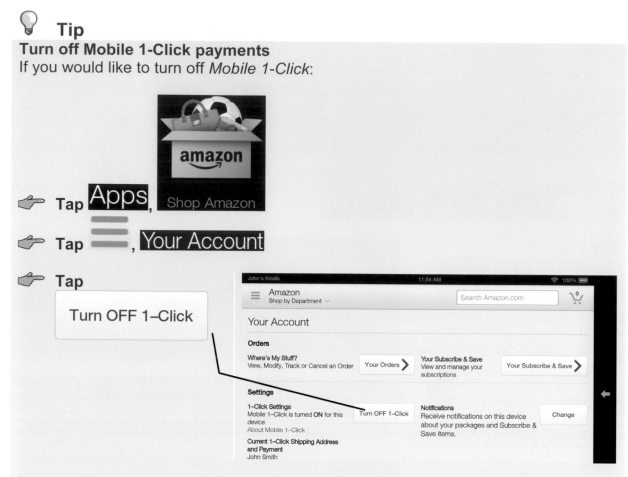

☞ Tap **Apps**, Shop Amazon

☞ Tap ≡, **Your Account**

☞ Tap **Turn OFF 1–Click**

From now on you can no longer purchase items and pay for them without signing in.

☞ **Go back to the Home screen** 👣³

Please note: it may take a little while for before the setting is activated and the *Mobile 1-Click* option is actually turned off.

Tip

Notifications

When you see a number in a circle in the status bar , there are messages for you. This could be an email message, or a message from an app. You can display the messages like this:

☞ **Open the *Quick Settings* menu**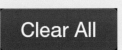

In this example there are three notifications:

When you tap a notification, the app that sent it will be launched.

To clear the notifications:

 Tap **Clear All**

You can select which apps are allowed to send notifications:

☞ **Open the *Settings* screen** ⸗**12**
☞ **Tap** 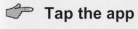 **Notifications & Quiet Time**

By default, all apps are allowed to send notifications:

To stop the notifications from an app:

👉 **Tap the app**

You see the notification options:

These options will differ for each app.

Tip

Force stop an app
There is no need to shut down apps you do not need for a while. They will not consume a noticeable amount of computing or battery power. But if an app does not work properly, you can force stop it like this:

☞ **Open the *Settings* screen** ✂️**12**

👉 **Tap** 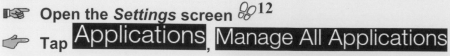 **Applications**, **Manage All Applications**

You see a long list of apps and services:

If you wish, you can filter the list here: ────

As soon as you see the app that does not work properly:

👉 **Tap the app** ────

👉 **Tap**

Force stop

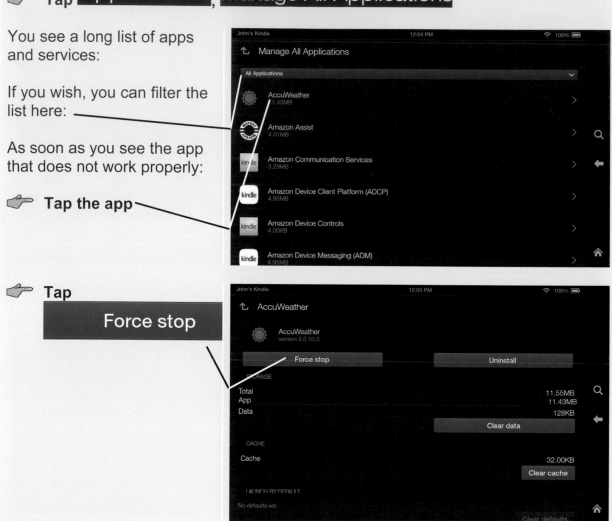

- Continue on the next page -

You see a warning message:

☞ **Tap**

> **Force Stop**

The app has been stopped.

Please note: only use this method for apps you started yourself, such as *Silk*, *Contacts*, *Calendar* or *Email*. Do not force stop other processes or services, as this may cause the Kindle Fire HDX to malfunction.

 Tip

Restart or reset the Kindle Fire HDX

Has an app become unresponsive? Or has your Kindle Fire HDX become inexplicably slow? Do you have trouble downloading? Then there are two things you can try. The first one is turning the Kindle Fire HDX off and then on:

☞ **Turn off the Kindle Fire HDX** 🦶[5]

☞ **Turn on the Kindle Fire HDX** 🦶[1]

If this does not solve the problem, you can restart the Kindle Fire HDX:

☞ **Press and hold the Power button**

After six to eight seconds, the screen will go blank. This is normal. Continue to hold the power button.

☞ **After twenty seconds, release the Power button**

☞ **Press the Power button again**

If you have successfully restarted your Kindle Fire HDX, you will see the start-up screen.

Tip

Mayday

When a problem occurs or you have a question, you can connect to an Amazon Tech advisor. This is called the Mayday option.

An Amazon Tech advisor can guide you through any feature on your Kindle by drawing on your screen, walking you through how to do something for yourself, or doing it for you.

Mayday is always available for free. Throughout your session, you will be able to see your Amazon Tech advisor live on your screen, but they will not see you.

Please note: when you connect, an Amazon Tech advisor will access your device. The session may be recorded for quality assurance.

☞ **Open the** *Quick Settings* **menu** ⚆²

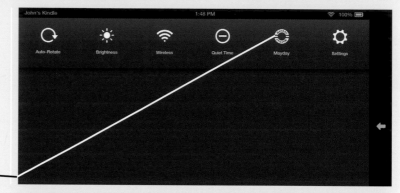

☞ **Tap** Mayday

You see the Amazon Assist screen:

At the bottom, you see some other options to ask for help:

To connect:

☞ **Tap**

At the bottom-right corner of your screen you see the Amazon Tech advisor on your screen:

You can ask your question by talking and the advisor will help you.

9. Using Skype, Facebook and Twitter

In addition to email, the Kindle Fire HDX offers more ways to stay in touch with your friends: *Skype*, *Facebook* and *Twitter*. *Skype* can be used to make free voice and video calls over the Internet from your Kindle Fire HDX to any *Skype* user with a desktop computer, laptop, tablet computer or smartphone. We will show you how to use the *Skype* app, add contacts and start a video call.

Facebook is a very popular social networking site intended to connect friends, family, and business associates. You can use the free *Facebook* app to post messages and photos and follow your friends. *Twitter* is another popular free online social networking and microblogging service. With the free *Twitter* app you can send tweets and follow tweets from friends or your favorite celebrity or organization that you are interested in. In this chapter you will get a short introduction to both of these social networking apps.

In this chapter you will learn how to:

- add contacts to the *Skype* app;
- make a video call;
- link your *Facebook* account to the Kindle;
- download your *Facebook* photos to the *Cloud Drive Photos* library;
- download and use the *Facebook* app;
- link your *Twitter* account to the Kindle;
- download and use the *Twitter* app.

➥ Please note:

You need a *Skype, Facebook and Twitter* account to be able to follow the examples in this chapter. If do not have any of the mentioned accounts, you can just read through this chapter, or you can create a free account with these services. For *Skype*, you can also use a *Microsoft* account to sign in. A *Microsoft* account is an email address ending with hotmail.com, live.com or outlook.com.

☞ For a *Skype* account, go to www.skype.com
☞ For a *Facebook* account, go to www.facebook.com
☞ For a *Twitter* account, go to www.twitter.com

9.1 Using Skype

You can use the *Skype* app to make free (video) calls and chat with other *Skype* users.

☞ **Unlock or turn on the Kindle** 🦶¹

The *Skype* app is stored on your Cloud Drive and needs to be downloaded first:

☞ Tap **Apps**, **Cloud**, Skype (Kindle Tabl...

You will see that the app is downloaded to your device. Once the download has finished:

☞ Tap Skype (Kindle Tabl...

If you already have a *Skype* account:

☞ Tap **Sign in with a Skype account**

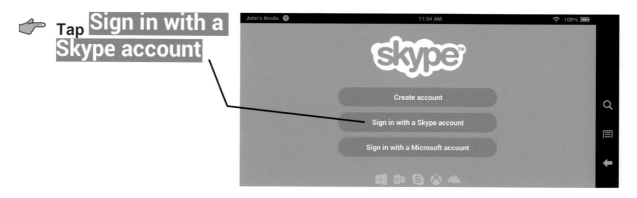

If you do not have a *Skype* account, you can also use your *Microsoft* account. That is an email address that ends with hotmail.com, live.com or outlook.com and the password that goes with it. In that case:

☞ Tap **Sign in with a Microsoft account**

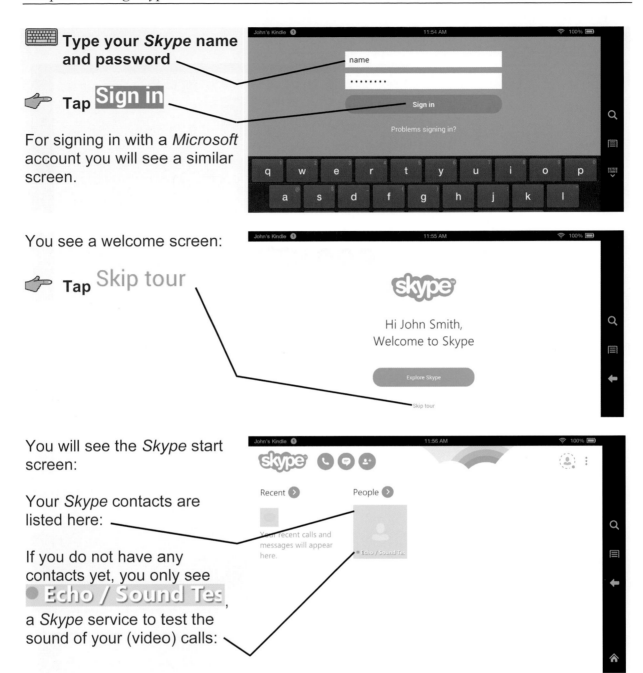

▦ **Type your** *Skype* **name and password**

☞ **Tap** Sign in

For signing in with a *Microsoft* account you will see a similar screen.

You see a welcome screen:

☞ **Tap** Skip tour

You will see the *Skype* start screen:

Your *Skype* contacts are listed here:

If you do not have any contacts yet, you only see ● Echo / Sound Tes, a *Skype* service to test the sound of your (video) calls:

You can add a contact like this:

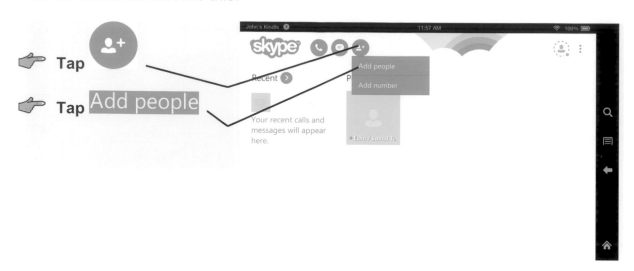

☞ **Tap**

☞ **Tap** Add people

In this example a fictitious *Skype* name is used. You can search the *Skype* directory for somebody you know that uses *Skype*:

⌨ **Type the name, *Skype* name or email address of the person you are looking for**

You will see search results appear while you are typing:

☞ **Tap** 🔍

☞ **Tap the name of the person you are looking for**

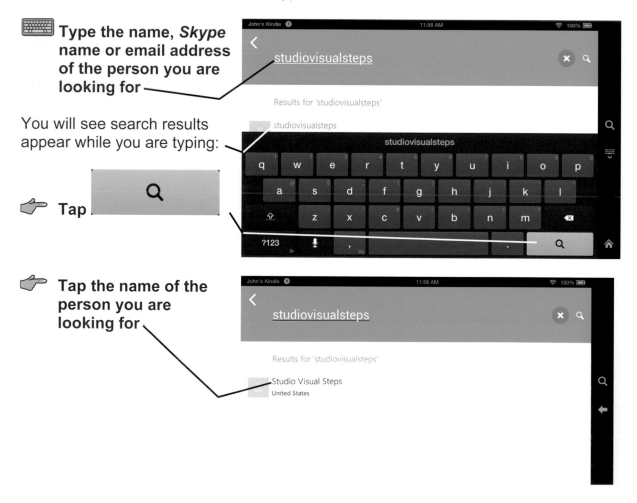

You will see the profile of this person. To add him or her as a contact:

☞ **Tap**

Add to contacts

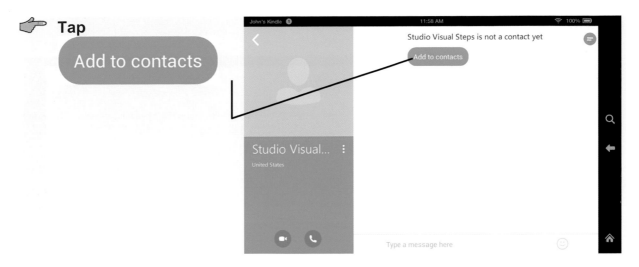

The person you want to add has to give permission before you can make a call. You can send him or her a contact request:

You see the standard contact request. You do not have to change the text for now:

Send

☞ **Tap**

You see the profile screen again:

☞ **Tap** ❮ **twice**

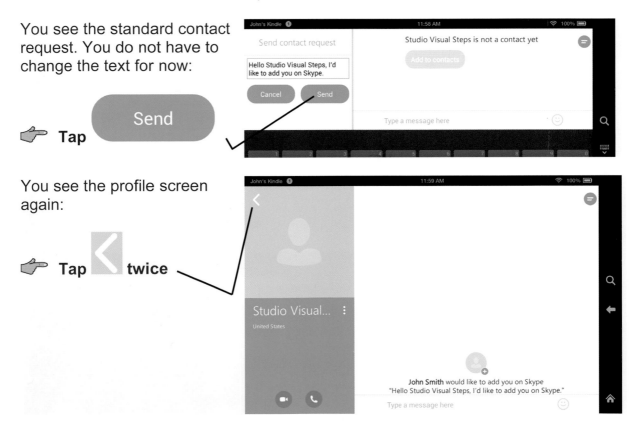

You see the list of contacts again. If the request has not yet been accepted, you see **Studio Visual Step**. As soon as the request is accepted, you will see

Studio Visual Ste. The green dot indicates that your contact is also online.

You can start a video call like this:

☞ **Tap**

The contact's page appears with different ways to interact with this person:

☞ **Tap**

As you wait for the other person to pick up, you see yourself on the screen:

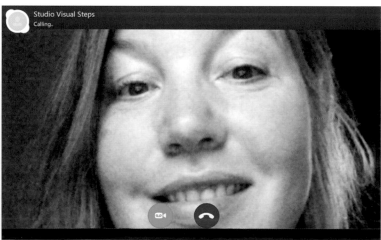

As soon as the connection is made, you can see and hear the person you called:

To end the video call:

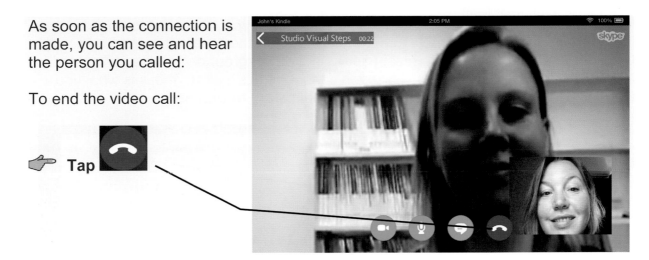

☞ **Tap**

The other buttons in the screen have the following functions:

Turn your camera off. The person you are calling will no longer see the images from your camera. You make a voice call.

Turn your microphone off. The person you are calling will no longer hear you.

Send a chat message or a file.

The connection is disabled. To go back to the *Skype* start screen:

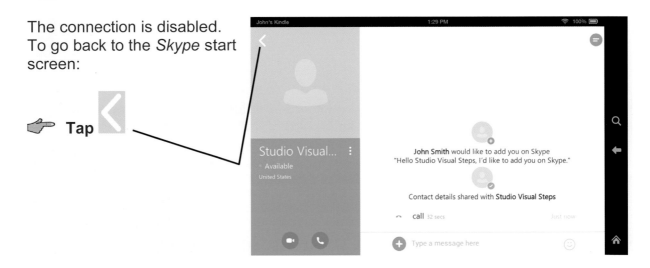

☞ **Tap**

You will see the *Skype* start screen again. To close *Skype*, you need to do more than just return to the Kindle Home screen. If you go to another app or begin to read a book, for example, *Skype* will remain active in the background. You are still signed in and are available for incoming calls, even if the Kindle is locked. If this is what you want, you can leave *Skype* open, but if you really want to sign out:

The app is now turned off and you are signed out. You can no longer receive calls. When you open the app again, you will be signed in automatically. If you want to prevent automatic sign in, see the *Tips* at the end of this chapter to learn how to adjust these settings.

You will see the Home screen again.

9.2 Linking Facebook With the Kindle Fire HDX

If you are a *Facebook* user, you can link your *Facebook* account to your Kindle. This will also enable you to download your *Facebook* photos to your *Cloud Drive Photos* library. This is how you link your *Facebook* account:

☞ **Open the *Settings* screen** ❡¹²

☞ **Tap**  Tap My Account, Social Network Accounts

Add your *Facebook* account:

☞ **Tap**

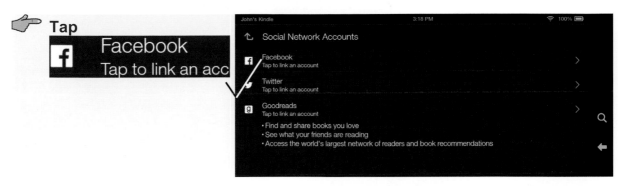

f Facebook
Tap to link an acc

⌨ **Type your email address and password**

☞ **Tap**

Done

Here you can read what happens when you link your *Facebook* account to Amazon:

☞ **Tap Connect**

You see that your *Facebook* account has been linked. If at any time you want to remove the link, you can do so with

the button :

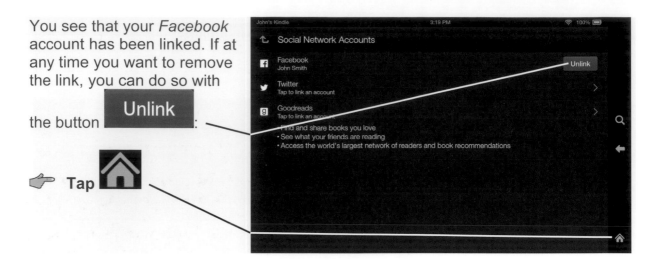

☞ **Tap**

You will see the Home screen. If you want to add the photos you posted to *Facebook* to your *Cloud Drive Photos* library, you can do so like this:

☞ **Tap Photos**

The *Photos* library is opened:

☞ **Tap** , **Add Photos**

☞ **Tap**
f Facebook

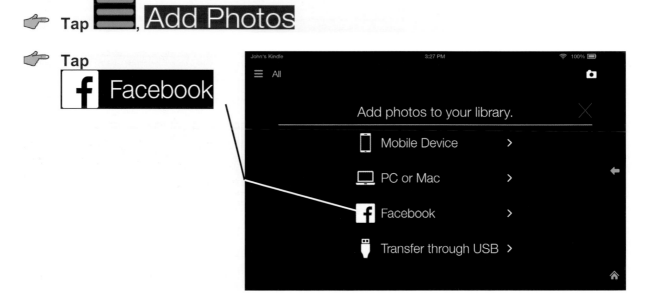

Tap to add the photos:

☞ **Tap Add Facebook Photos**

Allow Amazon to access
your photos:

☞ **Tap**

For a few seconds, you will see the message
. To go back to the *Photos* library:

☞ **Tap** ⬅️

After a while you will see the new folders appear in the *Cloud Drive Files* library:

☞ **Tap** ▤, **Cloud Drive Files**

You see the folders with the
pictures from your *Facebook*
page:

To go back to the Home
screen:

☞ **Tap** 🏠

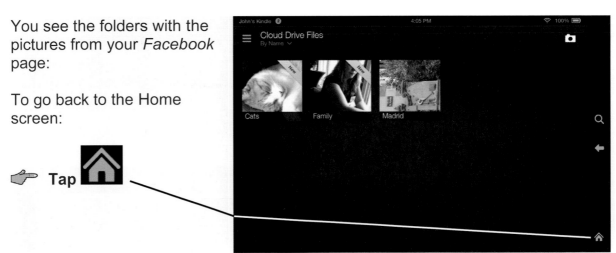

🖎 **Please note:**
You will need to repeat this process every time you add new photos to *Facebook*.
New photos are not added automatically.

9.3 Downloading and Using the Facebook App

You can download the free *Facebook* app from the *Amazon Appstore*:

🖎 **Download the *Facebook* app** 👣²⁴

To open the *Facebook* app:

☞ **Tap** Apps, Facebook

You linked your *Facebook* account to the Kindle, so you will sign in to the *Facebook* app automatically:

You will see your name here:

☞ **Tap your name, for example** **Continue as John Sr**

If you do not see your name, you will see a screen where you can sign in.

You see the news feed from your *Facebook* page:

With ☑ **Status** you can update your status by posting a message on your own *Facebook* page:

With ◉ **Photo** you can select a photo or take a picture and publish it to your page:

With ☒ **Check In** you can publish a message to your page to let your friends know where you are at the moment:

In the news feed you will see the messages posted by your friends, and by well-known people, celebrities or the organizations you follow. The messages you post on your own page will appear in your friends' news feeds.

If you want to comment on a message, tap **💬 Comment** and type a comment: ———

To 'like' a message, tap **👍 Like**: ———

To share a message with your friends, tap ➥ **Share**:

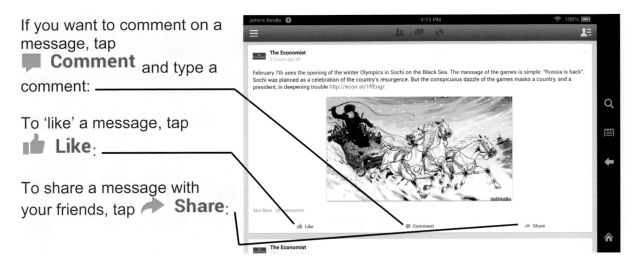

To view your own timeline:

👉 **Tap ▤** ———

👉 **Tap your name** ———

You will see the messages on your timeline.

With **Friends** you can access your list of friends: ———

With **Photos** you can view the photos you have uploaded to *Facebook*: ———

With **About** you can access the personal information you have shared on *Facebook*: ———

With **Activity Log** you can see your recent activities: ———

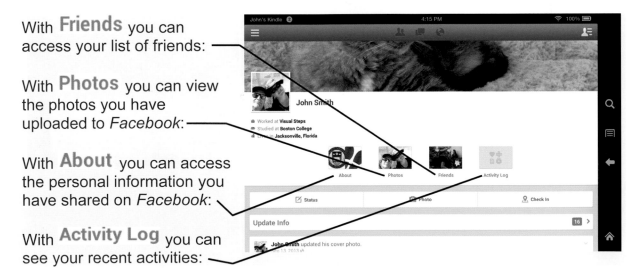

Kindle Fire HDX for Seniors

At the top of the screen you see ![icons]. If someone reacts to your status update, photo or check-in, or reacts to a message on which you have commented, the ![globe] button will turn into ![globe with 1]. In the same way you will be alerted of any friend requests by ![friends], and of private messages by ![message].

Take a look at the other menu options:

☞ **Tap** ![menu icon]

You can use the search box to search for acquaintances or specific pages: ——

Tap here to find new friends: ——

With the ![Messages] button you can access your private messages: ——

☞ **Swipe the page upwards**

With ![Like Pages] you can view some suggestions for pages you may like: ——

With ![Friends] you can look for friends and acquaintances in various ways: ——

With the ![Photos] app you can view and manage your photos in *Facebook*: ——

Swipe the page upwards ———

At the bottom of the screen you will find buttons for the Help Center and for editing the account and privacy settings:

If you remain logged in, new data will be retrieved as soon as you open the *Facebook* app. If you prefer to sign out, you can do that like this:

☞ **Tap** , Confirm

☞ **Go back to the Home screen** 👣³

9.4 Linking Twitter With the Kindle Fire HDX

If you are a *Twitter* user, you can link your *Twitter* account to your Kindle. This is how you link your *Twitter* account:

☞ **Open the Settings screen** 👣¹²

☞ **Tap**

Add your *Twitter* account:

☞ **Tap**

Type your username or email address and password

☞ **Tap**

Done

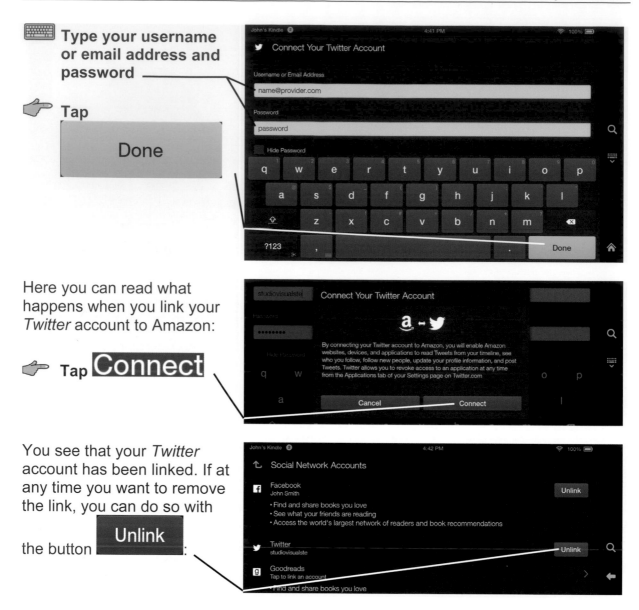

Here you can read what happens when you link your *Twitter* account to Amazon:

☞ **Tap Connect**

You see that your *Twitter* account has been linked. If at any time you want to remove the link, you can do so with

the button **Unlink** :

☞ **Go back to the Home screen** 🦶³

9.5 Downloading and Using the Twitter App

You can download the free *Twitter* app from the *Amazon Appstore*:

☞ **Download the *Twitter* app** 🦶²⁴

To open the *Twitter* app:

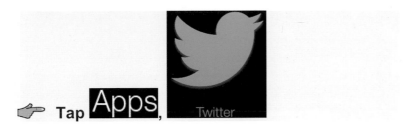

👉 **Tap** Apps , Twitter

Even though you linked your *Twitter* account to the Kindle, you will need to sign in for the *Twitter* app:

👉 **Tap** Sign In

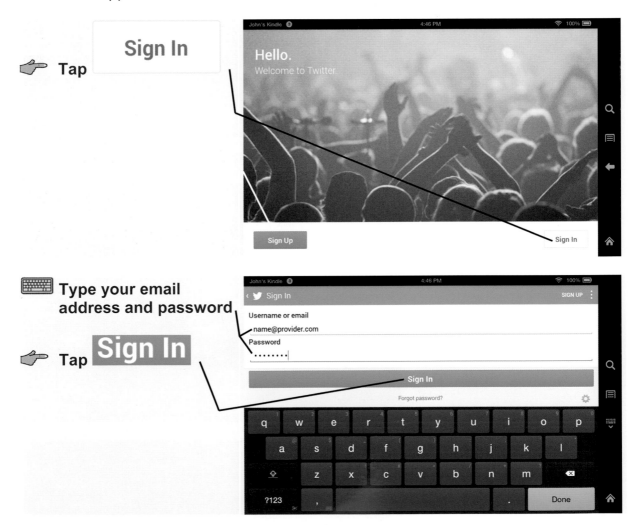

⌨ **Type your email address and password**

👉 **Tap** Sign In

Twitter wants to use your current location, if you would like to do this:

☞ Tap OK

☞ Tap Settings

☞ By
Location-Based Serv
tap On

☞ Tap Continue

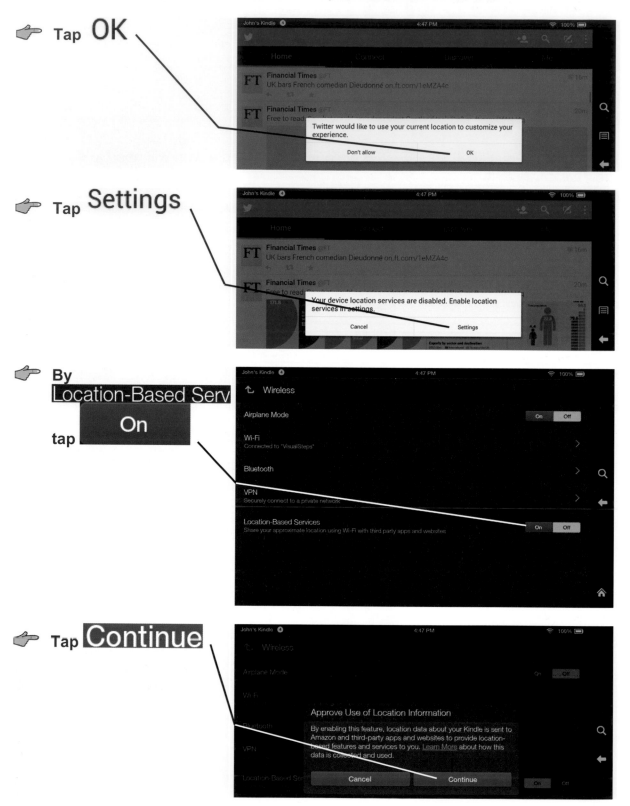

☞ **Go back to the Home screen** 👣³

👉 **Tap**

You will see your timeline, with the latest tweets from your friends, or the celebrities and organizations you follow. Your own tweets will appear in your followers' timelines:

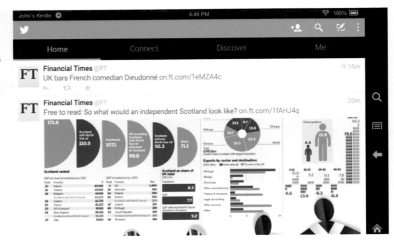

This is how you load new tweets:

👉 **Swipe downwards over the screen**

Here are the functions for the buttons in the menu:

Home   This opens the *Twitter* Home page. Here you see the latest tweets from the people or organizations you follow, and your own tweets as well.

Connect   This allows you to see the action that has taken place on your account. This includes the messages in which your user name is mentioned and those who have retweeted your tweets, and more.

Discover   This function displays 'personalized' content; it is dependent on your location settings and the people you follow. You are given suggestions regarding trends, events, whom to follow, etc.

Me   This opens the page containing your profile information. This page also contains links to the timeline with the tweets you have sent, the accounts you follow, and your own followers. This page is visible to everyone. Here you can also access your private messages. These will only be visible to you.

🔍   Search for tweets about a certain subject, or a certain name.

     See suggestions for people to follow on *Twitter* and find friends by importing your contacts.

This is how you send a new tweet:

☞ **Tap** [icon]

⌨ **Type your message**

☞ **Tap** TWEET

You can also add content to a tweet:

📍 Add a location to your tweet. For this you will need to enable *Location-Based services*, so the Kindle can use Wi-Fi to determine your location.

📷 Take a picture and add it to your tweet.

🖼 Add a photo from the *Photos* library to your tweet.

Your tweet appears at the top of your timeline. Your followers will also see your tweet appear in their timelines.

To sign out from the *Twitter* app:

☞ Tap ⁝

☞ Tap Settings

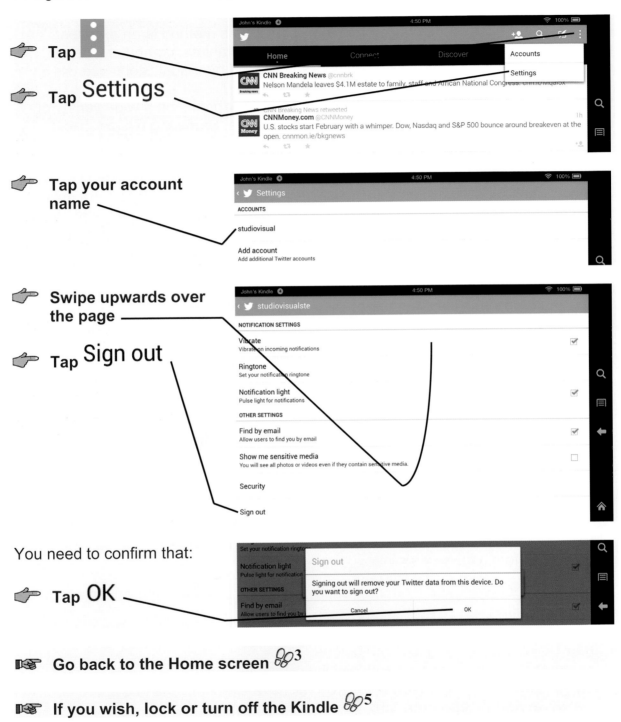

☞ Tap your account name

☞ Swipe upwards over the page

☞ Tap Sign out

You need to confirm that:

☞ Tap OK

☞ Go back to the Home screen 👣³

☞ If you wish, lock or turn off the Kindle 👣⁵

You have reached the end of this book. In this book you have learned how to work with the Kindle Fire HDX. Now you can start experimenting with all the apps and features this handy device has to offer.

9.6 Visual Steps Website and Newsletter

By now we hope you have noticed that the Visual Steps method is an excellent method for quickly and efficiently learning more about tablets, computers, other devices and software applications. All books published by Visual Steps use this same method.

In various series, we have published a large number of books on a wide variety of topics including *Windows*, *Mac OS X*, the iPad, iPhone, Samsung Galaxy Tab, Kindle, photo editing and many other topics.

On the **www.visualsteps.com** website you can click the Catalog page to find an overview of all the Visual Steps titles, including an extensive description. Each title gives you an extensive description and allows you to preview the full table of contents and a sample chapter in PDF format. In this way, you can quickly determine if a specific title will meet your expectations. All titles can be ordered online and are also available in bookstores in the USA, Canada, United Kingdom, Australia and New Zealand.

Furthermore, the website offers many extras, among other things:

- free computer guides and booklets (PDF files) covering all sorts of subjects;
- frequently asked questions and their answers;
- information on the free Computer Certificate that you can acquire at the certificate's website **www.ccforseniors.com**;
- a free email notification service: let's you know when a new book is published.

There is always more to learn. Visual Steps offers many other books on computer-related subjects. Each Visual Steps book has been written using the same step-by-step method with short, concise instructions and screen shots illustrating every step.

Visual Steps Newsletter
Would you like to be informed when a new Visual Steps title becomes available? Subscribe to the free Visual Steps newsletter (no strings attached) and you will receive this information in your inbox.

The Newsletter is sent approximately each month and includes information about

- the latest titles;
- supplemental information concerning titles previously released;
- new free computer booklets and guides;
- contests and questionnaires with which you can win prizes.

When you subscribe to our Newsletter you will have direct access to the free booklets on the **www.visualsteps.com/info_downloads** web page.

9.7 Background Information

Dictionary

Chat	Real-time transmission of text messages from sender to receiver. Chat messages are generally short, in order to enable other participants to respond quickly.
Facebook	Popular free social networking site intended to connect friends, family and business associates.
Location based service	When you enable location-based services, you provide location data about your Kindle that Amazon and third-party apps and websites can use to provide information based on the location you are in.
Mood message	A simple message you can add to your *Skype* profile to let your friends know what you are up to or what mood you are in.
Skype	Free program that enables free (video) calls over the Internet between desktop computers, laptops, tablet computers or smartphones. *Skype* also offers phone calls to land lines and cell phones all over the world at substantially lower rates. This is called *SkypeOut*. It works as a prepaid system, you have to buy *Skype Credit* before you can start making phone calls.
Skype name	Unique user name that you use to sign in to *Skype*.
Tweet	Text messages posted to *Twitter*. These messages are limited to 140 characters and revolve around the question 'What's happening?'.
Twitter	*Twitter* is a popular, free, online social networking and microblogging service that enables users to send and read *tweets*. It is an easy way to discover the latest news related to subjects you care about.
Video call	A call made from one computer or tablet computer with a camera to another, allowing the participants to see each other as they talk.

Source: Skype, Twitter and Facebook User Guide

9.8 Tips

 Tip

Status

Too busy to answer a *Skype* call? You can set your status to Invisible so that your contacts know you do not want to be called. This is how you do that:

☞ **Tap**

☞ **Tap** Invisible

You can also enter a *mood message* here, to let your contacts know what you are feeling or what you are doing:

 Tip

Disable automatic sign in when you open the Skype app

When you open the *Skype* app, you are automatically signed in. If you would like to prevent this from happening:

☞ **Tap**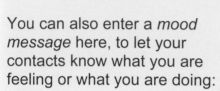

☞ **Tap** Settings

☞ **Check the box** ☑ **by** Sign in automatically

Appendix A. How Do I Do That Again?

The actions and exercises in this book are marked with footsteps:

Read how to do something once more by finding the corresponding number in the appendix below.

1 Unlock the Kindle Fire HDX or turn on

- Press the Power button ⏻

- Place your finger on the padlock 🔒

- Drag the padlock to the left

Turn on:

- Press the Power button ⏻ and keep it pressed in until you see the Kindle Fire logo

- Place your finger on the padlock 🔒

- Drag the padlock to the left

2 Open the *Quick Settings* menu
- Swipe your finger from the top of the screen downwards

3 Go back to the Home screen

- Tap 🏠

4 Turn Wi-Fi off
- Swipe your finger from the top of the screen downwards

- Tap Wireless

- By Wi-Fi, tap Off

5 Lock the Kindle Fire HDX or turn off
- Briefly press the Power button ⏻

Turn off altogether:

- Press the Power button ⏻ and keep it pressed in until you see the *Do you want to shut down your Kindle?* window

- Tap Power off

6 Open a book
- Tap Books

- Tap the book

7 Go to the next page
- Tap the right-hand side of the page

🐾8 **Open a web page in the *Silk* app**
- Tap

- Tap the address bar

- Type the web address

- Press

🐾9 **Go to a tab**
- Tap the desired tab

🐾10 **Unlock or lock page rotation**
- Swipe your finger from the top of the screen downwards

- Tap Locked or Auto-Rotate

- Swipe your finger from the bottom of the screen upwards

🐾11 **Open the *Email* app**
- Tap Apps

- Tap Email

🐾12 **Open the *Settings* screen**
- Swipe your finger from the top of the screen downwards

- Tap Settings

🐾13 **Add a contact**

- Tap New

- Tap the account you want to use

- If necessary, tap First name

- Type the name of the contact

- Tap Next

- Type the information in the fields you want to fill in

- Tap Save

🐾14 **Open the *Contacts* app**
- Tap Apps

- Tap Contacts

15 Open a web page on your computer

In Windows 8.1, on the desktop:

- On the taskbar, click

Or in Windows 7 or Vista:

- Click

- Click ▶ **All Programs**

- Click *e* Internet Explorer

To open the web page:
- Click the address bar

- Type the web address

- Press **Enter** ↵

16 Select text
- Click in front of the first word

- Drag the mouse over the word(s)

17 Close a window
- Click ✕

18 Go to the desktop
- On the Start screen, click the Desktop tile, for example

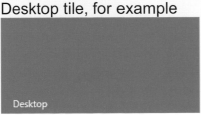

Desktop

19 Copy a file to the Kindle Fire HDX using a USB cable (sideloading)

- Drag   Wildlife   to

   Movies

- As soon as you see ⊕ Copy , release the mouse button

20 Let a window fill the right-hand or left-hand side of the screen
In Windows 8.1 or 7:
- Drag the window against the side of the screen

- As soon as you see a new window outline appear, release the mouse button

In Windows Vista:
- Move the windows next to each other manually

21 Move a file to the *Cloud Drive* folder

- Drag   Carrot cake   to

   Documents

- As soon as you see
  ⟶ Move to , release the
  mouse button

22 Sign in with your *Amazon* account

- If necessary, click
  Hello. Sign in
  Your Account ▾

- Click

  Sign in

- Type your email address and password

- Click

  Sign in using our secure server ▶

23 Open the *Appstore*

- Tap **Apps**

- Tap **Store** ⟩

24 Download an app

- Tap **Apps**

- Tap **Store** ⟩

- Tap 🔍

- Type the name of the app

- Tap 🔍

- Tap the app

- Tap **FREE**

- Tap **Get App**

Appendix B. Index

W

X

Y

Z

0